Y0-BEB-476

KINGSHIP AND POLITICS IN THE REIGN OF EDWARD VI

This book offers a reappraisal of the kingship and politics of the reign of Edward VI, the third Tudor king of England who reigned from the age of nine in 1547 until his death in 1553. The reign has often been interpreted as a period of political instability, mainly because of Edward's age, but this account challenges the view that the king's minority was a time of unstable political faction. It shows how Edward was shaped and educated from the start for adult kingship, and how Edwardian politics evolved to accommodate a maturing and able young king.

The book also explores the political values of the men around the king, and tries to reconstruct the relationships of family and association that bound together the governing elite in the king's Council, his court, and in the universities. It also, importantly, assesses the impact of Edward's reign on Elizabethan politics, both conceptually (the notion of what it was to be a monarch) and practically (the importance in Elizabeth's reign of men who had already shaped Edwardian politics).

STEPHEN ALFORD is Assistant Lecturer in History, University of Cambridge, and Fellow of King's College. His previous publications include *The Early Elizabethan Polity: William Cecil and the British Succession Crisis, 1558–1569* (Cambridge, 1998).

KINGSHIP AND POLITICS IN THE REIGN OF EDWARD VI

STEPHEN ALFORD

PUBLISHED BY THE PRESS SYNDICATE OF THE UNIVERSITY OF CAMBRIDGE
The Pitt Building, Trumpington Street, Cambridge, United Kingdom

CAMBRIDGE UNIVERSITY PRESS
The Edinburgh Building, Cambridge CB2 2RU, UK
40 West 20th Street, New York, NY 10011-4211, USA
447 Williamstown Road, Port Melbourne, VIC 3207, Australia
Ruiz de Alarcón 13, 28014 Madrid, Spain
Dock House, The Waterfront, Cape Town 8001, South Africa

http://www.cambridge.org

© Stephen Alford 2002

This book is in copyright. Subject to statutory exception
and to the provisions of relevant collective licensing agreements,
no reproduction of any part may take place without
the written permission of Cambridge University Press.

First published 2002

Printed in the United Kingdom at the University Press, Cambridge

Typeface Baskerville Monotype 11/12.5 pt.   *System* LATEX 2ε   [TB]

A catalogue record for this book is available from the British Library.

Library of Congress Cataloguing in Publication data
Alford, Stephen, 1970–
Kingship and politics in the reign of Edward VI / Stephen Alford.
p.   cm.
Includes bibliographical references and index.
ISBN 0 521 66055 6
1. Edward VI, King of England, 1537–1553.   2. Great Britain – Politics
and government – 1547–1553.   3. Monarchy – Great Britain – History – 16th century.
4. Great Britain – History – Edward VI, 1547–1553.   5. Great Britain – Kings and
rulers – Biography.   I. Title.
DA345 .A45   2002
942.05′3–dc21   2001043603

ISBN 0 521 66055 6 hardback

In memory of my grandparents, Phoebe and Harry Corbett

Contents

Wo be unto thee (O thou realm and land) whose king is but a child, and whose princes are early at their banquets. But well is thee (O thou realm and land) whose king is come of noblesse, and whose princes eat in due season, for strength and not for lust.

Ecclesiastes 10:16–17.

Illustrations

Acknowledgements

Research can be a solitary affair – but it rarely is, and I am deeply grateful to friends and colleagues who have supported and encouraged me in piecing together and writing *Kingship and politics*. John Guy has responded so patiently to energetic bursts of correspondence. He read a complete draft of the book at the busiest time of the academic year, and his comments, criticisms, and corrections were invaluable. John Cramsie, my trusty counsellor and great friend, lived with the curse of the unannounced e-mail attachment at a time when he had far more important things to do than to read drafts of chapters that barely made sense to their author. Tom Freeman is as encyclopaedic as he is generous, and I owe to him my account of the subtle but important changes in John Foxe's presentation of John Dudley between 1559 and 1570, and much more besides. Lisa Richardson very kindly allowed me to appropriate her fascinating exploration of the relationship between John Hayward's *The Life, and Raigne of King Edward the Sixt* and Richard Grenewey's *The annales of Cornelius Tacitus*. Elizabeth Evenden, whose work on the printer John Day is of critical significance to any historian working on the politics of the reigns of Edward and Elizabeth, helped me to pin down the relationship between Day and Richard Grafton. Natalie Mears pointed me in the direction of *The copie of a pistel or letter sent to Gilbard Potter*, and Alan Bryson, the author of an extremely important thesis on '"The speciall men in every shere": the Edwardian regime, 1547–53' (University of St Andrews, 2001), kindly sent me references to, and transcripts of, some documents that informed his own research. I suspect that Dale Hoak may disagree with some of the claims of *Kingship and politics*, but from the (as yet) unpublished papers he kindly sent me I am fairly certain that we are intrigued by many of the same features of Edwardian and Elizabethan political history. I am extremely grateful to William Davies of Cambridge University Press for his patience and encouragement in gently steering me in the direction of completion. Max has tolerated my

xi

historical ramblings with patience and humour, listened without choice to strange thoughts on the reign of Edward, and allowed a cast of historical characters to invade our marriage (Stephen Gardiner was her least favourite). Albert, Flash, and Zorro naturally did what cats do best: they tried to convince me of the folly of taking life so seriously and encouraged me to find more productive and exciting uses for piles of paper. They nearly succeeded.

This book began life as a Postdoctoral Fellowship project funded by the British Academy, hosted by the Cambridge Faculty of History, and complemented by a research fellowship at Fitzwilliam College. I am deeply grateful to the Academy, to its Assistant Secretary Ken Emond, and to the Master and Fellows of Fitzwilliam – Rosemary Horrox in particular, whose support has, and always will be, appreciated. King's elected me to an Ehrman Fellowship in 1999, and as a college community it has provided me with everything a historian could wish for: friendship, conversation, and the time and freedom to write a book on Tudor kingship yards away from one of the finest architectural legacies of the dynasty.

Peter Jones and Rosalind Moad of King's College deserve very special thanks for helping me to navigate the College Library and Archive. The staff of the Rare Books and Manuscripts Rooms of Cambridge University Library have been, as ever, extremely supportive. A number of librarians across the country – Nicholas Bennett (Cathedral Librarian at Lincoln), Gill Cannell (Corpus Christi College, Cambridge), Christina Mackwell (Lambeth Palace Library), Sarah Newton (Corpus Christi College, Oxford), and Elizabeth Rainey (Durham University Library) – checked references, traced editions, and answered frantic e-mails, and I am very grateful to them. Crown copyright documents in the Public Record Office are quoted by permission of the Controller of Her Majesty's Stationery Office, manuscripts in the British Library by permission of the Trustees, and those in Cambridge University Library by permission of the Syndics. Documents in the College Archives of King's College, Cambridge are quoted by permission of the Provost and Scholars, and papers in the Parker Library of Corpus Christi College, Cambridge by permission of the Master and Fellows. I am grateful to the Marquess of Salisbury for allowing me to quote from the Cecil Papers at Hatfield House, Hertfordshire. Quotations from the Portland Papers and the Seymour Papers are included by permission of the Marquess of Bath, Longleat House, Warminster, Wiltshire, Great Britain. The quotations from 'An ordre for redresse of the state of the Realme' (*c.* 1559) are reproduced by permission of the Huntington Library, San Marino, California.

Abbreviations and conventions

APC	*Acts of the Privy Council of England*, ed. J.R. Dasent: 3 vols. for Edward VI's reign (*1547–50, 1550–52, 1552–54*), published between 1890 and 1892 (HMSO; London)
CPR	*Calendar of the Patent Rolls preserved in the Public Record Office: Edward VI*, in 6 vols. (*1547–48, 1548–49, 1549–51, 1550–53, 1553*, and *Index*), published between 1924 and 1929 (HMSO; London)
fo(s).	folio(s)
Knighton	C.S. Knighton, ed., *Calendar of State Papers, Domestic Series, of the reign of Edward VI 1547–1553* (HMSO; London, 1992) [cited by entry number]
MS	manuscript
sig(s).	signature(s)
SP	Public Record Office, Kew, London, State Papers
STC	*A short-title catalogue of books printed in England, Scotland, & Ireland and of English books printed abroad 1475–1640*, ed. W.A. Jackson, F.S. Ferguson, and Katharine F. Pantzer, 3 vols. (Bibliographical Society; London, 1976–91)

All quotations are in original spelling, but I have transcribed the thorn as 'th', silently extended contractions, and modernized the Tudor habit of using 'u' for 'v', 'v' for 'u', and 'i' for 'j'.

Scriptural quotations are from *The Byble, that is to say all the holy Scripture*, edited by Edmund Becke from 'Thomas Matthew's Bible' (the translations of William Tyndale and John Rogers), published by John Day and William Seres in London in 1549 (*STC* 2077).

In giving dates, the Old Style has been retained, but the year is assumed to have begun on 1 January.

Introduction

The middle Tudor monarchs, sandwiched between the 'greatness' of Henry VIII and the 'glories' of Elizabeth I, often look like the poor relations of the dynasty, occupying (and indeed shaping) a decade beset by crisis and instability. The reign of Mary I presented (and, for historians, still presents) peculiar problems of its own. So did (and, again for historians, still does) the reign of Mary's half-brother Edward, the son of Henry VIII by his third wife Jane Seymour, and, at nine years of age, the only male Tudor heir to the throne after the death of his father in 1547. The five-and-a-half years of Edward's reign were marked by controversial and destructive Protestant Reformation. But they were also profoundly important to the construction and presentation of Tudor monarchy after Edward's death – critical, indeed, for our reading of the queenship and politics of the reign of Elizabeth I, and for our understanding of the men who inhabited the Elizabethan political scene, many of whom had served their apprenticeships between 1547 and 1553. That at least is the argument of this book.

Kingship and politics in the reign of Edward VI is, I think, the book I wanted to write. I have just reread the proposal I submitted to Cambridge University Press in 1998, and the projected structure of *Kingship and politics* matches the end result fairly well. The proposal also captures the essence of the book's purpose as I imagined it three years ago, because my intention was to try to look at Edward's reign from a new perspective. It seemed to me that studies of the English polity of the late 1540s and early 1550s were standardly written as high political narratives of a politics conceived institutionally, structurally, and even morally. The key political players of Edward's reign had often been written of as 'good' or 'bad', and this tradition, deeply embedded in the historiography, persisted in new and different forms. Privy Council and 'constitution' dominated accounts of political life in the 1540s and 1550s.[1] Only a few historians had worked on the culture of Edwardian politics and religion and the visual presentation of monarchy in art and iconography.[2] No real effort had been made to take Edward's kingship expressed both conceptually and practically – and the commitment of the men governing in the king's name – seriously. Two of the other themes I wanted to explore back in 1998 were, first of all, the close relationship between the Edwardian and Elizabethan political elites (here Winthrop Hudson's study of *The Cambridge connection* was influential) and, second, the impact of the 'acephalous' political conditions of Edward's reign on the Elizabethan response to the challenge of unmarried female monarchy (an issue I had scratched the surface of in my doctoral work on the 'succession crisis' of the 1560s).[3]

'What kingship?' is a question that people have been asking me, in a gently critical way, for some time. The point is a fair one. Can we talk about kingship in a personal or possessive sense for the years between 1547 and 1553? Did Edward VI, dead at fifteen, really *have* a kingship? The answer is, I think, yes. The practical dimensions of Edwardian kingship were certainly beginning to form by his middle teenage years, but even more coherent and superficially impressive were the grand claims and aspirations of middle Tudor Protestant monarchy. The Henrician royal supremacy became a vehicle for the evangelical Reformation. Edward was presented as a godly prince, a second King Josiah (2 Kings 22–23) guided by providence to extinguish once and for all the influence of the papal Antichrist of Rome in England. Although this kingship was

---

[1] The principal texts from the last thirty-five years are W.K. Jordan, *Edward VI: the young king. The protectorship of the duke of Somerset* (London, 1968); W.K. Jordan, *Edward VI: the threshold of power. The dominance of the duke of Northumberland* (London, 1970); Michael L. Bush, *The government policy of Protector Somerset* (London, 1975); and Dale E. Hoak, *The King's Council in the reign of Edward VI* (Cambridge, 1976). More recent additions are David Loades, *John Dudley duke of Northumberland, 1504–1553* (Oxford, 1996); and Jennifer Loach, *Edward VI*, ed. George Bernard and Penry Williams (New Haven and London, 1999).

[2] Margaret Aston, *The king's bedpost: reformation and iconography in a Tudor group portrait* (Cambridge, 1993); John Guy, 'Tudor monarchy and its critiques', in John Guy, ed., *The Tudor monarchy* (London, 1997), esp. pp. 89–91; Dale Hoak, 'The iconography of the crown imperial', in Dale Hoak, ed., *Tudor political culture* (Cambridge, 1995), pp. 54–103; Dale Hoak, 'The coronations of Edward VI, Mary I, and Elizabeth I, and the transformation of Tudor monarchy', in Richard Mortimer and Charles S. Knighton, eds., *Reformation to revolution: Westminster Abbey 1540–1660* (Stamford, 2002); and John N. King, *Tudor royal iconography: literature and art in an age of religious crisis* (Princeton, 1989).

[3] Winthrop S. Hudson, *The Cambridge connection and the Elizabethan settlement of 1559* (Durham, NC, 1980); Stephen Alford, *The early Elizabethan polity: William Cecil and the British succession crisis, 1558–1569* (Cambridge, 1998); cf. Patrick Collinson, 'The Elizabethan exclusion crisis and the Elizabethan polity', *Proceedings of the British Academy*, 84 (1994), pp. 51–92.

constructed on Edward's behalf, he understood and accepted its implications: a strong and compelling theme of Diarmaid MacCulloch's *Tudor
church militant*.[4] But to what extent was this model of kingship promoted
to mask the realities of Edwardian governance? How did the subjects of
the Tudor crown cope with the practical and the theoretical implications
of royal minority?

The answer is, predictably, rather complex. On one level Edwardians
could certainly accommodate a male minor, surrounded and supported
by a male political establishment at court and in the Privy Council. The
model of the Edwardian court as a factional battleground of the great
subjects of the realm, fighting for control of the king and the governance
of the kingdom, is profoundly distorted. The men around Edward were
fallible and his reign certainly experienced periods of stress and upheaval.
But historians have not generally given the Edwardian political establishment the credit it deserves: continuity, effectiveness, service, and cohesion
are often missing from accounts of the politics of the reign. And yet, at the
same time, there were some serious problems in reconciling royal minority with the core notions of Tudor monarchy. The location of sovereign
authority was not really at issue. Few subjects of the crown in 1547 could
deny that Edward was legitimate and acknowledged heir to Henry VIII's
throne. But the exercise of power was a rather different matter. It was difficult to disguise the essential fact that, before the king's majority, sovereign
power had to be exercised collaboratively – a notion that threw into silhouette the behaviour of the men around Edward during six years of
active, unsettling, and controversial Protestant Reformation.

After 1558, Elizabeth I and her councillors had to contend with a powerfully stated and distinctive Edwardian inheritance – an inheritance
many Elizabethans had helped to shape. The reign of Edward was a
bridge between the political establishments of the 1540s and the 1560s –
a remarkably stable governing group marked by close associations of
family, religion, and political office. Intellectually, the Edwardian legacy
was just as formative but rather more ambiguous. Protestant Marian
exiles like John Aylmer, Christopher Goodman, John Knox, and John
Ponet inherited from the late 1540s and early 1550s strong notions of
what those in political authority should and should not do. Tudor monarchy became ideologically measurable, and the monarch, in effect, an
accountable public officer. But these ideas were widely held, and established themselves at the heart of the political culture of the second half of

---

[4] Diarmaid MacCulloch, *Tudor church militant: Edward VI and the Protestant Reformation* (London, 1999).

the sixteenth century, articulated by Elizabeth's bishops in parliament in 1572, for example, and embedded in the Geneva Bibles produced by the queen's printer in the 1570s and 1580s. This potentially radical critique of political power grew out of the culture of Edwardian kingship, powerful, providential, and driven by Old Testament texts and exemplars. At the same time, the Edwardian years helped to shape mechanisms for the governance of the kingdom during the effective absence of a king (although the creation of a truly operational king was always the goal of the men around Edward), and, arguably, prepared the way for the notion that Privy Council and parliament had an important part to play in unlocking the power of the Tudor crown and supporting the queen in the governance of her realm.

In his 'devise' for the succession of 1553, Edward VI distinguished between the kingship of a male minor below the age of fourteen and a teenage king between the ages of fourteen and eighteen. For a king younger than fourteen, the realm would be governed entirely on his behalf; older, and the king should participate, working with his Council (see below, chapter 5, pp. 171–3). Edward's 'devise' may have as much to say about perceptions of Elizabeth's (limited and constrained?) queenship as it did about Edward and the nature of his authority. When, in 1559, John Aylmer wrote of the queen's Council at her elbow, supervising the execution of law – and when Francis Knollys, ten years later, told Elizabeth that it was not possible for her councillors to govern her state well until she began resolutely to follow their opinions – was this Elizabethan politics and political culture in an authentically Edwardian context?[5] Did the Edwardian years give courtiers and councillors the confidence and experience to shape (or at least try to shape) female rule? Was the political legacy of Edward's years a powerfully stated, but potentially limited, monarchy?

Many readers will find this book selective and, in places, even speculative. It probably asks too many questions – certainly more than it satisfactorily answers – and it cannot claim to be exhaustive. But if *Kingship and politics* encourages its readers to think more seriously about the nature of the first half of the middle Tudor decade – and goes some way to making the case that the reign of Edward VI is a reign Tudor historians cannot afford to ignore – then it will have achieved much of what I wanted it to achieve.

---

5 John Aylmer, *An harborowe for faithfull and trewe subjectes* ([London,] 1559; *STC* 1005), sig. {H3v}; Alford, *Early Elizabethan polity*, p. 33.

I

Constructing the reign of Edward VI

If no man had written the goodnesse of noble Augustus, nor the pitie of mercifull Trajan, how shoulde their successours have folowed ther steppes in vertue and princely qualities: on the contrarie parte, if the crueltie of Nero, the ungracious life of Caligula had not beene put in remembrance, young Princes and fraile governors might likewise have fallen in a like pit, but by redyng their vices and seyng their mischeveous ende, thei bee compelled to leave their evill waies, and embrace the good qualities of notable princes and prudent governours: Thus, writyng is the keye to enduce vertue, and represse vice, Thus memorie maketh menne ded many a thousande yere still to live as though thei were present: Thus Fame triumpheth upon death, and renoune upon Oblivion, and all by reason of writyng and historie.[1]

For Edward Hall, in the dedication of the first edition of *The union of the two noble and illustre famelies of Lancastre & Yorke* (1548) to Edward VI, historical writing was a critical point of contact between the past and the present, an active dialogue between princes and governors living and dead, and a mirror for the successes and the failures of historical actors. History was live; it was neither antiseptically academic (Hall himself could be called a journalist as well as a chronicler) nor necessarily rooted in what a modern historian would recognize as 'historical fact'. Since the sixteenth century commentators on the reign of Edward VI had worked with a craft that often had as much to do with rhetoric and polemic as it did with veracity. And understandably so, because the notion of history as a professional discipline committed to 'historical truth' is a comparatively recent one. Modern historians do their best to understand the past, and, in doing so, impose on historical events and forces an order of their own. But even

---

[1] Edward Hall, *The union of the two noble and illustre famelies of Lancastre & Yorke* (London, 1548; *STC* 12722), sig. ❧2r.

the work of a professional historian – ideally sensitive, imaginative, and authentic – bears the complex and unique imprint of personality and environment. Transparent, timeless, 'objective' history is very probably a myth: a historian often bears the medals – and the scars – of his or her own generation, and history as subject is all the richer for the diversity. So exploring the construction and presentation of the reign of Edward VI over 450 years is a serious, surprisingly difficult, but extremely important challenge.

How have Tudor evangelicals, Jacobean courtiers, Reformation polemicists, Anglican clergymen, gentleman antiquarians, and professional historians from the late nineteenth century to the closing years of the twentieth probed, explained, and constructed the reign of Edward VI? To what extent were they influenced by the political and cultural environments in which they wrote or the prevailing notions of how the Tudor polity functioned? What beliefs or preconceptions did they bring to six years of Tudor minority? Unpicking this historiography is vital in a study of the kingship and the politics of 1547–53 because accounts of Edward's reign have served so many different purposes and reflected so many different assumptions. The skill of critically decoding the reign and its historians is certainly still important. The most recent biography of Edward, for example, reconstructs an aristocratic, luxurious, and martial royal court, and uses it to challenge the conventional account of the young king as a 'godly imp', committed, in a serious and rather precocious way, to the Reformation of his kingdom.[2] The distinction was a false one; false too was the assumption that the presentation of Edward was the fault of John Foxe writing in an Elizabethan tradition. Godly kingship was one of the great Edwardian constructions (see below, chapter 2, pp. 50–6; and chapter 4, pp. 112–15). But there are other preconceptions readers and students bring to the reign of Edward. Factional conflict, the manipulation of a boy-king, the sacrifice of Jane Grey in 1553 by the 'wicked' John Dudley, and even the determination of some historians to measure the reign against the constitutional perfection of Thomas Cromwell's 'revolution' – an exercise rather like using a piece of string to measure volume – have all absorbed historians and, in spite of some valiant efforts, continue to feed the imaginations of readers.

---

[2] Jennifer Loach, *Edward VI*, ed. George Bernard and Penry Williams (New Haven and London, 1999), pp. 180–1; cf. Stephen Alford, 'Between God and government', *Times Literary Supplement*, 11 Feb. 2000, p. 28.

FROM POORE PRATTE TO DAVID HUME

Historiography is a complex business, but in the construction and presentation of the posthumous reputation of the reign of Edward VI one thing is certain: it began within weeks, if not days, of the king's death. *The copie of a pistel or letter sent to Gilbard Potter* appeared in the shop of the London printer Hugh Singleton soon after 1 August 1553, eight days after the arrest of John Dudley at Cambridge and the definitive collapse of the Edwardian regime.[3] Its putative author was 'Poore Pratte', who had sent the letter to comfort his friend Potter, a true subject of 'Mary quene of England, not only by wordes, but by deedes'.[4] In July Potter had heard the proclamation of Jane Grey as queen but instead declared his allegiance to Mary. His punishment was public and brutal: Potter's ears were nailed to the pillory in Cheapside and then cut off.[5] So *The copie of a pistel or letter* is a testament to the dangers and uncertainties of the days following the death of Edward. But it is interesting for two other important reasons. The first is that the pamphlet records the instinctive response of the crown's subjects – even Edwardian evangelicals – to declare loyalty to Mary I as the legitimate successor to her brother. Both Singleton and the printer he sub-contracted to produce the book, Richard Jugge, were Protestants. *The copie of a pistel or letter* allowed them, indirectly but clearly, to condemn the Edwardian regime's effort to preserve itself in the name of Jane Grey. The second important feature of the book is even more striking. There was an immediate and violent reaction against the regime of John Dudley – a reaction that scarred his historical reputation for 400 years.

Many commentators in the sixteenth century condemned Dudley, and at times their hatred was visceral.[6] Poore Pratte wrote that the 'great devell Dudley ruleth, Duke I shuld have sayde'.[7] John Ponet called him

---

3 *The copie of a pistel or letter sent to Gilbard Potter in the tyme When he was in prison, for speakinge on our most true quenes part the Lady Mary before he had his eares cut of. The .xiij. of Julye* (London, 1 Aug. 1553; *STC* 20188).

4 *Copie of a pistel*, sig. {A1 v}.

5 For an account of Potter's punishment 'for words speaking at time of the proclamation of ladie Jane', see Raphael Holinshed, *The First and second volumes of Chronicles*, 2 vols. (London, 1597; *STC* 13569), II, p. 1084. The proclamation was printed by Richard Grafton as printer to the queen (*STC* 7846).

6 Barrett L. Beer, 'Northumberland: the myth of the wicked duke and the historical John Dudley', *Albion*, 11 (1979), pp. 1–14; David Loades, *John Dudley duke of Northumberland, 1504–1553* (Oxford, 1996), pp. vii–ix.

7 *Copie of a pistel*, sig. {A7v}.

England's Alcibiades, recalling the Athenian general whose actions had led to military defeat by Sparta: an appropriate reference, given Dudley's power, reputation as a soldier, and betrayal of the Protestant cause.[8] That was in 1556. But *The copie of a pistel or letter* suggests that John Dudley became a figure of public hatred only days after the breath was out of the body of the Edwardian regime. In the pamphlet the Dudley arms of the bear and the ragged staff became a coded but clear reference to a regime dominated by one man. Poore Pratte wrote to Gilbert Potter as one who had offered himself 'into the handes of the ragged beare most rancke, with whome is nether mercy, pitie, nor compassion, but his indignation present death'.[9] If Mary 'oure lawfull quene' were taken from her subjects, Dudley would represent the punishment of providence, the 'ragged beare' as a cruel pharoah who would rule, 'pul & pol', spoil, destroy, and bring to calamity and misery the queen's subjects.[10] And even by the beginning of August 1553 the suggestion that John Dudley had benefited from the death of Edward was in the public domain. Mary, wrote Poore Pratte, was 'more sorowful' for her brother than glad that she was queen: 'she would have bene as glad of her brothers life, as the ragged beare is glad of his death'.[11] The ground was well prepared for *Leicester's commonwealth*, the great Elizabethan libel of the Dudley family.[12]

John Ponet's *Shorte treatise of politike power* was, in many ways, a classically Edwardian book written in the context of Marian exile (see below, chapter 6, pp. 177–9). Ponet was an Edwardian insider, a protégé of Archbishop Thomas Cranmer of Canterbury and one of Edward's favourite preachers. His presentation of key moments in the regime's history – moments he experienced, one suspects, in a fairly indirect way – is patchy. But there is still a grittiness to his reconstruction of the events of July 1553, when 'the innocent Lady Jane contrary to her will, yea by force, with teares dropping downe her chekes, suffred her self to be called Quene of Englande'.[13] His account of the behaviour of Cranmer in

---

[8] John Ponet, *A shorte treatise of politike power, and of the true Obedience which subjectes owe to kynges and other civile Governours, with an Exhortacion to all true naturall Englishe men* ([Strasburg,] 1556; *STC* 20178), sig. 13r.

[9] *Copie of a pistel*, sig. {A1 v}; cf. sig. A4r.   [10] *Copie of a pistel*, sig. {A5r}.

[11] *Copie of a pistel*, sig. {A5v}.

[12] Dwight C. Peck, ed., *Leicester's commonwealth: the copy of a letter written by a Master of Art of Cambridge (1584) and related documents* (Athens, OH and London, 1985); Simon Adams, 'Favourites and factions at the Elizabethan court', in Ronald G. Asch and Adolf M. Birke, eds., *Princes, patronage, and the nobility: the court at the beginning of the modern age c. 1450–1650* (Oxford, 1991), pp. 267–76.

[13] Ponet, *Shorte treatise*, sig. {D7r–v}. For an account of Cranmer's response to the plan to divert the royal succession in 1553, see Diarmaid MacCulloch, *Thomas Cranmer* (New Haven and London, 1996), pp. 540–2.

1553 trod on sensitive ground, but it succeeded in balancing his mentor's initial refusal to endorse the Grey claim against the archbishop's eventual subscription – only, of course, 'to content the kinges minde and commaundement, yea in dede to save the innocent king from the violence of most wicked traiterous tirannes'.[14] Ponet also presented perhaps the first high-political narrative of the fall of Protector Somerset in 1549. Thomas Wriothesley earl of Southampton, Henry fitz Alan earl of Arundel, and Richard Southwell had conspired with John Dudley to remove Protector Somerset 'out of his authoritie'. To do this, Ponet explained, they had forged letters and lies to make Edward Seymour hated.[15] Equally, the men who had 'conspired' to kill Lord Admiral Thomas Seymour and his brother Protector Somerset did so that they could rob the king and spoil the realm at their pleasure.[16] Ponet was a bitter man, and it must have seemed to him, writing from Strasburg, three years into Mary's reign, that the godly commonwealth of Edward VI had been subverted and consumed by ambitious men determined merely to secure power and line their own pockets. The same theme was explored in Geneva by the Marian exile Anthony Gilby, who wrote that the Lenten preachers before the king in 1553 were denounced by John Dudley: 'the libertie of the preachers tonges would cause the counsile and nobilitie to ryse uppe against them: for they could not suffer so to be intreated'.[17] Promoting the godly commonwealth, so the argument went, conflicted with self-interest. The true religion had been used to cloak the feeding frenzy of the Reformation.[18]

Noble faction, rapacity, the manipulation of the king: three of the classic themes of accounts of Edward's reign written in the seventeenth and eighteenth centuries emerged in their earliest forms from the polemically charged political environment of the 1550s. The Elizabethan response to the Protestant calamity of 1553 was, predictably, rather different. Sixteenth-century accounts of Edward's reign swung between the brutal polemic of Ponet and relatively neutral, rather formal, narrative. Elizabethan authors naturally lauded Edward's evangelical zeal, highlighted the godliness of his uncle Edward Seymour, and were generally careful when it came to exploring the career, fall, and execution of John Dudley – principally because his son Robert, after 1564 earl of Leicester,

---

[14] Ponet, *Shorte treatise*, sig. {D7v}.　　[15] Ponet, *Shorte treatise*, sig. I3r.
[16] Ponet, *Shorte treatise*, sig. {E1v}.
[17] Anthony Gilby, 'An admonition to England and Scotland to call them to repentance, written by Antoni Gilby', in John Knox, *The appellation of John Knoxe* (Geneva, 1558; *STC* 15063), p. 71v.
[18] Gilby, 'Admonition', p. 71r.

was a major force in Elizabethan politics. John Foxe was a rich source for later writers and editors like Richard Grafton and Raphael Holinshed, but his *Acts and Monuments* reflected the complexity of the Edwardian legacy.[19] In the 1570 edition of *Acts and Monuments* 'the Actes and thynges done in the reigne of kyng Edward the 6' were displayed in dramatic visual and allegorical form. The volume's printer, John Day, presented the Edwardian Reformation in a single woodcut, with images of the purging of the temple and the departure of Catholics from the realm – 'Shippe over your trinkets and be packing ye Papistes' – and the replacement of the altar by a communion table set on a north–south axis. The woodcut emphasizes preaching and sets Edward, handing the Bible to his subjects, at the heart of this kingly Reformation.[20] Foxe's text was just as effusive. The goodness of Christ led him into the mild and halcyon days of Edward 'as into a haven of fayrer and calmer whether'. In the margin of the edition of 1563 he rather neatly summarized the relationship between the reformations of Henry VIII and Edward: 'King Henry unhorsed the Pope: but king Edward toke awaye sadle, trappers and al.'[21]

Acts and Monuments was a great resource for later writers but it did not, for the most part, present a narrative account of Edward's reign. The first edition of 1563 reproduced the Edwardian regime's injunctions, instructions to bishops, and correspondence with Bishop Edmund Bonner of London, and recounted Edward's efforts to encourage his half-sister Mary to conform to Edwardian doctrine. Foxe spent well over a hundred pages reconstructing the 'history and the doings and the attempts' of Stephen Gardiner, from the sermon he preached at court on St Peter's Day 1548 to his trial and removal from the bishopric of Winchester (see below, chapter 2, pp. 57–9; and chapter 3, pp. 83–5). Perhaps the most important single contribution Foxe made to the later historiography was 'The tragicall History of the moste noble and famous Lorde, Edwarde Duke of Somerset, Protector of kyng Edward, and of hys Realme'.[22] He accepted that Protector Somerset had colluded in the execution of his brother Thomas in 1549 but blamed the breakdown of their relationship on 'slaunderous tongues'. More strangely, he presented

[19] John Foxe, *Actes and Monuments of these latter and perillous dayes* (London, 1563; *STC* 11222); 1570 (*STC* 11223); 1576 (*STC* 11224); 1583 (*STC* 11225); 1596–7 (*STC* 11226, 11226a).

[20] *STC* 11223 (1570), p. 1483, reproduced in John N. King, *Tudor royal iconography: literature and art in an age of religious crisis* (Princeton, 1989), pp. 97–9; also Margaret Aston, *The king's bedpost: Reformation and iconography in a Tudor group portrait* (Cambridge, 1993), p. 160; Diarmaid MacCulloch, *Tudor church militant: Edward VI and the Protestant Reformation* (London, 1999), p. 10.

[21] *STC* 11222 (1563), p. 675.   [22] *STC* 11222 (1563), pp. 880–4.

the two Seymour brothers as the key to the preservation of 'bothe them-selves, the king theyr Nephew, and the whole common wealth, from the violence and feare of al daunger'.[23] But the key to early Edwardian success was clearly Protector Somerset and, like Hugh Latimer in 1549, *Acts and Monuments* compared him to other protectors in English history in general and Humphrey of Lancaster, duke of Gloucester, protector dur-ing the minority of Henry VI, in particular – an important and positive association.

For Elizabethan writers like John Foxe, the history of the Edwardian regime in its broader context was not set in stone. Foxe certainly massaged his text, and between 1559 and 1570 he altered it in subtle, but signifi-cant, ways. Like Richard Grafton he had to reconcile critical accounts of John Dudley with the Elizabethan pre-eminence of the earl of Leicester. In *Rerum in ecclesia gestarum* (1559), Foxe explained that *some had said* Dudley had sought to poison Edward, and he strongly implicated the duke in the deaths of Edward Seymour duke of Somerset and Ralph Vane. Four years later, in the first English edition of *Acts and Monuments*, Foxe recounted that after his surrender at Cambridge in 1553 Dudley had been taken to the Tower of London as a traitor to the crown, and he prudently (but rather ambiguously) explained that the duke had recanted his Protestant faith 'of his own mynd, or els having before some promise and hope geven of pardon'.[24] In 1570 these passages were altered to present Dudley in a more positive light. Dudley was taken at Cambridge as a traitor to the crown 'notwithstanding that he had there proclaimed her Queene before' – in other words he was not technically guilty of treason.[25] Dudley recanted, Foxe explained, after 'having a promise and being put in hope of pardon'.[26] Equally, the edition of 1570 tried to mod-erate the enthusiasm for Edward Seymour of 1563. Foxe explained that his description of Somerset's death should not be confused with accounts of the death of Christ. Similarly, he asked his readers not to misunder-stand his presentation of Protector Somerset's godliness. As editor he did not 'ever meane to derogate or empayre the martiall prayse or factes of other men, which also are to be commended in such thynges where they wel deserved' – a subtle but decodable reference to Dudley.[27]

---

[23] *STC* 11222 (1563), p. 880.   [24] *STC* 11222 (1563), p. 902.
[25] *STC* 11223 (1570), II, p. 1569. I owe this account of Foxe's texts to the generosity of Dr T.S. Freeman.
[26] *STC* 11223 (1570), II, p. 1569.
[27] *STC* 11223 (1570): 'Certeine Cautions of the Author to the Reader, of thynges to be considered in readyng this story.'

Richard Grafton's account of Edward's reign similarly shaped itself to the political environment of the 1560s. In *A Chronicle at large and meere History of the affayres of Englande* (1569) he dropped the name of William Cecil from the group of men arrested and detained in October 1549 because of their association with Protector Somerset.[28] Cecil, Elizabeth I's principal secretary, was the dedicatee of Grafton's volume. Raphael Holinshed chose the same path. His source was not Grafton – Holinshed mentioned in addition the names of William Gray, Michael Stanhope, John Thynne, and Edward Wolf – but he too decided that it was preferable to avoid an uncomfortable detail from Cecil's early career.[29] John Dudley received similar treatment. Grafton described him as 'a valiant and hardie Gentleman, but also wise and pollitique', his part in the *coup d'état* of 1549 was merely hinted at in the text, and his political pre-eminence after the collapse of the protectorate – a sentence on Dudley's 'highest aucthoritie' – was mentioned only once.[30] Raphael Holinshed emphasized the 'manlie courage of the earle of Warwike' during Protector Somerset's Scottish campaigns, followed Grafton's lead in the account of October 1549, and reproduced Grafton's rather enigmatic line on Dudley's 'highest authoritie'.[31] In *The Annales of England* (1592), by John Stow, there was nothing on John Dudley's manipulation of his colleagues over the succession to the throne in 1553.[32] Grafton and Holinshed had taken a similar line. In *A Chronicle at large* Grafton recorded that, because Edward was 'sore' sick, 'dyverse of the kinges counsayle and other of the nobilitie of the realme, and also by certaine of the Judges and Lawyers' argued for Jane as rightful queen.[33] Holinshed's text gave the king a more central role in trying to establish 'a meet order of succession' by noble marriage, but he blamed the Council and others for subverting the succession.[34] John Dudley faded into the background.

Was this accident or design? A co-ordinated effort on the part of Elizabethan writers to present fairly neutral accounts of a sensitive reign? Probably not: authors and editors like Grafton and Holinshed compiled their volumes by freely borrowing, reproducing, and re-editing the work

---

[28] Richard Grafton, *A Chronicle at large and meere History of the affayres of Englande and Kinges of the same, deduced from the Creation of the worlde, unto the first habitation of thys Islande: and so by contynuance unto the first yere of the reigne of our most deere and sovereigne Lady Queene Elizabeth* (London, 1569; *STC* 12147), p. 1313.

[29] Holinshed, *Chronicles*, p. 1059.   [30] Grafton, *Chronicle*, pp. 1309, 1313.

[31] Holinshed, *Chronicles*, pp. 982, 1061.

[32] John Stow, *The Annales of England, faithfully collected out of the most autenticall Authors, Records, and other Monuments of Antiquitie, from the first inhabitation untill this present yeere 1592* (London, 1592; *STC* 23334), p. 1031.

[33] Grafton, *Chronicle*, pp. 1324–5.   [34] Holinshed, *Chronicles*, p. 1083.

of others. This meant, however, that when Richard Grafton airbrushed and tidied aspects of Edward's reign he affected later derivative – but in the case of Holinshed extremely popular – accounts quite profoundly. More interesting, perhaps, is the model of Edwardian political life men like Grafton and Holinshed promoted: relatively consensual, fairly stable, and capable of surviving political upheaval. These Elizabethan accounts of Edward's reign certainly borrowed freely from John Foxe, but they also imposed on the reign something that a reader would have to fight hard to find in *Acts and Monuments*: clear moral and narrative shape. Both Grafton and Holinshed began, naturally enough, with accounts of Edward's accession and the establishment of the protectorate. Holinshed reproduced Grafton's discussion of the Edwardian iconoclasm and Protector Somerset's military campaign in Scotland. The assault against enclosures and the rebellions of 1549 came next, followed by the collapse of the protectorate and the eventual execution of Edward Seymour. Grafton and Holinshed recounted Nicholas Ridley's sermon before the king on the hardships of the London poor. Grafton in particular emphasized Ridley's amazement at the wisdom and earnest zeal of his young king, but both Holinshed and Grafton recorded the establishment of charitable foundations for the poor in London.[35] Grafton and Holinshed followed Foxe in recounting Edward's final prayer, perhaps the definitive expression of the young king's godliness: 'Oh Lorde God, save thy chosen people of England. Oh my Lord God defend this Realme from papistry, and maintain thy true religion, that I & my people maye praise thy holy name.'[36]

So although *A Chronicle at large* and Holinshed's *Chronicles* very occasionally wandered off in slightly different directions – and in spite of John Stow's rather breathless account in *The Annales* – Edward's reign had acquired by the end of the sixteenth century a familiar, even rhythmical, narrative form. The main features of the years between 1547 and 1553 as these popular and accessible Elizabethan books presented them are certainly interesting in the context of the polemical rage of the 1550s and the preoccupation with political faction and discord in the seventeenth and eighteenth centuries. Richard Grafton recorded that for the honour and surety of the king, Edward earl of Hertford, one of Edward VI's uncles on his mother's side, 'was by order of the Counsaylors aforenamed, or the more part of them, with the assent of the kinges Majestie'

[35] Holinshed, *Chronicles*, pp. 1081–2; Grafton, *Chronicle*, pp. 1321–2.
[36] *STC* 11222 (1563), p. (888); Grafton, *Chronicle*, p. 1324; Holinshed, *Chronicles*, p. 1084.

created duke of Somerset and governor of the king's person and protector of his realms, dominions, and subjects. This was 'well allowed'
of all the noblemen, with the exception of Thomas Wriothesley earl of
Southampton; Wriothesley was removed from the lord chancellorship
because of 'his overmuch repugnyng to the rest in matters of Counsaile' –
an assault on the corporate group responsible for the governance of the
realm.[37] Holinshed agreed.[38] John Foxe sidestepped the technicalities
and explained instead that the king needed support because he 'was but
of grene & tendre age comming to his crowne'. For Foxe Somerset's
principal qualification for the office of governor and protector was his
godliness, 'his favour to Gods word, worthy of his vocation and calling'.[39]
The establishment of the protectorate, then, was neither controversial
nor politically corrosive. It was presented by the Elizabethan writers as
a natural consequence of Edward's minority. The year 1547 became a
triumph of consensus.

Richard Grafton and Raphael Holinshed managed to balance a careful and measured presentation of John Dudley against a positive portray-
al of Edward Seymour. Grafton recorded Seymour's humility during
his trial, and even his speech on the scaffold managed to say something extremely constructive about the Edwardian achievement, deftly
sidestepping the issue of why he had to die at all.[40] On the day of his death,
Seymour declared, 'the state of Christian religion seemeth to drawe most
nere unto the forme of an order of the Primative Church', and in a second oration from the scaffold he exhorted the crowd to quietness and
obedience and wished the king's councillors the grace and favour of
God.[41] Richard Grafton and Raphael Holinshed presented a man loved
and mourned by the people – but not at the expense of the reputation of
John Dudley. Richard Grafton chose to remain silent on Dudley's trial
and execution. But even his fall could be presented in a rather positive
light. Holinshed recorded that John Dudley treated his judges with great
reverence, and professed his faith and allegiance to Mary, 'whome he
confessed greevouslie to have offended'. One element of his defence was
he had acted 'by authoritie of the princes councell, & by warrant of the
great seale of England', but his judges maintained that he should still be
tried for treason. Found guilty, he declared his 'earnest repentance', and
submitted himself to punishment with four requests: that he might have
the death of a nobleman; that Mary would be gracious to his children;

---

[37] Grafton, *Chronicle*, p. 1283.   [38] Holinshed, *Chronicles*, p. 979.   [39] *STC* 11222 (1563), p. 675.
[40] Grafton, *Chronicle*, p. 1316.   [41] Grafton, *Chronicle*, pp. 1318–19.

that a learned man could be appointed for the instruction and quieting of his conscience; and that the queen would 'send two of the councell to commune with me, to whome I will declare such matters as shall be expedient for hir and the common-weale'.[42] John Stow offered the same account in 1592.[43] The three Elizabethan chroniclers failed to mention Dudley's recantation of Protestantism, and Grafton clearly stated that the duke had been pardoned by Mary.[44]

For all the Elizabethan writers, the godliness of King Edward was beyond question. Holinshed explored indirectly the notion that if God had 'spared' Edward with a longer life 'he should have so governed this English common-wealth, that he might have beene comparable with any of his noble progenitors'.[45] Edward's death was the work of providence, of the 'secret counsell' of God; the king was translated from his own kingdom to God's because 'he was too good a prince for so bad a people'. For Holinshed, like John Foxe, Edward's care for his subjects was indistinguishable from 'the reformation of religion, wherin the kings care was exceeding great, as his desire to establish Gods glorie was zealous'.[46] It was the king, by the advice of his uncle the protector and his Privy Council, who 'myndyng first of all to seeke Gods high honour and glory, did therefore entend a reformation in religion'.[47] Edward sat at the centre of his kingdom, supported by godly men and a godly precociousness. His reputation for kindness, clemency, respect for justice, complemented by skills in Latin, French, Greek, Italian and Spanish, logic, natural philosophy, and music was established within ten years of Edward's death. But this represented more than godly saintliness: agency and responsibility were at stake. Holinshed condemned the subjects of the crown who had challenged royal authority because of the king's 'tender yeares' and believed, falsely, that Edward's 'roiall authoritie' had been 'usurped by others against his will and pleasure'.[48] England was *Edward's* kingdom and the Reformation definitively royal.

In the context of these pious and rather opaque Elizabethan accounts of Edward's reign, John Hayward's *The Life, and Raigne of King Edward the Sixt* (1630) must have struck its readers as a merciless dissection of Edwardian politics.[49] It was anything but hagiography. If Richard Grafton's account of the years between 1547 and 1553 was rather

---

[42] Holinshed, *Chronicles*, p. 1090.   [43] Stow, *Annales*, p. 1039.   [44] Grafton, *Chronicle*, p. 1326.
[45] Holinshed, *Chronicles*, p. 1084.   [46] Holinshed, *Chronicles*, p. 1082.
[47] Grafton, *Chronicle*, p. 1283; cf. the identical text in Holinshed, *Chronicles*, p. 979.
[48] Holinshed, *Chronicles*, p. 1084.
[49] John Hayward, *The Life, and Raigne of King Edward the Sixt* (London, 1630; *STC* 12998).

mechanical, and *Acts and Monuments* so dense as to be virtually unread-
able, Hayward explored faction, intrigue, and violence with the pace
of a political journalist. He subjected the reign to Tacitean dissection –
quite literally, because the model for Hayward's account of Edward's
reign was the English translation of *The annales of Cornelius Tacitus* edited
by Richard Grenewey and printed in 1598.[50] Dr Lisa Richardson has
reconstructed in fascinating detail the intimate relationship between
Hayward's text and Grenewey's translation, and she has argued that
Edward the Sixt was a Tacitean, rhetorical, political history of invented
speeches and borrowed characterizations.[51] Richard Grafton freely used
the proclamations, injunctions, statutes, and pamphlets he had produced as royal printer between 1547 and 1553. Hayward, on the other
hand, pieced together *Edward the Sixt* from Foxe, Holinshed, Stow, John
Speed, *The Expedicion into Scotlande* (1548) by William Patten, and even the
Catholic polemic of the Elizabethan exile Nicholas Sanders.[52] Hayward
incorporated two of his own publications: *A treatise of Union of the two
Realmes of England and Scotland* (1604) and *A Reporte of a Discourse Concerning
Supreme power in affaires of Religion* (1606). *The Life, and Raigne* was, after all,
an early Stuart book written in a seventeenth-century context.[53] But to
this imaginative – even eccentric – mix Hayward did actually add important Edwardian sources from the manuscript library of his friend Robert
Cotton. The most significant was Edward's journal, now part of the
Cotton collection in the British Library; another was a volume of papers
on the Anglo-French negotiations of 1550.[54]

   It may have been a coincidence that the journal of a king compared
by John Hayward to Nero was shelved in Robert Cotton's library near
the bust of that emperor, but according to Dr Richardson it was analogy
and context that guided Hayward in his deployment of Tacitus, and not
historical personality.[55] All the same, the result was the presentation of a
complex and rather brutal middle-Tudor court of self-interest, greed, ambition, and dissimulation. Hayward presented a composite John Dudley
of Tacitus' Nero, Sejanus, and Tiberius. Protector Somerset's tyranni-
cal characteristics were taken from, among others, Nero and Tiberius.
His wife Anne assumed the characterizations of the Roman imperial

---

[50] *The annales of Cornelius Tacitus. The description of Germanie*, trans. Richard Grenewey (London, 1598;
    STC 23644).
[51] Lisa J. Richardson, 'Sir John Hayward and early Stuart historiography', 2 vols., PhD dissertation,
    University of Cambridge (1999), pp. 192, 218–20.
[52] Richardson, 'Hayward', I, pp. 183–5.   [53] Richardson, 'Hayward', I, pp. 207–9, 212–13.
[54] Richardson, 'Hayward', I, pp. 183–4.   [55] Richardson, 'Hayward', I, p. 192.

consorts Livia, Messalina, Poppaea, and Agrippina.[56] William Cecil, John Cheke, and Richard Cox all took, at different times and in different forms, the characters of Seneca and (in the cases of Cheke and Cox) Sextus Afranius Burrus, both of whom were Nero's tutors.[57] This rhetorical matching of character to character and situation to situation was rather subtle – Hayward was not comparing Edward VI to Nero in a conventional sense, merely taking from Tacitus situation and dialogue – but it was political nevertheless. The account of Edwardian politics in *The Life, and Raigne of King Edward the Sixt* marked an important change in perceptions of the reign and its political dynamics. Hayward himself disapproved of the Edwardian Reformation, its iconoclasm, and (as far as he was concerned) its precarious legal standing. Unlike Foxe, Grafton, and Holinshed, he saw at the root of Reformation in the late 1540s and early 1550s factious councillors.[58] This was a king heavily dependent on – even restrained by – the political establishment around him. Edward was 'so farre from governing his Lords that he was scarce at his owne liberty'.[59]

Some later commentators challenged the accuracy of John Hayward's presentation of the reign of Edward. One editor reprinted *Edward the Sixt* in 1706 as part of *A Complete History of England*, but he corrected mistakes, pointed out problems with Hayward's chronology, tried to challenge the wrong done to Protector Somerset, blamed *Leicester's commonwealth* for a distorted characterization of John Dudley, and even suggested that 'our Author' had 'dressed up and improved by his own Eloquence' Edward's speech to the French ambassador in 1551.[60] John Strype agreed, complaining that Hayward was 'apt to give ill Characters, especially of Protestant Church-men, and others that were chief Favourers of the Reformation'.[61] But other writers embraced Hayward's account of the reign. For Jeremy Collier, in *An Ecclesiastical History of Great Britain* (1708–14), Hayward was a historian of the first rank. So was Peter Heylyn, the biographer of Archbishop William Laud, whom Collier quoted with assurance. Unlike Hayward's eighteenth-century editor Heylyn failed to notice that the source for an account of vicious competition between Catherine Parr, the queen dowager, and Anne Seymour duchess of

---

[56] Richardson, 'Hayward', I, pp. 194–6.   [57] Richardson, 'Hayward', I, p. 198.
[58] Richardson, 'Hayward', I, p. 221.   [59] Richardson, 'Hayward', I, p. 223 and n. 239.
[60] White Kennett, *A Complete History of England: with the Lives of all the Kings and Queens thereof; From the Earliest Account of Time, to the Death of His late Majesty King William III*, 3 vols. (London, 1706), II, pp. 276–319; cf. Hayward, *Edward the Sixt*, p. 127.
[61] John Strype, *Historical Memorials, chiefly Ecclesiastical*, 3 vols. (London, 1721), II, p. 20.

Somerset was actually difficult to discover.[62] Hayward had constructed it from two sources: from Tacitus, modelling the struggle for precedence between the two women on the quarrel of Agrippina and Domitia Lepida; and from Nicholas Sanders' hostile *De origine ac progressu schismatis Anglicani* (1587).[63] Similarly, Hayward's account of John Dudley's sinister 'diligence' about the sick king 'to espie . . . the state of his health' influenced eighteenth-century accounts of Edward's death, which began to hint that Dudley was responsible for his demise.[64] The line came from Tacitus' account of the emissaries sent by Piso 'to espie' the condition of Germanicus.[65]

For the most part late seventeenth- and eighteenth-century writers found the Edwardian political world created by John Hayward both familiar and accessible. Their vocabulary was a contemporary one, and they imposed it fairly indiscriminately on the politics of the 1540s and 1550s. Court 'Grandees', 'open Factions', 'the Opposite Party', 'Impeachment', 'Ministry', 'Creatures', 'Interest' were all commonly used by commentators like Peter Heylyn and Jeremy Collier. According to Heylyn both Edward Seymour and John Dudley built parties at court and led open factions. The king, as a consequence, was 'prey' to party.[66] Court and Council became battlefields of faction. Collier had Dudley establishing a party 'Interest' in the Council, and wrote of him as a man in the ascendant at court.[67] Even John Strype, critical of the veracity of Hayward's *Edward the Sixt*, described John Dudley's use of the 'King's Cost' to build up his 'Interest'.[68] The Edwardian court was rapacious. Courtiers and 'politicians' enriched themselves, and this 'spoil' and 'rapine' soon became, in the minds of writers from Heylyn to David Hume, closely associated with the opportunities and abuses of royal minority. Jeremy Collier did his best to present a serious constitutional critique of the establishment of Edward Seymour's protectorate in January 1547, but a page later he argued that the kingdom had divided itself into

---

[62] Peter Heylyn, *Ecclesia Restaurata; or the History of the Reformation of the Church of England* (London, 1661), pp. 70–2; Kennett, *Complete History of England*, II, p. 301.

[63] Hayward, *Edward the Sixt*, pp. 82–3; Richardson, 'Hayward', I, p. 198; II, pp. 205–6.

[64] Peter Heylyn commented that Dudley discharged the king's physician and chose instead a woman to treat the king; David Hume reported that the king's health declined 'from the time that lord Robert Dudley had been put about him, in the quality of gentleman of the bedchamber'. Heylyn, *Ecclesia Restaurata*, p. 139; David Hume, *The History of England under the House of Tudor*, 2 vols. (London, 1759), I, p. 343.

[65] Richardson, 'Hayward', I, pp. 199–200.   [66] Heylyn, *Ecclesia Restaurata*, p. 142.

[67] Jeremy Collier, *An Ecclesiastical History of Great Britain, Chiefly of England*, 2 vols. (London, 1708–14), II, p. 312.

[68] Strype, *Historical Memorials*, p. 423.

two parties, one 'willing Religion should continue upon the present Foot; the other press'd for a farther *Reformation*'.[69] Heylyn was less forgiving. 'Next comes a *Minor* on the Stage, just, mild and gracious; whose Name was made a Property to serve turns withall, and his Authority abused (as commonly it happeneth on the like occasions) to his undoing.'[70]

For Heylyn the reign of Edward was 'sufficently remarkable for the Progress of the *Reformation*; but otherwise tumultuous in it self, and defamed by Sacrilege, and so distracted into Sides, and Factions'.[71] It was religion, just as much as politics, that helped to form the response of seventeenth- and eighteenth-century writers to the Edwardian halfdecade, and even to the king himself. Edward's reputation became a weapon in the armoury of religious polemic. Although Heylyn included in his *Ecclesia Restaurata* all the classic elements of praise for the king – his final prayer, Jerome Cardanus' enthusiastic character sketch, references to Edward's 'Publick Works of Piety' – his 'excellent Abilities' were measured against the sacrilegious destruction and 'Unfortunateness of his Condition' during his minority.[72] A reasonable assessment, perhaps; but in 1682 one writer took exception to Heylyn's comments and likened them 'to the ravings of one of *Baal*'s *Priests*'.[73] Heylyn was Laud's man, and *Ecclesia Restaurata* was read by some – quite correctly – as an open attack on the Edwardian Reformation and the godliness of the king.[74] Edward's own words – his manuscript treatise against the papal supremacy – were used to demonstrate that 'This Pious King was the true *Defender of our Faith*, and under God and his Christ, the *Captain* of our Reformation'.[75] What followed was an exploration of Edward's 'well manag'd Zeal against Popery, and his full purpose of reforming the Nation from Idolatry, and Superstition'.[76]

One eighteenth-century writer who drew heavily on commentators like Heylyn and Collier, but found what they had to say about the nature of religion and politics in Edward's reign rather distasteful, was David Hume. In *The History of England under the House of Tudor* (1759) Hume cast

---

[69] Collier, *Ecclesiastical History*, p. 218.   [70] Heylyn, *Ecclesia Restaurata*, sig. a1v.
[71] Heylyn, *Ecclesia Restaurata*, p. 142.   [72] Heylyn, *Ecclesia Restaurata*, pp. 131, 140–1.
[73] *K. Edward the VIth His Own Arguments Against the Pope's Supremacy. Wherein several Popish Doctrines and Practices, contrary to God's Word, are animadverted on; and the Marks of Anti-Christ are applied to the Pope of Rome. Translated out of the Original, written with the King's own Hand in French, and still preserved. To which are subjoined some Remarks upon his Life and Reign, in Vindication of his Memory, from Dr. Heylin's severe and unjust Censure* (London, 1682), p. 107. Cf. MacCulloch, *Tudor church militant*, p. 210.
[74] MacCulloch, *Tudor church militant*, p. 210.
[75] *K. Edward the VIth His Own Arguments Against the Pope's Supremacy*, sig. {A5r}. MacCulloch, *Tudor church militant*, pp. 25–31.
[76] *K. Edward the VIth His Own Arguments Against the Pope's Supremacy*, p. 103.

his critical eye over a period of religious superstition and bigotry, fiscal rapacity and political violence, marked by the absolute and arbitrary power of the Tudor monarchs and, for Edward's minority, factional and party conflict. For Hume, the executors of 1547 were men who had been so reliant on the person of Henry VIII that they 'had no pretensions to govern the nation by their own authority' and accepted Somerset's protectorate as a proposal 'which seemed calculated for preserving public peace and tranquillity'.[77] This did not mean an absence of faction. Quite the opposite, in fact, because even during the arbitrary conditions of Henry VIII's reign factions had 'secretly prevailed'. It was unlikely that faction 'should be suppressed in the weak administration, which usually attends a minority'.[78] And yet Hume also used the events and personalities of 1547–53 to map important cultural forces. The repeal of statutes on treason, felony, and heresy in 1547 represented 'some dawnings, both of civil and religious liberty'.[79] Here the late eighteenth century met the late nineteenth. In his classic and popular *History of England* (1856–70), James Anthony Froude called Edward Seymour 'a believer in liberty' who 'imagined that the strong hand could now be dispensed with, that an age of enlightenment was at hand when severity could be superseded with gentleness and force by persuasion'.[80] A.F. Pollard may have taken issue with Froude on a number of serious methodological and historical matters – his reading of Edward's reign in the context of the Henrician inheritance, his refusal to acknowledge the 'sanctity of inverted commas', and his treatment of the Edwardian Church – but they united in their presentation of Protector Somerset as a lover of liberty.[81] Edward Seymour became a liberal hero, a subtle and complex mutation of the model of godliness John Foxe had promoted so enthusiastically.[82]

POLITICS AND CONSTITUTION

Historians of Edward's reign in the late nineteenth and early twentieth centuries inherited a complex historiography. A number of themes and

---

[77] Hume, *House of Tudor*, p. 289.   [78] Hume, *House of Tudor*, p. 290.

[79] Hume, *House of Tudor*, pp. 304–5.

[80] James Anthony Froude, *History of England from the fall of Wolsey to the death of Elizabeth*, 12 vols. (London, 1856–70), V, p. 3.

[81] A.F. Pollard, *England under Protector Somerset: an essay* (London, 1900), p. 319; on Froude and his methods, pp. 338–9.

[82] Ethan H. Shagan, 'Protector Somerset and the 1549 rebellions: new sources and new perspectives', *English Historical Review*, 114 (1999), pp. 34–63; and the subsequent debate between Shagan, Michael Bush, and George Bernard in *English Historical Review*, 115 (2000), pp. 103–33.

assumptions were deeply embedded in the literature. Perhaps the most important – and one that is deceptively easy to forget – is that royal minority was different from adult monarchy, and that the dynamics of politics assumed a distinctive form all of their own. This was a reign of divided, factional, and confessional politics, marked by the principal subjects of the king fighting for political power. But the work of historians like Froude and Pollard suggested that the reality was more complex than this, because helping to shape their model of Edwardian political life were three other forces or features. The first was the temptation still to read the reign in strongly moral terms, considering the individual reputations of key players like Protector Somerset who, for Froude, was ambitious but harnessed that ambition 'to do good'.[83] Some of these writers found it difficult to reconcile the appearance of religious liberty in the late 1540s and the destructive power of Reformation. 'Amidst the wreck of ancient institutions, the misery of the people, and the moral and social anarchy by which the nation was disintegrated', commented Froude, 'thoughtful persons in England could not fail by this time to be asking themselves what they had gained by the Reformation.'[84] Equally, forty years earlier, John Lingard had commented on the 'zeal' of the king's councillors 'stimulated by the prospect of reward'.[85] Were Edwardians liberal heroes or (to use a phrase familiar to Edwardians) 'caterpillars of the commonwealth'?

The second feature of the late nineteenth-century reading of the politics of Edward's reign was thoroughly Victorian in conception. In 1829 Sharon Turner had written of the Privy Council as a 'cabinet', with the protector 'and state counsellors' carrying on 'the efficient business of the government'.[86] Courtiers and councillors became (for Froude and Pollard) statesmen with policies to achieve, endowed with a notion of politics as the rational pursuit of effective government. Froude commented that for Protector Somerset 'to accomplish' his 'great purposes, he required a larger measure of authority'.[87] The account of Seymour's disposal of political opposition in the earliest days of the protectorate was sanitized to make it look, if not entirely acceptable, then certainly understandable, enabling the protector 'to make a more considerable innovation in the structure of the government'.[88] For Froude, the period

[83] Froude, *History of England*, V, p. 14. [84] Froude, *History of England*, V, p. 437.
[85] John Lingard, *A history of England*, 8 vols. (London, 1819–30), IV, p. 384.
[86] Sharon Turner, *The history of the reigns of Edward the Sixth, Mary, and Elizabeth*, 2 vols. (London, 1829), II, pp. 284, 224.
[87] Froude, *History of England*, V, p. 3. [88] Froude, *History of England*, V, p. 12.

after 1549 represented 'The Reformed Administration' because, as he
saw it, Somerset was the bad manager of an 'administration' marked by
waste and expense.[89] Even Pollard, whose 'essay' on Edward Seymour
was in part written as a response to Froude's reconstruction of the protectorate, presented the 'Principles and Methods of Government' as an
entirely rational business, marked by a movement towards 'constitutional
liberty'. The 'spirit' of this 'new administration' after 1547 could be found
in statute – principally in the Treasons Act of 1547 – and Protector
Somerset's relationship with the English parliament.[90] Somerset had
dealt with treason and heresy in a way that represented 'nothing less
than a revolution', but, like a good Victorian statesman, his 'administration' recognized the powers of parliament and protected freedom of
debate.[91] For Pollard, there was a connection between 'Government and
Parliament', with considerable overlap in membership of the Commons,
the king's chamber, 'and others who held important posts in what would
now be called the Civil Service, the Foreign Office, or the War Office'.[92]
The Privy Council was 'the pivot of the administration', comprehending
'every department of administration proper' and legislative and judicial
functions.[93] In his Stanhope Essay, published seven years after Pollard's
study, Lord Eustace Percy was tempted 'to pass over in silence' the actions of the Council between 1547 and 1553, but he recognized that,
in managing financial retrenchment and the defence of the realm, it
had done something to redeem itself.[94] Pollard was less critical. Unlike
late Victorian cabinets the Privy Council met very regularly, and its administrative and bureaucratic shape was clearly defined.[95] And yet the
'industry of the Council' was 'trifling' compared with that of Seymour,
who was 'guiltless of neglecting his public duties or of preferring his own
ease to the demands of the State'.[96]

A third feature of the Victorian historiography was the exploration of
the relationship between the king and the political establishment set up
around him. By the nineteenth and early twentieth centuries, the precocious godliness of Edward had transformed itself into an appreciation
of his exceptional intellectual ability. Froude sketched the character of a
king quite capable, in the closing years of his reign, of engaging himself in

[89] Froude, *History of England*, V, p. 224.
[90] Pollard, *Protector Somerset*, pp. 59–74; quotation at p. 59.
[91] Pollard, *Protector Somerset*, pp. 67–8.
[92] Pollard, *Protector Somerset*, pp. 74–5; quotation at p. 75.
[93] Pollard, *Protector Somerset*, pp. 76, 82.
[94] Eustace Percy, *The Privy Council under the Tudors* (Oxford and London, 1907), pp. 31, 34.
[95] Pollard, *Protector Somerset*, pp. 88–9.   [96] Pollard, *Protector Somerset*, p. 89.

the business of governance, 'gaining an insight beyond his years into the diseases of the realm, which threatened danger to those who had abused his childhood'. His interests extended to the realm's currency, debts, and the limiting of expenditure; scrutinizing the administration of the revenues, punishing fraud, and engaging with the business of the Privy Council. All of this was a fair reflection of the king's surviving writings in English, but as read by historians who judged kingship by the standards of bureaucracy.[97] Three years before the publication of Froude's volume on Edward, John Gough Nichols had offered an account of the king's exercise books in Latin and Greek, the key to his thoroughly classical and rhetorical education.[98] For the most part, however, historians have tended to consider Edward's intellectual and political maturity in the context of his introduction to the business of Council or the texts read by Froude. These have been edited as 'political papers' and yet, with one or two exceptions, they are rather uninspiring texts.[99] But Edward's education certainly introduced him to a political world beyond the administrative and the bureaucratic. One of the characters who helped to do this was, rather ironically, a clerk of the institutional Privy Council called William Thomas. Thomas was also an expert on the language and history of Italy, and he prepared for Edward some short written discussions strongly reminiscent of the themes of Machiavelli's *The prince*.[100]

A.F. Pollard wrote of a king 'released from the trammels of minority' in the early 1550s, but free only because of John Dudley's domination of 'the boy-king's mind' in a political 'scheme' subtler and more efficient than the protectorate.[101] For the Cambridge historian G.R. Elton, in *England under the Tudors* (1955), Edward was an inconvenience who, as king, 'could not be ignored and had to be persuaded'. His 'character and

[97] Froude, *History of England*, v, pp. 479–80.

[98] John Gough Nichols, ed., *Literary remains of King Edward VI*, 2 vols. (Roxburghe Club; London, 1857), I, pp. xl–xliv, 93–143; Loach, *Edward VI*, ed. Bernard and Williams, pp. 12–13.

[99] W.K. Jordan, ed., *The chronicle and political papers of King Edward VI* (Ithaca, NY, 1966), pp. xxiv–xxxiii, 159–90, mainly from British Library, Cotton MS Nero C 10, but also British Library, Lansdowne MS 1236 (fos. 19r–21r).

[100] William Thomas, *The historie of Italie, a boke excedyng profitable to be redde: Because it intreateth of the astate of many and divers common weales, how thei have ben, & now be governed* (London, 1549; *STC* 24018); and his *Principal rules of the Italian grammer, with a dictionarie* (London, 1550; *STC* 24020); British Library, Cotton MS Titus B 2 fos. 85r–90r. Thomas completed three written discussions, all of which survive in British Library, Cotton MS Vespasian D 18: 'Wheather it be expedient to varie with tyme' (fos. 2r–11v); 'What Princes Amitie is best' (fos. 12r–19r); and 'Wheather it be better for a common wealthe, that the power be in the nobilitie or in the commonaltie' (fos. 20r–27v). Cf. E.R. Adair, 'William Thomas', in R.W. Seton-Watson, ed., *Tudor studies* (London, 1924), pp. 143–4.

[101] A.F. Pollard, *The history of England from the accession of Edward VI to the death of Elizabeth (1547–1603)* (London, 1910), pp. 59–60.

views mattered a little' but 'his so-called opinions were those of his advisers, and his so-called acts were his endorsements of accomplished fact'.[102] Dale Hoak was just as dismissive: Edward may have been bright, even precocious; but his 'speeches' and papers, read by Jordan as the work of a boy on the 'threshold of power' in 1553, actually presented 'the somewhat pathetic figure of an articulate puppet far removed from the realities of government'.[103] 'Government' is the key word here. For many historians, the true test of the maturity of Edward's kingship was whether it could accommodate itself to the formal processes of government administration. Edward had to be introduced to established structures of a bureaucracy and a government that could operate with or without his direct supervision. In some accounts he appears almost as a nuisance (see below, chapter 5, pp. 164–5). This historiographical legacy has meant that our sense of Edward's operational kingship often depends heavily on accounts of his interaction with the institutional Privy Council. It has also meant that accounts of 1547–53 emphasize 'government' at the expense of politics (or, more usually, confuse them) and even tend to write Edward out of his own reign. The latest biography of the king, published in 1999, contends that Edward VI 'was obviously too young to rule himself and the history of his reign must therefore be the history of those who ruled in his name'.[104]

This has been one of the great assumptions of books on the politics of the reign. In *The government policy of Protector Somerset*, by Michael Bush (1975), Edward barely makes an appearance. It is a book that reads rather like a modern Civil Service account of the formal relationship between Downing Street, Whitehall, and local government. It explores the 'machinery' of a 'government' operating in a relatively harmonious and consensual political environment – for Bush, Protector Somerset shared the same political values as his colleagues – directed by one man with a 'government policy'. Or, rather, policies: Scotland, social policy in two parts (social reform and the 'government' response to the rebellions of 1549), religious policy, and 'The Policy towards Government'. This last chapter is perhaps the most telling. Bush conceived the governance of the localities in terms of 'the conciliar system of regional government'

---

[102] G.R. Elton, *England under the Tudors* (London, 1955), p. 202.
[103] Dale Hoak, 'Rehabilitating the duke of Northumberland: politics and political control', in Jennifer Loach and Robert Tittler, eds., *The mid-Tudor polity c. 1540–1560* (London and Basingstoke, 1980), p. 43; cf. W.K. Jordan, *Edward VI: the threshold of power. The dominance of the duke of Northumberland* (London, 1970), pp. 532–5; D.E. Hoak, *The King's Council in the reign of Edward VI* (Cambridge, 1976), pp. 120–5.
[104] Loach, *Edward VI*, ed. Bernard and Williams, p. 39.

and lords lieutenant. Because of Edward's minority the Privy Council 'became, inevitably, more formalized in its procedure and larger in its membership'.[105] 'In the history of governmental development' the years between 1547 and 1549 could not compare to the achievements of Elton's 1530s, but the foundation on which the 'Somerset government' rested was still one of law.[106] For Bush 'the declaration and enforcement of the government's will' came from the centre, shaped by parliamentary statute and proclamation.[107]

The King's Council in the reign of Edward VI, published a year after Michael Bush's study, is just as important in, and expressive of, the recent historiography. Elton had presented a reign beset by virulent 'faction struggles' resulting from 'the decay of good royal government in Edward VI's minority'. John Dudley was 'exceedingly ambitious of power and very greedy', and for Elton his regime demonstrated 'that the evils of factious magnate rule were reviving under this upstart nobility'.[108] Dale Hoak openly challenged this interpretation, classifying it as one of 'the fossilate remains of Tudor historiography'.[109] Although 'factiousness' still had a part to play in this revised model of Edwardian politics, it was a model shaped primarily by an appreciation of what, for Hoak, became the critical point of reference: the institutional Privy Council. During Edward's minority the Council made policy, governed, and exercised judicial power, so in Professor Hoak's thesis it played a central role in understanding the king's affairs.[110] It was the key to politics and governance for the reign in general but the years between 1549 and 1553 in particular. And yet the road was not an easy one to travel. Professor Hoak contended that Protector Somerset virtually abandoned the Privy Council and informally dispatched the king's business in his own household.[111] But after 1550, with the collapse of the protectorate, the Tudor Privy Council began to work to a fixed administrative routine.[112] The architect of this transformation was John Dudley, a man who, in understanding 'the requirements of the successful governor', recognized that the future of governmental reform lay in a Council possessed of full authority – and a Council closely controlled and managed.[113] In turn, the key to Dudley's dominance of the Privy Council was the office of lord president. As lord president he could act as the 'lieutenant' of

---

[105] M.L. Bush, *The government policy of Protector Somerset* (London, 1975), p. 127.
[106] Bush, *Government policy*, p. 128.   [107] Bush, *Government policy*, p. 131.
[108] Elton, *England under the Tudors*, p. 209.   [109] Hoak, *King's Council*, p. 3.
[110] Hoak, *King's Council*, pp. 1–2.   [111] Hoak, *King's Council*, p. 260.
[112] Hoak, *King's Council*, p. 265.
[113] Hoak, *King's Council*, p. 266; cf. Hoak, 'Northumberland', p. 36.

the crown in the institutional body, ordering, directing, and organiz-
ing, with William Cecil as his operational manager.[114] But in 1982, in
the light of the work of David Starkey, Professor Hoak recognized that
the Edwardian Privy Chamber held the key to John Dudley's seizure
of 'the machinery of government' and not, as he had originally argued,
Dudley's presidency of the Council – at least in the very early days of his
ascendancy.[115]

Dale Hoak's approach to the politics of Edward's reign – even politics
with the Privy Chamber put back – was essentially structural. Verbal
contact with the king and access to the royal apartments became institutional issues in a model of kingly governance that appeared on the
surface to acknowledge the notion of personal monarchy but stripped it
of its mystical and cultural resonances. Edwardian politics became bu-
reaucratized, with politics effectively limited to Council and conceived
almost exclusively as opposition to, and the control of opposition by, the
regime.[116] Although the shape of the Privy Council was affected by these
'political' forces – and of course the determination of John Dudley to
control the machinery of government – the business of governance was
essentially institutional in nature. Politics was the awkward bit, bureaucratic efficiency the great achievement. This was part of a governmental narrative for the sixteenth century. After all, John Dudley restored
and reorganized 'methods of government-in-council in England', and in
doing so he established 'administrative precedents' that would later be
followed by Elizabeth I's privy councillors.[117]

These institutional and structural explorations of the politics of
Edward's reign shared a common faith in the Eltonian orthodoxy that,
in England's transformation from 'a medievally governed kingdom' to
a modern sovereign state, the sixteenth century in general – and the
1530s in particular – played a critical role.[118] Elton's thesis (particularly
its association of Thomas Cromwell with the 'revolutionary' 1530s) was
profoundly controversial and shaped the landscape of Tudor historiography for nearly half a century.[119] The vocabulary used by Elton to

---

[114] Hoak, 'Northumberland', pp. 37–8; Hoak, *King's Council*, pp. 97–8, 104–6, 142–4.
[115] Dale Hoak, 'The king's Privy Chamber, 1547–1553', in DeLloyd J. Guth and John W. McKenna,
eds., *Tudor rule and revolution* (Cambridge, 1982), p. 87.
[116] Hoak, *King's Council*, pp. 231–58; Hoak, 'Privy Chamber', pp. 92–4, 100–2.
[117] Hoak, 'Northumberland', pp. 30–1.
[118] G.R. Elton, *The Tudor revolution in government* (Cambridge, 1953), p. 3.
[119] Christopher Coleman and David Starkey, eds., *Revolution reassessed: revisions in the history of Tudor
government and administration* (Oxford, 1986); John Guy, 'General introduction', in John Guy, ed.,
The Tudor monarchy (London, 1997), pp. 1–8.

describe this process of governmental revolution dominated the lexicon of Tudor political history, as the work of historians like Michael Bush and Dale Hoak demonstrated very clearly. Elton explored a 'machinery of government' that operated on the principle of 'bureaucratic organiza-tion' in the place of the personal control of the king, and 'national man-agement' rather than the 'management of the king's estate'.[120] Beneath personal monarchy, Elton argued in 1953, there lay a 'national foun-dation' – 'a nation at last fully conscious of its nationhood' – that ex-pressed itself in administrative or bureaucratic form.[121] Although Elton subtly revised his position over the course of the next thirty years, the essential features of this constitutional model remained unchanged. According to Elton, the Council governed the kingdom on behalf of the crown, and so the interaction between the monarch and his council-lors could be read, if necessary, in exclusively administrative terms.[122] Because the king asked the institutional Council for advice, and the in-stitutional Council enforced policy on his behalf, governance became a bureaucratic exercise that subordinated kingship and politics to a formal, legally coherent, and recognizable 'Tudor constitution'.[123] In-deed, for Elton, royal counsel-taking – arguably Tudor politics at its source – was properly limited to the sworn members of the institutional body.[124]

So for many years historians of Tudor politics worked with two basic assumptions. The first was that the notion of what it was to be a king, or to exercise monarchical authority, could be defined almost exclusively in terms of the bureaucratic machinery of a developing English state. The second assumption was that the key to understanding the nature of Tudor politics lay in the reconstruction of an institutional 'framework' of government: in statics rather than dynamics and in the 'formal' dimen-sions of government rather than the 'informal'.[125] This is an issue that late medievalists, as well as early modernists, have had to contend with historiographically. John Watts has pointed out that for 'administrative' historians of the fifteenth century 'who discuss it in detail, government

---

[120] Elton, *Tudor revolution in government*, p. 4.   [121] Elton, *Tudor revolution in government*, p. 4.
[122] G.R. Elton, ed., *The Tudor constitution: documents and commentary* (Cambridge, 1982 edn), pp. 88–94, 102–5.
[123] Elton, ed., *Tudor constitution*, p. 102.
[124] G.R. Elton, 'Tudor government: the points of contact. II. The Council', *Transactions of the Royal Historical Society*, fifth series, 25 (1975), p. 197. Cf. John Guy, 'The rhetoric of counsel in early modern England', in Dale Hoak, ed., *Tudor political culture* (Cambridge, 1995), pp. 292–310.
[125] David Starkey, 'Tudor government: the facts?', *Historical Journal*, 31 (1988), p. 931; Stephen Alford, 'Politics and political history in the Tudor century', *Historical Journal*, 42 (1999), pp. 535–9.

tends to be seen as an essentially uncontroversial and bureaucratic exercise, carried out to a large extent by professional administrators under the king's general command'.[126] One expression of this 'administrative history' of the middle ages was the work of T.F. Tout in the 1930s. Tout, in turn, had informed Elton's reading of the centuries before 1500 and his appreciation of the operation of government. In a discipline dominated in the post-war years by Elton, Tudor politics became extremely difficult to separate from the institutional and administrative structures of 'central government'.[127]

One result of this has been that for fifty years historians of the fifteenth and sixteenth centuries have worked on their subjects in radically different ways. Another is that Tudor historians have inherited an excessively institutionalized model of how government *should* have worked in the sixteenth century, even to the point of distorting our understanding of what 'politics' actually was. This 'constitution' has forced on the complex, sophisticated, and multilayered culture of politics and governance the straitjacket of bureaucracy, and, as a result, Tudor historians have developed some bad habits. The king's (or queen's) principal secretary is often referred to in secondary literature as a 'Secretary of State', and holders of crown office are sometimes described as 'civil servants'. Institutions at the centre – parliament, Privy Council, the courts of finance and of justice – have tended to overshadow the nature of local governance in county and parish.[128] Historians can also forget that in spite of the institutional identity of the monarch's privy councillors, the principal role of these men was to offer counsel to their monarch, affecting and shaping the royal will as well as supervising the governance of the realm. And yet, at the same time, kingship both in theory and in practice was not an exact science and could very easily extend beyond the administratively and bureaucratically definable. There was more to counsel than a signature on a Council warrant, just as there was more to politics – political relationships and conventions or expectations of political behaviour – than Council. Political historians of the Tudor century should disabuse themselves of the notion that institutional structures can tell the whole story.

---

[126] John Watts, *Henry VI and the politics of kingship* (Cambridge, 1996), p. 81.

[127] For a discussion of the historiographical inheritances of the fifteenth and sixteenth centuries, see S.J. Gunn, *Early Tudor government, 1485–1558* (Basingstoke and London, 1995), pp. 2–5.

[128] Two distinguished exceptions are Steve Hindle, *The state and social change in early modern England, c. 1550–1640* (Basingstoke and London, 2000), and Penry Williams, *The Tudor regime* (Oxford, 1979).

How, then, should we reconstruct the politics of Edward VI's reign? The intention of *Kingship and politics* is to sketch some of the directions in which historians might wish to go, but, like any book, it cannot hope to provide all the right answers – or even ask all the right questions. Again, like any book, it does have a duty to respond to the existing historiography, both in its exploration of the dynamics of the reign – *Kingship and politics* emphasizes continuity and stability rather than factional instability – and in its presentation of how Tudor politics actually worked. English politics in the sixteenth century was not solely, or even primarily, institutional. Formal bureaucracies undoubtedly played an important part in the governance of the realm; but, as the medievalist K.B. McFarlane wrote, institutions 'are born, develop, change, and decay by human agencies. Their life is the life of the men who make them.'[129] Politics was a point of interaction, the point at which the men who governed the Tudor polity, the beliefs and assumptions that informed their political lives, and their institutional inheritance actually met. Politics was shaped by character and personality, expectations of political behaviour, and the complex relationship between the vocabulary of politics as expressive of thought and belief and the practice of politics.

One good example is the nature of Edward Seymour's protectorate. Historians have often argued that between 1547 and 1549 the Privy Council lost its policy-making role to Edward Seymour and the men around him in his household. In part this thesis is an extension of the Eltonian orthodoxy that the Council sat (or *should* have sat) at the centre of politics and governance, but it is also a reflection of the notion of the 'corporate' supervision of the realm proposed by Henry VIII for his son's minority. Here, a *political history* of 1547–49 can clash with an institutional or administrative account of government. Somerset was the governor of the king's realm, dominions, and subjects, empowered by the king and the king's councillors to exercise monarchical authority: this power, in itself, has been difficult for some historians to reconcile with the formal provisions of the Tudor constitution. The Council certainly claimed that, as the 'body' and 'state' of the king's 'counsel', the protector's power was conditional on their authority.[130] But just as significant in the breakdown of trust between Protector Somerset and his colleagues was his unwillingness to take coun*sel* rather than his practice of acting without the Coun*cil*, because Seymour had 'litle ... esteamed

---

[129] K.B. McFarlane, *The nobility of later medieval England* (Oxford, 1997 edn), p. 280.
[130] SP 10/9 fos. 59r–61v (9 Oct. 1549; Knighton 405); cf. *A Proclamacion, set furth by the body and state, of the Kynges Majest[y]s privey Counsayle* (London, 10 Oct. 1549; *STC* 7829).

the grave advise of all his Majesties good and faithfull Counsailors'.[131] 'Constitutionally', Somerset's powers as protector were seriously ambiguous, shaped by his colleagues' expectations of good governorship. Underpinning the claim of Somerset's colleagues that they merely wanted Edward put back in the proper context of kingship was the notion that the governor and protector had betrayed his duty of tutorial care to the king. He had failed to exercise power properly and definitively, and broken a code of political behaviour – a cultural code of depth and resonance (discussed in greater detail below, chapter 3, pp. 69–75). Comparable is John Dudley's remarkable exploration of the nature of his service to king, commonwealth, and country, written in part as an appreciation of his father's service to Henry VII.[132]

Reading Edwardian politics in strictly formal, constitutional terms does have its limitations. In his biography of John Dudley, David Loades contrasted Protector Somerset, who relied 'upon the constitutional powers bestowed by his letters patent', with Dudley, who had 'no patent, and no defined constitutional position'.[133] The difficulty here is that Dudley's ascendancy looks so much more constitutionally acceptable than the protectorate. (The conventional response to this, of course, is that Dudley formalized his position during his lord presidency of the Council.) Loades' study of John Dudley is a hybrid, in which the insights of historians of noble affinity and clientele are grafted on to a traditional high political narrative.[134] For Professor Loades, Dudley was a financial and political opportunist, skilful and amoral. He was not a dangerous and overmighty subject. And yet, in spite of being a man who relied on the strength of his own personality, Dudley finally and fatally miscalculated his political environment and underestimated 'the forces of conventional morality'.[135] But the political world of David Loades' *Northumberland* is still the world of Elton and Hoak, driven by a politics conceived institutionally and constitutionally.

[131] *A Proclamacion set forth by the state and bodie of the Kynges Majesties Counsayle now assembled at London, conteinyng the very trouth of the Duke of Somersets evel Government, and false and detestable procedings* (London, 1549; *STC* 7828).
[132] SP 10/15 fos. 137v–138r (to William Cecil, 7 Dec. 1552; Knighton 779).
[133] David Loades, *John Dudley, duke of Northumberland, 1504–1553* (Oxford, 1996), pp. 192–3.
[134] See, for example, Simon Adams, 'Baronial contexts? Continuity and change in the noble affinity, 1400–1600', in John L. Watts, ed., *The end of the middle ages? England in the fifteenth and sixteenth centuries* (Stroud, 1998), pp. 155–97; Simon Adams, 'The Dudley clientele, 1553–1563', in G.W. Bernard, ed., *The Tudor nobility* (Manchester and New York, 1992), pp. 241–65; and G.W. Bernard, 'The downfall of Sir Thomas Seymour', in Bernard, ed., *Tudor nobility*, pp. 212–40.
[135] Loades, *Northumberland*, p. x.

The latest explorations of Edward's reign are, in quite different ways, rather more sensitive to the culture of politics and religion in Edward's reign, but Jennifer Loach's biography of Edward, edited by George Bernard and Penry Williams, still offers a conventional narrative account of the reign. One of the limitations of the book is its assumption that the aristocratic and material culture of the Edwardian court – a culture impressively reconstructed – is somehow incompatible with the presentation of Edward as an authentically 'godly' king.[136] Here, Diarmaid MacCulloch is more persuasive, and his *Tudor church militant* presents a convincing and impressive account of Edward as a thoroughly committed evangelical monarch supported by men in church and state who shared similar aims. Continuity is one of the themes of Professor MacCulloch's account of the reign. So too is the legacy of the Edwardian Reformation.[137] I have tried to position *Kingship and politics in the reign of Edward VI* somewhere between *Edward VI* and *Tudor church militant*. The book tries to pay serious attention to the cultural dimensions of the politics of 1547–53, but does so without the narrative drive of *Edward VI* and the instinctive need to define politics solely in institutional terms.

Kingship and politics will, I hope, complement the existing literature and offer some new insights into the importance of the Edwardian half-decade. The book tries to sketch some of the networks of kin, friendship, and association that can be used to explain the distinctive shape of the Edwardian polity, at court, in the household of Protector Somerset, in the universities, in the legal establishment, or in the printing profession. Sometimes it has been difficult for historians to take the reign seriously because of its reputation for faction or rapacity, but this is an issue of historiography rather than history. The profound limitations of the historiography are thrown into dramatic silhouette by the depth and sophistication of Edwardian political culture – at times too sophisticated, falling short of the practical realities of minority monarchy, but rich and diverse nevertheless, conscious of the potential of kingship both in theory and in practice. This was a political world in which culture and governorship, kingship and practical politics *did* meet, with profound implications for the second half of the sixteenth century. And at the core of this sophisticated and complex polity was the person and office of the king.

[136] For example, Loach, *Edward VI*, ed. Bernard and Williams, pp. 180–1.
[137] MacCulloch, *Tudor church militant*, esp. pp. 21–36.

King and kingship

Few monarchs in English history could have been more aware of what their subjects expected of them than Edward VI, a king who was given a formidable classical and rhetorical education, surrounded by counsellors and preachers committed to impressing upon him the duties of his office. Royal minority certainly had its problems – the second half of this chapter examines some of the issues Edwardians faced in matching their boy-king to the authority of Tudor monarchy – but the conditions of childhood also allowed the governing elite to mould Edward in their own image. Court preaching certainly played a central role in Edwardian culture, although not to the exclusion of other influences – Edward was a king whose social and educational experiences were rich and varied – but still absolutely formative in shaping expectations of what it was to be king. Some of the sources for a reconstruction of Edwardian kingship have been lost (or indeed never were sources in the way that historians understand them): Edward's notes on the sermons he heard at court, for example, or conversations in the king's Privy Chamber and private readings with his tutors. Nevertheless, this chapter seeks to answer three questions. How would Edward have understood the nature of the office he held? How did Tudor kingship adapt to confront the practical and intellectual challenges of royal minority? And did the regime convince the subjects of the crown that reforming, Protestant monarchy was a legitimate proposition?

KINGSHIP

Edwardian kingship was not a limited, court-centred affair. Worshippers in parish churches, and assiduous readers of English Bibles and cheap editions of sermons preached at court or at Paul's Cross, were left in no doubt of the nature of their society and the powers and responsibilities of their governors – and the contribution they themselves were expected to make in the great corporate endeavour of returning England to the true religion. Godly Reformation became inseparable from kingship, and governance could be understood scripturally. John Day's Bible (1549) included 'A Table of the principall matters conteyned in the Byble, in which the readers maye fynde and practise many commune places', working from 'abhomination' through to 'zeal'. A careful reader would find that the commonwealth flourished when the righteous reigned (Proverbs 28:12), and was kept by good counsel, and not by tyranny and force (Proverbs 11:14). A righteous king was the strength of his realm (Proverbs 29:2). Subjects should honour the king (1 Peter 2:17), and kings, in turn, should use mercy. But it was clear from the example of Jeroboam that there were disastrous consequences for a king who countenanced idolatry (2 Kings 17:18–23).[1] Print put kingship in the public domain. Bishop Hugh Latimer's editor, Thomas Some, explained in his introduction to Latimer's sermons that they were 'frutefull and godlye documentes, directing ordinatly not only the steps, conversacyon, and lyving of kynges: but also of other mynisters and subjectes under him'.[2] Some revealed that the texts of many philosophers had been saved from 'the tyrannye of oblivion, to the great and hygh profette of countryes, of commen wealthes, of empyres, and of assemblies of men', and Latimer's sermons were no exception.[3]

Printed sermons are some of the best sources on the Edwardian ideal of kingship, precisely because godly editors like Thomas Some recognized the importance of the preaching of men like Latimer, John Hooper, Thomas Lever, and John Ponet at court, from Paul's Cross, and in their dioceses. Latimer, famously, preached in Lent 1549, very specifically on the office of king. The preachers 'before the kynges majestye' in Lent 1550 were Hooper on Wednesdays, Ponet on Fridays, William Bill, Latimer, and Thomas Lever of St John's College, Cambridge.[4] These were men

---

[1] *The Byble, that is to say all the holy Scripture: In whych are contayned the Olde and New Testamente* (London, 1549; *STC* 2077), sigs. {bb3v}, {bb6v}.

[2] Hugh Latimer, *The fyrste Sermon of Mayster Hughe Latimer, whiche he preached before the Kynges Majest[y] wythin his graces palayce at Westmynster M.D.XLIX. the viii. of Marche* (London, 1549; *STC* 15270.7), sig. a3r.

[3] Hugh Latimer, *The seconde Sermon of Maister Hughe Latimer, whych he preached before the Kynges majestie, within his graces Palayce at Westminster the .xv. day of Marche. M.ccccc.xlix.* (London, 1549; *STC* 15274.7), sigs. {a1v}–{a2v}; quotation at sig. {a1v}.

[4] Susan Brigden, ed., 'The letters of Richard Scudamore to Sir Philip Hoby, September 1549– March 1555', *Camden Miscellany XXX* (Camden Society, fourth series, 39; London, 1990), p. 124 (2 Mar. 1550). All seven of Hooper's sermons survive (19 Feb.–2 Apr. 1550): John Hooper, *An oversight, and deliberacion upon the holy Prophete Jonas: made, and uttered before the kynges majestie, and his moost honorable councell, by Jhon Hoper in lent last past. Comprehended in seven Sermons. Anno .MD.L.* (London, 1550; *STC* 13763). Hugh Latimer preached on 2 Mar. 1550: *A moste faithfull Sermon preached*

on the fast track to impressive careers in church and college – Ponet was consecrated bishop of Rochester in June 1550, Hooper nominated for Gloucester that July, and Lever master of St John's from 1551 – and the sermons they preached were important and popularly attended occasions at Whitehall. Some of the texts were printed, often with letters of dedication to the king and epistles of explanation for the reader, and so they really worked on two levels. The first, of course, was that Edward and his court experienced them directly. The second, just as significantly, was that these remarkably powerful sermons were available to the king's subjects to read and discuss privately or in small groups. When Edwardian preachers spoke on the duties of king and councillors their audience extended far beyond Whitehall and Paul's Cross.

To understand these preachers' vision of commonwealth and king – and to offer just a flavour of the sermons Edward experienced from his seat overlooking the preaching place at Whitehall Palace – it might be interesting to travel on a short textual journey through some of the sermons preached by Hooper, Latimer, Ponet, and Lever in the three weeks between Wednesday 26 February and Friday 14 March 1550. The scriptural foundation for Hooper's seven sermons (5 February–2 April) was the Book of Jonah, which describes the eventual success of a flawed man, the preacher Jonah, in convincing the people of the Assyrian metropolis of Ninevah of the desperate need for their repentance. In his second sermon, on 26 February, Hooper preached on the nature of vocation, and used his text to explore 'the office of the kyngs magestye, hys councell, and al his Magistrates' in seeing 'the true boke of God the holye Byble to be tawghte and receyved of hys magesties subjects' as a protection against idolatry. The regal prototypes for this sort of reforming, supervisory kingship were Moses, Joshua, David, Jehoshaphat, and Josiah, all 'Noble Princes of goddes people'.[5] Here, Hooper compensated for one of the limitations of the Book of Jonah as a text – Jonah was a reluctant but

---

before the Kynges most excellente Majestye, and hys most honorable Councell, in hys Courte at Westminster, by the reverend Father Master Hughe Latimer (London, 1550; *STC* 15289). Thomas Lever's sermon of 9 Mar. 1550 was printed as *A Sermon preached the thyrd Sondaye in Lente before the Kynges Majestie, and his honorable Counsell, by Thomas Leaver* (London, 1550; *STC* 15548). And Ponet's sermon of Friday 14 Mar. 1550 (the only volume in the Lenten series of 1550 not printed by John Day and William Seres): *A notable Sermon concerninge the ryght use of the lordes supper and other thynges very profitable for all men to knowe preached before the Kynges most excellent Mayestye and hys most honorable counsel in hys courte at Westmynster the 14. daye of Marche, by Mayster John ponet Doctor of dyvinity. 1550.* (London, 1550; *STC* 20177). For the significance of the Lenten sermons, see Peter E. McCullough, *Sermons at court: politics and religion in Elizabethan and Jacobean preaching* (Cambridge, 1998), pp. 52–3, 56–7.
[5] Hooper, *Oversight*, sig. {DIV}.

effective preacher rather than a reforming king – but he also used Jonah the sinner to expose the dangers of sin to a commonwealth. The men who cast lots to detect Jonah's sin realized that the 'desperate daunger' they faced could come only from the anger of God.[6] Detecting and removing sin meant peace, joy, and quietness in the commonwealth. The commonwealth was Jonah's ship, and so, when the ship of the commonwealth was troubled, its master – 'the Kynge with his counsell' – should 'inquire deligentelye of the authours of the trouble, or else the tempeste of trouble shal never cease'.[7]

John Hooper pointed to many Jonahs who were aboard the ship of the English commonwealth: idle noblemen, rich lawyers, bishops and priests who defended superstition and neglected their true duties, and an idle commonalty.[8] 'Repent and amende', cried Hugh Latimer four days later. 'But how long hast thou England thou England?'[9] Covetousness was the root of all evil and the root of rebellion, in an England scarred by the sins of adultery, whoredom, and lechery.[10] But there were many Jonahs to reveal to 'declare unto you gods threatnings'.[11] For Latimer it was Jonah the preacher who secured the repentance of the Ninevites, living in a city threatened with destruction for its sin. In England preachers preached many long sermons 'and yet the people wyl not repent nor convert'.[12] Jonah's sermon was short, and yet the Ninevites 'beleved Gods Preacher, Gods Offycer, Gods Minister Jonas, & wer converted from theyr syn'.[13] It was the duty of the preacher to warn the people of God's wrath and hold them to account – a notion that had important implications for the relationship between king and preacher (see below, pp. 41, 43).

The examples of Jonah's preaching, and the repentance of the Ninevites, worked their way into the sermon of the third Sunday of Lent (9 March) 1550 preached by Thomas Lever, 'For the tyme is even nowe comynge, when as God muste needes eyther of his mercy here in Englande, worcke suche a wonderfull miracle unto our conforte . . . or els of his righteousnes take such vengeaunce of this land to thexample of all other landes.'[14] Plagues destroyed men when God's Word truly preached was not believed, received, and followed. At the preaching of Jonah, the Ninevites 'repented wonderfully'. And when the book of the Law was read to King Josiah, he and his people speedily repenting found

[6] Hooper, *Oversight*, sig. {D2v}.   [7] Hooper, *Oversight*, sig. {D3v}.
[8] Hooper, *Oversight*, sigs. {D5r–v}, {D6r–v}.   [9] Latimer, *Moste faithfull Sermon*, sig. B3r.
[10] Latimer, *Moste faithfull Sermon*, sig. B4r, B1r.   [11] Latimer, *Moste faithfull Sermon*, sig. {B4r}.
[12] Latimer, *Moste faithfull Sermon*, sig. {A3r}–A3v.   [13] Latimer, *Moste faithfull Sermon*, sig. A3r.
[14] Lever, *Sermon preached . . . before the Kynges Majestie*, sig. A2r.

mercy, blessing, and grace.[15] For Lever – as for Hooper and Latimer – national repentance rested with the rulers and governors of the kingdom. 'The wynges of God be stretched abrode here in Englande, by the kinges gracious majestye and hys honorable counsel . . . their ordynaunce, rule, & governance . . . is the power, the wings & the honor of god.'[16] Lever believed that Edward, endowed with the faithful diligence of King David, was ordained by God to govern, cherish, and feed the people of his realm.[17] But it was the responsibility of all the 'heade Rulers and governors' of England, *Principes Anglie*, first to amend their own faults and then to see to all 'under offycers'.[18] Repentance (and Reformation) had to be total and led by the example of governors.

The duties of the king and his subjects were conceived nationally, internationally, and providentially. In the epistle to Edward that prefaced the published sermons on Jonah, John Hooper underlined the importance of kings and princes who 'set forthe unto their subjectes the pure, and sincere religion of the eternal God'.[19] Jehu's removal of idolatry and idolatrous priests (2 Kings 9) was one of the scriptural examples Hooper presented to a king and his counsel seeking 'the glorye of God and the restitucion of hys holye and Apostolycall churche'.[20] The king's age – and here Hooper exposed one of the most important and sensitive issues facing the Protestant governors of the kingdom (see also below, pp. 49–50) – did not matter. Evil men might say that 'As long as the kynge is in hys tender age hys councell shulde do nothinge in matters of religyon', but that was foolishness and malice. God's Word taught that a king 'in hys younge age wyth hys wyse and godlye counsell shoulde abolyshe Idolatrye, and sette forthe the true, & godly religyon of the living God'. The prototypes were Josiah (2 Kings 22–23) and Joash (2 Kings 11–12).[21] The people of England had been – but were no longer – 'oppressed wyth the vyolente and cruel tyrannye of Antychryste' because young Edward had continued the work of his father.[22]

John Hooper wrote those words in September 1550; before the king, on 14 March, five days after Lever's Lenten sermon, John Ponet had preached before the king on the Antichrist of Rome and the nature and purpose of the Tudor royal supremacy. God's holy Word had been

[15] Lever, *Sermon preached . . . before the Kynges Majestie*, sig. A2v.
[16] Lever, *Sermon preached . . . before the Kynges Majestie*, sigs. {a3v}–{a4r}.
[17] Lever, *Sermon preached . . . before the Kynges Majestie*, sig. B4r{–v}.
[18] Lever, *Sermon preached . . . before the Kynges Majestie*, sig. C3r.   [19] Hooper, *Oversight*, sig. {✠2v}.
[20] Hooper, *Oversight*, sig. {✠3v}.   [21] Hooper, *Oversight*, sigs. {✠4v}–{✠5r}.
[22] Hooper, *Oversight*, sigs. ✠4r, {✠5v}–{✠6r}.

trodden under foot, and 'The chefe & arche capitayn tread worde is the Antichristian Bushope of Rome', who trod on the Bible as he said mass as a token that he and his ministers had an authority greater than that of scripture (see also below, chapter 4, pp. 105–15).[23] Ponet exposed the arguments of the treaders and stampers of the Word of God. He balanced the false papal claims of authority against scriptural endorsement of Edward's title of supreme head of the Church. Working from the notion that the Roman Church could not err, he treated his royal and noble audience to a logical syllogism of the sort he had once used at Paul's Cross.[24] Whoever believed that the king was not supreme head of the Church was a traitor; but whoever argued that the Roman Church could not err concluded that the king was not supreme head. *Ergo*, whoever said that the Roman Church could not err was a traitor. Similarly, whoever believed the bishop of Rome to be supreme head of the Church was a heretic; but whoever said that the Roman Church could not err concluded that the bishop of Rome was its supreme head. *Ergo*, whoever claimed that the Roman Church could not err was a heretic.[25] This was logical proof both of Edward's supremacy and of the false claims of Rome. Men should not be blinded by Antichristian talk devised by Romish ministers.[26]

In those three weeks of Lent 1550, Edward VI was exposed to the duties, obligations, implications, and historical and providential dimensions of his own kingship. His part in the great battle against Antichrist had been explored in a book translated by John Ponet in the autumn of 1549, a book which, like *An oversight, and deliberacion upon the holy Prophete Jonas*, sat on the shelves of the royal library (see below, chapter 4, pp. 114–15). The Lenten sermons clearly established that Edward's kingly duty was to extend to his people the Word of God, and in doing this he was supported by the godly men around him and by the regal prototypes of the Old Testament, as scriptural proof of God's endorsement of Reformation. There was no room for complacency. England had to repent of its sins, but it was reformable (Ninevah, of course, was saved). The English commonwealth was a society out of order, and its restoration – and repentance – depended on a king who led by godly example. Although the preaching of men like Lever and Latimer, powerful in its condemnation of sin and private gain before common good, may look modern, social, and radical, it actually 'underwrote the social

---

[23] Ponet, *Notable Sermon*, sigs. {E4v}–E5r.   [24] Ponet, *Notable Sermon*, sig. {F6r}.
[25] Ponet, *Notable Sermon*, sig. {F6v}.   [26] Ponet, *Notable Sermon*, sig. {F7r}.

and political order, offering no challenge to it'.[27] Restoration was the key, not social revolution. Little wonder that Edward himself wrote in English (like the preachers he heard) on his spiritual and temporal responsibilities as king, his encouragement of an active, preaching ministry for bishops, and his duty to restore order and hierarchy to the commonwealth.[28] But there was a tension. The Homily on Obedience of 1547 explained to Edward's subjects that 'Every degre of people, in their vocacion, callyng, & office, hath appoynted to them, their dueties & ordre'.[29] It also called on them to pray for kings and rulers who followed 'the moste faithfull kynges and capitaines in the Bible, David, Ezechias, Josias, & Moses, with such other'.[30] This was a conservative vision of a hierarchical and ordered society, working efficiently and effectively, but governed by a radically reforming, active, godly king.

The purpose of society was to worship God properly. In the year he preached before the king (but in a book that had a distinguished printing history) John Hooper explained that the second Table of the Ten Commandments 'prescrybed howe, and by what meanes, one man may lyve wyth an other in peace and unyte, in thys Civile lyfe'.[31] Although many writers had prescribed laws to govern and keep the people 'in a politike felicite' – Lycurgus the Spartan, the Greeks Solon, Plato, and Aristotle, the Romans Numa, Pompey, Cicero, and others, the Christians Constantine and Justinian – the origins and nature of society were best understood scripturally.[32] God had gathered together His people into one company and multitude, brought them out of Egypt, and given to them a land and cities 'where they shoulde lyve, as membres of one commune wealthe'. God had prescribed two laws 'wythoute the whych, no commune wealthe, can long indure'. The first was that the people should

---

[27] Patrick Collinson, *The birthpangs of Protestant England: religion and cultural change in the sixteenth and seventeenth centuries* (New York, 1988), p. 18. Three of the best examples of this critique of a commonwealth 'out of order' were preached by Hugh Latimer in 1548 and Thomas Lever in 1550: *A notable Sermon of the reverende father Maister Hughe Latemar, whiche he preached in the Shrouds at paules churche in London, on the .xviii. daye of January. 1548* (London, 1548; *STC* 15291); *A fruitfull Sermon made in Poules churche at London in the shroudes the seconde daye of February by Thomas Lever: Anno .M.D & fiftie.* (London, 1550; *STC* 15543); and *A Sermon preached at Pauls Crosse, the .xiiii. day of December, by Thomas Lever. Anno .MD.L.* (London, 1550; *STC* 15546.3).
[28] British Library, Cotton MS Nero C 10 fos. 113r–117v, printed in W.K. Jordan, ed., *The chronicle and political papers of King Edward VI* (Ithaca, NY, 1966), pp. 159–67.
[29] 'An exhortacion, concernyng good ordre and obedience, to rulers and magistrates', in *Certayne Sermons, or Homelies, appoynted by the kynges Majestie, to be declared and redde, by all persones, Vicars, or Curates, every Sondaye in their churches, where they have Cure* (London, 1547; *STC* 13640), sig. R1r.
[30] *Certayne Sermons, or Homelies*, sig. {S4r}.
[31] John Hooper, *A Declaratyon of the ten holy commaundementes of almyghtye God ... with certayne newe addisions made by the same maister Houper* (London, 1550; *STC* 13750.5), sig. {H4v}.
[32] Hooper, *Ten holy commaundementes*, sig. {H4v}.

know how to reverence and honour Him as 'the presidente, & the defender' of all cities and realms.[33] The second law was that the people should live in peace and concord without discord and dissension.[34] In order to protect against disorder, the Law of God instituted 'a certayne Imperye, and dominion, to be had among hys people'.[35] This superior power, in England, was the king, whose duty it was to love the members of the commonwealth as a father loves his children.[36] Civil governance lay in the king living well himself, observing mercy and justice, punishing vice, and extolling virtue.[37] 'The princes ar called reges, a regendo, that is to say. They are called kynges whych name commith of a verbe that sygnifyeth to governe, they must lead the people, and them selfes by the law, and not agaynst the lawe.'[38]

Edwardian writers and preachers agreed with John Hooper that the exercise of governing authority was made possible by the obedience of subjects to it. The king was God's lieutenant, His representative on earth.[39] As St Paul put it, in the most ubiquitous text on obedience to rulers, every soul had to submit himself to the authority of the higher powers because the 'powers that be are ordeyned of God'. Resisting governors meant resisting God; and resisting God meant damnation. The 'power' was the minister of God for the wealth of His people, and he bore the sword to take vengeance on those that did evil.[40] The power of kings and rulers was unequalled, and because of this magistrates were called gods (Psalm 82:1, 6–7).[41] But this was not unlimited or unaccountable power, because the exercise of authority was indistinguishable from the king's responsibilities both to God and to his realm. The superior power was appointed to govern to be God's vicar, to execute *His* law, *His* will, *His* pleasure, and to bring men to God. God could, and did, punish governors who failed properly to execute their duties because, as ministers, they were the earthly representatives of divine power. If a king became arrogant and proud, wrote Hooper, 'let hym remember Sainte Paules wordes, that he is *but* a minister'.[42] Thomas Lever concluded a long epistle to Edward's privy councillors by reminding them that it

---

[33] Hooper, *Ten holy commaundementes*, sig. {H5r}.   [34] Hooper, *Ten holy commaundementes*, sig. {H5v}.
[35] Hooper, *Ten holy commaundementes*, sigs. {H5v}–{H6r}.
[36] Hooper, *Ten holy commaundementes*, sig. I2r.   [37] Hooper, *Ten holy commaundementes*, sig. {I3r}.
[38] Hooper, *Ten holy commaundementes*, sig. {I3v}.
[39] William Thomas, *The vanitee of this world* (London, 1549; *STC* 24023), sig. B6r–v.
[40] Romans 13:1–7: *The Byble*, New Testament, sig. N2r. Cf. John Hooper, *Godly and most necessary Annotations in the .xiii. Chapyter too the Romaynes: Set furthe by the right vigilant Pastor, Jhon Hoper, by gods calling, Busshop of Gloucestre* (Worcester, 1551; *STC* 13756).
[41] Hooper, *Annotations*, sig. {B6v}.   [42] Hooper, *Annotations*, sig. {C4v}, with my emphasis.

was not their own worthiness 'but Goddes grace' that had placed them 'in hygh authority, and in the same aucthoritye not your owne powers and polycy, but the myght and wisdome of God'.[43] The Homilies of 1547 quoted Proverbs 8:15–17, which identified God as the 'onely aucthor and provider' of order in society: 'through me, kynges do reigne: through me counsailors make just lawes, through me, doo princes beare rule, and all judges of the yearth execute judgement: I am lovyng to them, that love me'.[44] Earthly authority was under constant supervision. Anthony Gilby (later one of the translators of the Geneva Bible) reminded the readers of his commentary on the Prophet Micah that God witnessed the 'dooynges' of the king in his private apartments and councillors in their chamber. 'No Kynge, no Courte, no Emperoure, no Poope, Prelate shal woorcke so pryvelye, but thys Lord shal espye and se, shal both wytnes and judge al their doinges.'[45]

So kings were accountable, but not to their subjects. In the Tower of London, on Christmas Day 1549, John Hooper preached a sermon on responsible government, 'entreatyng upon a salme of kyng Davyd, havyng occasyon therby to speke ageynst governours that mysordered theyr vocacyons, perswadyng that God punysshed rulers for theyr synnes'. Sometimes God allowed the ungodly to replace rightful rulers because of the sins of the people, and subjects' 'unjuste and unfaythfull dealynge' with princes caused the plagues of hunger, dearth, and pestilence.[46] And yet obedience was more or less unconditional, and Edwardian commentators maintained, as Hooper put it in 1551, 'let the king & Magistrate be as wicked as can be devysed and thought, yet is his offyce & place the ordinaunce & appointment of god, and therfore to be obeyed' – a notion that exercised the minds and pens of Protestants during the years of Marian exile (see below, chapter 6, pp. 177–84).[47] But even passive disobedience was ambiguous. Latimer argued that if the king made an unjust request for taxation, his subjects were 'bounde to paye it, and not resyste nor rebel against the king'. The king put his soul in peril if he made unjust demands on his subjects, and God would 'in his due tyme reken with him for it'. But the monarch had to be obeyed because it was God, rather than subjects, who judged the king.[48] St Paul may have hated Nero and Caligula, explained John Hooper, but he 'loved

[43] Lever, *Sermon preached at Pauls Crosse*, sig. {A8r}.   [44] *Certayne Sermons, or Homelies*, sig. R2r.
[45] Anthony Gilby, *A commentarye upon the Prophet Mycha. Wrytten by Antony Gilby* (London, 1551; *STC* 11886), sig. B1r–{v}.
[46] Hugh Latimer, *A Sermon of Master Latimer, preached at Stamford the .ix. day of October* (London, [1550]; *STC* 15293), sig. {E2v}.
[47] Hooper, *Annotations*, sig. {B7r}.   [48] Latimer, *Sermon . . . preached at Stamford*, sig. E2r–{v}.

the polycie and lawes of Rome and never taught sedicion'. Obey the superior powers, he added, 'where they commaund the[e] nothing agaynst
Goddes lawes' – an ambiguous statement with implications for the later
1550s.[49]

The king possessed full temporal authority, complemented and reinforced by the obligation he had to remove false and superstitious practices, plant true and godly religion, and maintain those who profited the
Church and Christ's flock.[50] Royal power was absolute and it could not
be limited in a physical sense. In 1551 Hooper suggested that 'the king
him self, is bound to be obedient unto the lawe, & unto God, where as
the lawes be not contrary to the law of god and the lawe of nature' but
this law was God's Law, communicated through scripture.[51] A familiar
and important text was Deuteronomy 17:14–20, in which 'Moyses him
selfe, speaking of the institucion of a kynge saieth, that he ought to be
with the law, and to reade in it all the daies of his life'.[52] Edmund Becke
discussed Deuteronomy 17 in the epistle to Edward in John Day's Bible
of 1549. Day's 'Table' of commonplaces explained that 'The kyng ought
to read the boke of Deuteronomye, that is to say, the lawe of God, and
to kepe hym to that only.'[53] John Hooper treated it as a text in which
it was written what the king should be and what he should and should
not do.[54] Deuteronomy 17 underpinned Hugh Latimer's sermons before the king and his court in Lent 1549.[55] It was a text which illustrated
and defined the godly kingship of Edward VI (see Fig. 1; also chapter 6,
pp. 179–82).

Although royal power was unlimited, it was necessarily defined and
shaped by the Word of God. Edwardian preachers argued that it was
part of their ministry to hold God's temporal ministers to account for
their actions. For Hugh Latimer, preaching before Edward in 1549, God
had two swords, one temporal and the other spiritual. The temporal
sword rested in the hands of kings and magistrates, and their authority
extended over all their subjects, 'as wel the Cleargy as the laite'. The
spiritual sword was in the hands of ministers and preachers 'wher unto all
Kynges, Majestrates, Rulers oug[h]te to be obediente, that is, to here, and
folowe, so longe as the ministers syt in Christes chayre, that is speakynge

---

[49] Hooper, *Ten holy commaundementes*, sig. 11 r. [50] Hooper, *Annotations*, sigs. C4v–C5r.

[51] Hooper, *Annotations*, sig. B2v. Cf. William Thomas: 'he that governeth accordyng to the lawes,
is trulie a kyng and lawfull lorde' and that the king who departed from the laws was a tyrant.
Thomas, *Vanitee of this world*, sig. B6v.

[52] Thomas, *Vanitee of this world*, sig. B7r. [53] *The Byble*, sig. AA5r; Table, sig. BB5v col. 1.

[54] Hooper, *Ten holy commaundementes*, sigs. 12r–{13v}.

[55] Latimer, *Fyrste Sermon*, sigs. B1 r–{D8r}; Latimer, *Seconde Sermon*, sig. B1 r–{v}.

Fig. 1   The frontispiece to Thomas Cranmer's Catechism (1548), showing Edward
enthroned, handing the Bible to his bishops. The text above the woodcut reads
'The Kyng ought to be feared as the roaryng of a Lyon, who so provoketh him unto
anger, offendeth against his owne soule' (Proverbs 20:2). And below it: 'Let not the
booke of this law depart out of your mouthes. But recorde there in daye and nyghte, that
you maye do accordynge to all that is wrytten therin' (Joshua 1:8; Deuteronomy 17:19).

out of Christes boke'. The preacher could correct the king with the spiritual sword, 'fearynge no man, settinge God only before hys eyes under whom he is a minister to supplante and roote up all vice and myschyefe by Goddes worde'.[56] 'It should not offende the Magistrates to bee reprehended by the preacher of the lawe of God', explained Hooper, 'but rather take it in good parte, and thanke God that he hath one, to admonyshe hym of yle in tyme.'[57]

It is a profoundly significant comment on the kingship of Edward VI that arguments like Latimer's and Hooper's were acceptable, even standard, in the late 1540s and early 1550s but anathema to his half-sister Elizabeth twenty or thirty years later.[58] This was kingship at its most complex, absolute but accountable, unlimited but underpinned and informed by the written Word of God (scripture) and by the spoken (the preacher). Kingship was a ministry of God, which made it at once immensely powerful and utterly accountable. But accountable to whom? Hooper, Latimer, and their colleagues claimed to God only. And yet although the king's preachers spoke from Christ's Chair, they were still men. So was it possible to place human limits on what kingship was or could and should achieve? Arguably so, but the full implications of a kingly power accountable to the true Word of God in the form of Protestantism were worked out only in the later 1550s. But the ambiguities do not end there. The English political system of the sixteenth century depended for its survival on the willingness of one man to perform the duties of monarchy, and to exercise monarchical power definitively but also responsibly. How could a king be trusted? What, apart from the punishment of God, could possibly encourage him to discharge his duty of care? How could the profound burden of monarchy be shared?

The preachers before Edward in 1549 and 1550 regularly referred to the king and his Council (or counsel) collaboratively performing the necessary duties of governance and Reformation. Counsel was a critical component of Tudor, and especially Edwardian, kingship (see below, pp. 46–8, 63–4). But a king was expected to govern and regulate himself, guided by God's Word, which 'shalbe wyth him and he shall read therin all dayes of hys life that he may learne to feare the lord his God for to kepe al the wordes of this lawe' (Deuteronomy 17:19). This was an issue of public record, both in scripture and, more indirectly, in the Homilies

---

[56] Latimer, *Fyrste Sermon*, sig. A6r–{v}, with some punctuation added. Cf. the notes to Latimer's text, Matthew 23:1–3, in *The Byble*, New Testament, sig. c4r (col. 1).

[57] Hooper, *Ten holy commaundementes*, sig. {13v}.   [58] McCullough, *Sermons at court*, pp. 48, 76–8.

of 1547. Governing subjects involved effort and application. Temporal authority was ordained by God, and it was the duty of governors to act with suitable responsibility: 'therfore they are here diligentely taught, to apply themselfes, to knowledge & wisedom, necessary for the orderynge of Gods people, to their governaunce committed'.[59] The foundation of this self-governance was education, and Edward VI's tutors – John Cheke, Richard Cox, Jean Belmaine, and (more informally) Anthony Cooke – believed that it was impossible to separate learning from the duties of kingship. Nicholas Udall, the Edwardian editor of Erasmus, agreed. The ideal was a realm blessed by the government of philosophers or of kings who had given themselves to philosophy. Kings dedicated to philosophy were committed 'to the due knowledge of God, to the discipline of vertue, and to that upryght execucion of their office towards all people'.[60]

Edward received a formidable education in classical literature and rhetoric. Not all the sources survive – his notes on Aristotle's *Rhetoric* and *Politics*, for example, or his thoughts on Sallust and the other historians his tutors read to him – but a good number do.[61] The course of study Edward pursued mirrored the curriculum of the best contemporary grammar schools and Cheke's teaching at Cambridge in the 1530s.[62] The king was, naturally, grounded in Latin grammar and vocabulary (1544–45), concentrated very closely on Cicero (1548–50), learned Greek (1549–50), read Plato and Demosthenes (1551–52), and began to write on theology (1552). His work brought him into close contact with the leading humanists of the time. In 1552 Roger Ascham reminded William Cecil that 'by myn especiall good master Cheekes means, I have bene caulled to teache the king to write in his privie chambre'.[63] Cecil, himself a pupil of Cheke in Cambridge and a former lecturer in Greek at St John's College, had worked with Edward on a rhetorical exercise on paper only four days earlier.[64] This rhetorical component of Edward's education was critical. After spending the first five months of 1548

[59] *Certayne Sermons, or Homelies*, sig. R2r.
[60] Desiderius Erasmus, *The first tome or volume of the Paraphrases of Erasmus upon the newe testament, conteinyng the fower Evangelistes, with the Actes of the Apostles* (London, 1551; *STC* 2866), sig. *2r.
[61] Some of the contents of Edward's exercise books were printed by John Gough Nichols, ed., *The literary remains of King Edward VI*, 2 vols. (Roxburghe Club; London, 1857), I, pp. 93–143, and are reconstructed in fascinating and intricate detail by Paul S. Needham, 'Sir John Cheke at Cambridge and court', 2 vols., PhD dissertation, Harvard University (1971), I chapter 4, 'Educating the King' (pp. 172–230).
[62] Needham, 'Cheke', I, p. 175.   [63] British Library, Lansdowne MS 3 fo. 3v (27 Sept. 1552).
[64] British Library, Cotton MS Nero C 10 fo. 73r–v (23 Sept. 1552).

working through Cicero's *De officiis*, and the summer and autumn reading *De amicitia, Paradoxa Stoicorum*, and the *Tusculan disputations*, Edward began to write *chreias*, or moral essays.[65] These were the preliminary exercises, *progymnasmata*, outlined by the ancient Greek rhetorician Aphthonius: carefully structured – from praise of an author to arguments for and against the author's dictum – and the essential grounding for an orator to declaim *in utramque partem*, 'in two parts' *pro* and *contra*.[66] By 1550, in his early teens, Edward was working through Greek and Latin texts, taking notes on Thursdays and delivering orations on Sundays.[67] In February 1551 he delivered an oration on Plato's *Republic*, and spent the rest of the year reading Demosthenes (*First Olynthiac, First Philippic*, and *Peace*) and the Cicero canon.[68]

What were the benefits of this classical and rhetorical education? Cheke was in no doubt. He reminded Edward of his training in virtue and good learning, complemented, Cheke hoped, by the service of men who would 'faithfullye, trewlye, and playnlye' give him counsel.[69] Tutor and pupil had read together 'dyvers discourses of dyvers sortes, as well of stories, as of philosophie', and these had given Edward grave and wise rules for the good governance of his realm. For Cheke, the principal guide was Aristotle, 'to whome I beseach you, for those matters, often to resorte'. Particularly relevant were two chapters from the *Politics*, 'the one *de mutatione regni*, etc. and the other *per quae regna servantur*'. The tenth and eleventh chapters of Book Three outline types of kingship and critique the king who acts according to his own will.[70] Learning, Cheke told Protector Somerset, should be a quality in men who entered the service of the king. But just as (if not more) important was the king whose wisdom could be complemented by an education of practical relevance. Edward had learned that the ground of all error was 'that self-pleasing which the Greekes do call *pilautia*; when a man delighteth in his own reason, and despyseth other mens conseill, and thincketh no mans foresight to be so good as his, nor no mans judgment compared to his owne'. Wisdom lay in 'conferringe with many wise heads, and of divers good counsells'. This was an important lesson for all but

---

[65] Needham, 'Cheke', I, pp. 180–7.
[66] Needham, 'Cheke', I, pp. 188–9; Quentin Skinner, *Reason and rhetoric in the philosophy of Hobbes* (Cambridge, 1996), pp. 29–30, 35.
[67] Needham, 'Cheke', I, p. 207.   [68] Needham, 'Cheke', I, pp. 214–16.
[69] John Harington, *Nugae Antiquae: being a miscellaneous collection of original papers, in prose and verse; written during the reigns of Henry VIII, Edward VI, Queen Mary, Elizabeth, and King James*, ed. Thomas Park, 2 vols. (London, 1804), I, pp. 17–18.
[70] Harington, *Nugae Antiquae*, ed. Park, I, p. 20.

particularly for Edward, because faults were greater in a king than in 'meane men'.[71] Cheke wanted his king to be an academic: slow to judge, glad to hear all men, mistrusting his own reason, taking truth to be hidden and so not to be found at first sight, realizing that wisdom lay in men of experience.[72] Edward learned that the sure safeguard of wisdom and happiness was the avoidance of the fault pointed out by Cicero in *De officiis*: taking things on trust and flattering ourselves that we know more than we really do.[73]

COUNSEL, SUPREMACY, AND SOVEREIGNTY

Moulding and shaping Edward as king was one of the more prominent features of Edwardian political culture. As important, but far more problematic, was the nature of the relationship between the king and his counsellors or ministers. Counsel, the process of advising the monarch, was a major element in the practical governance of kingdoms.[74] In western European political culture and thought, counsel represented a crucial point of contact between governor and governed, even sanctioning the exercise of political power. In the early fourteenth century, for example, it was possible to argue that public power could not be exercised legitimately without the advice of the principal men of the community.[75] But how could the subjects of the middle Tudor crown offer advice? And was the Tudor model of counsel, underpinned by the notion of a single sovereign individual, profoundly unsuited to the practical and intellectual limitations of royal minority?

Counsel meant participation, because offering advice to the king influenced the exercise of royal power. So the key to counsel, at least for a monarch, was balancing the need for advice against the importance of preserving the independence of royal power: counsel had to work on terms that suited the king. Consequently, important conventions governed its presentation. One of the best statements of this form of presentation survives in a book owned by Edward, *A tragoedie or Dialogue of the unjust usurped primacie of the Bishop of Rome* (1549). The book's author, Bernardino Ochino, presented a fictional scene from the reign of Henry VIII. In it Henry talks to a 'papist' and asks for the advice of Thomas

---

[71] Harington, *Nugae Antiquae*, ed. Park, I, pp. 44–5.
[72] Harington, *Nugae Antiquae*, ed. Park, I, p. 45.   [73] Harington, *Nugae Antiquae*, ed. Park, I, p. 46.
[74] John Guy, 'The rhetoric of counsel in early modern England', in Dale Hoak, ed., *Tudor political culture* (Cambridge, 1995), pp. 292–310.
[75] J.H. Burns, *Lordship, kingship, and empire: the idea of monarchy, 1400–1525* (Oxford, 1992), pp. 50–1.

Cranmer, who explains the reasons for England's separation from Rome. In need of counsel, Henry declares:

> We have sent for you in to oure presence . . . to resolve us of a dout, that is come to our minde. Therefore two thynges we requier of you, the one that everye of you saye hys mynde frankelye and frely, what he thinketh, without respecte of favoure or displeasure to any manne lyvynge. And the other, that ye kepe it secrete, and disclose not one worde of the thinges, that shalbe here reasoned. For it is a matter of great weight, & toucheth our honour, wherfore we charge you so longe to keepe counsell untill the truethe bee knowen, and that you have lycense of us to open it.[76]

This was the conventional vocabulary of counsel. Freedom of speech was balanced by confidentiality. Counsel touched the king's 'honour' because it could influence the king's exercise of his monarchical power and estate, so the royal invitation for counsel played a crucial part in the ritual. Unsolicited advice affected the delicate balance between subject and monarch: between the subject's duty to obey and the duty of the king to exercise sovereign authority. Counsel allowed the principal subjects of the king to participate in the affairs of his realm but only on conditions that allowed the crown to govern independently.

There are two other interesting Edwardian explorations of the nature of counsel. In 1548 Bishop Stephen Gardiner of Winchester offered one of the clearest conventional accounts of the relationship between the sovereign power of the king and the influence of the men around him. Gardiner explained that although 'the Kynges majestie or other supreme magistrates' used the advice of their 'Counsell', 'yet it may not be said that the Counsell is above the kynge'. The king should take the advice of his counsel 'above the rest'; but, once again, 'it may not be said that the counsaylles is of equall authoritie with the Kynge for ther is but on[e] Kynge'. Carpenters, physicians, and soldiers could all offer advice to the king, but the king was not bound by that advice. And yet, argued Gardiner, the 'regall dignitie' was always reserved. Although counsellors 'do take upon them to execute, the superioritie remayneth in the king'.[77] For Gardiner, even the controversies of national Reformation could be dealt with by asking for counsel. But the royal counsel he recommended was *papal* counsel in the settlement of the kingdom's religion, and this was one of the bishop's most unpalatable arguments. At Gardiner's trial

---

[76] Bernardino Ochino, *A tragoedie or Dialoge of the unjust usurped primacie of the Bishop of Rome*, trans. John Ponet (London, 1549; *STC* 18770), sig. Y2r.

[77] Corpus Christi College Cambridge, Parker MS 127 fos. 24–25. Cf. the text of the sermon in John Foxe, *Actes and Monuments of these latter and perillous dayes* (London, 1563; *STC* 11222), p. 774.

in 1550, William Cecil deposed that the king's supremacy and the bishop of Rome's authority were subjects the bishop should have avoided.[78]

The second exploration of the dynamics of counsel was sketched by the king himself in October 1551, weeks before his fourteenth birthday. Lord Chancellor Richard Rich had questioned the legitimacy of a letter from the Privy Council because it had been signed by only eight councillors. The Council's letter had accompanied a royal commission signed by Edward, and the king interpreted Rich's action as an assault on his sovereign authority and a distortion of the relationship between a monarch and his counsellors. In a draft letter to Rich prepared for the king, Edward explained that his authority was such 'that what so ever we shall do by the advise of the nombre of our Counsell attending upon our person' – even fewer than eight – had 'more strength and efficacye than to be put into question or doubt of the validite therof'. Although 'advise and good counsell necesserely becommeth the same wherunto also we will ever inclyne our selfe', the number of councillors did not make the king's authority.[79] Edward recorded privately that he 'marveled' that Rich had refused to deliver a letter 'willed by any on[e] about me to write'. Edward found it 'a great impediment for me, to send to al my councell, and i shuld seme to be in bondage'.[80]

Edward's exchange with Rich suggests that by 1551 he understood the relationship between counsel and sovereign power and could deploy its vocabulary in the politics of his reign. And yet, even here, some of the problems Edward's subjects faced begin to reveal themselves. For the model of counsel to work properly – for a healthy relationship to exist between the monarch and his political elite – the king had to preserve his independence and his integrity. This may have been (and I would argue actually was) increasingly possible in the early 1550s, but the years immediately after 1547 were a very different matter. Because of the peculiar conditions of Edward's minority in its earliest form, the king's uncle, rather than the king himself, held the key to the political dynamics of 1547–49. In October 1549 Protector Somerset's colleagues judged that he had acted inappropriately in discharging his duty to his royal charge and to the kingdom. Edward Seymour's failure to take counsel was one of the major themes of the war of words between the protector and his colleagues (see also below, chapter 3, pp. 70–2).

In the vacuum of minority Protector Somerset exercised authority as king. If the practice of offering advice to a monarch represented the key

<hr />

[78] Foxe, *Actes and Monuments*, p. [805].   [79] Knighton 555.
[80] British Library, Cotton MS Nero C 10 fo. 43r (Jordan, ed., *Chronicle*, p. 85).

to a healthy, consensual relationship between king and his subjects, it was even more incumbent on Edward Seymour to take counsel. A 'Discourse' prepared by William Paget in August 1549 offered humble counsel to the protector in the 'discharge both of my dewtie of conscience and also bond of service to my soveraigne and countrey'.[81] On Christmas Day 1548 he had tentatively offered advice to further Seymour's 'course in service until the Kings majesty be ready to receive the administration of his own things'; the aim was to encourage a wealthy and flourishing kingdom.[82] A week later, following the 'fashion of the world' by offering a New Year's gift to 'a personage of your estate', Paget presented Seymour with a 'scedule', 'wherein as in a glasse if your grace will dayly loke, by yt youe readye youe shall so well apparell your selfe as eche man shall delight to behold youe'. The schedule offered short *sententiae*, emphasizing mature deliberation, swift execution, impartial justice, the wisdom of ministers, punishment of the disobedient, and liberal rewards for the king's servants. Seymour was advised (among other things) to hear suits quickly, to accept rewards only from the king, to ensure that ministers were not corrupted, and to follow advice 'in counsaile'.[83] The protector's failure to act upon Paget's advice turned the counsellor into a Cassandra, a theme Paget introduced in February 1549 and referred to again in July of the same year. He would be sorry 'to lyve to be suche a one', he told Seymour: 'that is to saie, one that told the trouthe of daungers before and was not beleved'.[84] By summer, and with a grim sense of inevitability, he admitted his failure to counsel the protector. 'I was a Cassandra, I told your grace the trouthe, and was not beleved.'[85]

The king's subjects were certainly aware that Edward's minority did not put them in a unique historical position. One short and undated note in the Edwardian archives explained that Henry III had been six years of age at his accession, and Richard II ten. Henry VI was 'nott a yere olde', and so, at the beginning of his reign, parliament 'stablyched' the duke of Bedford as regent of France and the duke of Gloucester protector. Two men, the duke of Exeter and the bishop of Winchester, 'had the governanc[e] of hyme'.[86] Henry VI's minority did raise some uncomfortable issues for Edward's subjects. In 1548 Lord Thomas Seymour,

---

[81] Barrett L. Beer and Sybil M. Jack, eds., 'The letters of William Lord Paget of Beaudesert, 1547–63', *Camden Miscellany XXV* (Camden Society, fourth series, 13; London, 1974), p. 76.

[82] Barrett L. Beer, ed., 'A critique of the protectorate: an unpublished letter of Sir William Paget to the duke of Somerset', *Huntington Library Quarterly*, 34 (1971), p. 280.

[83] Beer and Jack, eds., 'Letters of William Lord Paget', pp. 19–20 (2 Jan. 1549).

[84] Beer and Jack, eds., 'Letters of William Lord Paget', p. 22 (2 Feb. 1549).

[85] SP 10/8 fo. 8r (7 July 1549).

[86] Hatfield House Library, Hertfordshire, Cecil Papers 150 fo. 33r–v.

the brother of Edward duke of Somerset, pointed to the fact that the powers of Henry's protector had been distinct from those of the governor of the king's person (see below, chapter 3, p. 95). But it was still possible to use the minority of Henry VI to positive effect. Edward Hall, for example, recorded a smooth and effective political transition from the royal majority of Henry V into the minority of his son. Henry VI's reign was a 'troubleous season', but the child was proclaimed king 'to the great rejoysyng and comfort of all the Englishe nacion'. According to Hall, the 'politike Princes and sage Magestrates of the realme of Englande' remembered the past, pondered the present, 'but moste of al prudentlye forseynge chaunces iminent and perels at hand, to thentent to set the membres of the body stedfast under the hedde'. Humphrey of Lancaster, duke of Gloucester became protector. Conscious of his responsibilities he 'called to hym wyse and grave counsaylers, by whose advise he provided and ordeined for all thynges whyche ether redounned to the honor of the realme, or semed profitable to the publique welth of the same'.[87]

And so, once again, counsel was the key: not in the conventional sense of advice requested by an independent and operational adult king but in the sense of structured, caring, and responsible support for a minor. This still sidestepped the lurking danger of manipulation and misgovernance. In his second court sermon of Lent 1549 Hugh Latimer explored the implications of the scriptural quotation 'Woo be to the Lande, to the Realme: whose Kynge is a childe' (Ecclesiastes 10:16). Some, he explained, maintained that this meant 'childish condicions', others that it referred to the 'age & yeres of Childehod'. When a king was in his minority, argued Latimer, the men who had governance about him had 'much lybertie to live voluptuously and licenciousli, & not to be in fear how they govern as they wold be yf the king wer of ful age, & then commonly they governe not wel'.[88] Latimer reconstructed the argument of the regime's opponents in their condemnation of godly Reformation carried out during a minority: 'Tushe, thys geare [matter] wyll not tarye, it is but my Lorde Protectours, and my Lord of Canterburyes doynge. The Kynge is a chyld, he knoweth not of it . . .'[89]

For Latimer and the regime, Edward VI's precocious godliness became one of the most significant buttresses in the defence of his authority as king. In 1549 Protector Somerset answered the first of Reginald

[87] Edward Hall, *The union of the two noble and illustre famelies of Lancastre & Yorke* (London, 1550; *STC* 12723), Henry VI sig. A1r–v.
[88] Latimer, *A moste faithfull Sermon*, sig. E7v.   [89] Latimer, *Seconde Sermon*, sig. C3r–v.

Pole's 'terrours', 'that the kinges Majeste is a child'. In age, it was true; but the young king was endowed with grace, supported by providence and the gift of God, and strengthened by 'faithfull, true, lovinge and well agreinge, counsellers and Subjectes'.[90] Somerset defended his nephew on two grounds. First, that God's punishment of England had been reflected in the failure of adult kings like Harold Godwinesson, Edward II, Richard II, and Henry VI. And second, Edward's subjects had put their trust in God, who was able to defend His 'elect vessell' against all his enemies 'aswell in Childhode as we trust his grace shall do in his Majestes mannes estate'.[91] The godly young king counselled, reforming his realm and ministering to his subjects, became a central feature of the political and religious culture of the reign.

Representations of the king in books and pamphlets served to underpin the principle that he was personally, but collaboratively, involved in Reformation. In the first edition of Hall's *Union of the two noble and illustre famelies*, the king's printer, Richard Grafton, shows Edward enthroned and taking counsel (see below, chapter 5, Fig. 10, p. 165). In John Bale's *Illustrium maioris Britanniae* (1548), a woodcut showed the author presenting his book to the king. The biblical translator Edmund Becke was similarly represented in John Day's Bible of 1551: Edward enthroned and surrounded by his courtiers and councillors accepted the text from Becke himself.[92] Even more significant was the frontispiece to Archbishop Cranmer's Catechism (1548), in which the king as emperor handed the Bible to his bishops (Fig. 1). Reinforced by scriptural texts from Proverbs (20:2), Joshua (1:8), and Deuteronomy (17:19), the woodcut held a double message. The king's duty lay in handing to his subjects the Word of God but, just as importantly, the Word defined and disciplined the king himself (see below, chapter 6, pp. 179–82). Edward was a godly monarch because he gave the Word of God to God's people *and* because he lived by it himself.

Comparisons with boy-kings of the Old Testament were particularly common.[93] Anthony Gilby wrote of the providential fashioning and

---

[90] SP 10/7 fo. 74v (4 June 1549; Knighton 265), printed in Nicholas Pocock, ed., *Troubles connected with the Prayer Book of 1549* (Camden Society, new series, 37; London, 1884), pp. vii–viii.
[91] SP 10/7 fo. 75r.
[92] Margaret Aston, *The king's bedpost: reformation and iconography in a Tudor group portrait* (Cambridge, 1993), pp. 86 (Bale), 159 (Becke).
[93] Aston, *King's bedpost*, pp. 26–36, 49–53; Christopher Bradshaw, 'David or Josiah? Old Testament kings as exemplars in Edwardian religious polemic', in Bruce Gordon, ed., *Protestant history and identity in sixteenth-century Europe*, 2 vols. (Aldershot, 1996), II, pp. 77–90; Diarmaid MacCulloch, *Tudor church militant* (London, 1999), pp. 62–3.

preservation of Edward in his mother's womb, and explained how, during the king's infancy, idols had been beaten down by the clear light of the gospel. Gilby compared Edward to 'the good yong King Josiah'.[94] At Edward's coronation, Thomas Cranmer addressed his king as 'a second Josiah', whose duty it was to promote the true worship of God, banish the tyranny of Rome, and destroy idolatry.[95] For Hugh Latimer, Josiah and his counterparts in the Old Testament proved that 'a kynge in hys chyldehode is a kynge, as well, as in any other age'. Boys of eight or twelve years of age had been called to kingship by the Holy Spirit.[96] Latimer argued that 'Josias & one or two mo though they wer chyldren yet had their realmes well governed and raigned prosperouslye'.[97] Nobility rather than age mattered: and nobility, in turn, depended on counsel and education.[98]

Intimately bound up with the model of Edward as a second Josiah was the Tudor royal supremacy. Cranmer explicitly linked the king's office as Christ's vicar within his own dominions to the second Josiah's reformation of the Church of God.[99] Edward VI inherited from his father three principles of kingship with profound implications for the governance of the polity. First, that a king of England exercised secular *imperium*. Second, that the English king was vicar of God in his own realm. And third, that the Church in England could separate itself from Rome.[100] Precedent was used in 1530 to argue that the spiritual and temporal power of the papacy had been granted by the emperor, and not by God; similarly, the argument ran, the sixth Council of Carthage (AD 419) had declared that no bishop could be called the 'universal bishop'.[101] The common lawyer Christopher St German chipped away at the notion of the Church's jurisdiction over more than spiritual matters.[102] Edward Foxe, in *De vera differentia* (1534), maintained that bishops were subject to

---

94 Gilby, *Commentarye upon the Prophet Mycha*, sig. LIv–L2r.
95 Henry Jenkyns, ed., *The remains of Thomas Cranmer*, 4 vols. (Oxford, 1833), II, pp. 118–20.
96 Latimer, *Seconde Sermon*, sig. C2r. His other example was Joash: 2 Kings 12.
97 Hugh Latimer, *A moste faithfull Sermon preached before the Kynges most excellente Majestye, and hys most honorable Council, in his Court at Westminster, by the reverende Father Master. Hughe Latymer* (London, [1553]; *STC* 15290), sigs. E7v–E8r.
98 Latimer, *Seconde Sermon*, sig. C2v.   99 Jenkyns, ed., *Cranmer*, II, pp. 118–20.
100 John Guy, 'Thomas Cromwell and the intellectual origins of the Henrician Reformation', in Alastair Fox and John Guy, *Reassessing the Henrician age: humanism, politics and reform 1500–1550* (Oxford, 1986), pp. 159–61; John Guy, 'The Henrician age', in J.G.A. Pocock, ed., *The varieties of British political thought, 1500–1800* (Cambridge, 1993), pp. 35–9.
101 Guy, 'Thomas Cromwell', p. 161; Graham Nicholson, 'The Act of Appeals and the English Reformation', in Claire Cross, David Loades, and J.J. Scarisbrick, eds., *Law and government under the Tudors* (Cambridge, 1988), pp. 22–3.
102 Guy, 'Thomas Cromwell', pp. 168–9.

kings. One of the major texts he deployed in defence of kingly authority was Romans 13:1–7.[103] Edwardian court preachers similarly emphasized the power of the king over all his subjects. Ecclesiastical laws that exempted 'ony spirituall' from the general rule that 'Every man be obediente to the higher power' were damnable and heretical, condemned by God's Word. Christ and his apostles had paid tribute 'and other dutyes' to the higher powers of the earth.[104]

Edward was an emperor. Printers used every opportunity to emphasize the power of imperial kingship in their editions of sermons, homilies and injunctions, and bibles, inheriting from the reign of Henry VIII the presentation of the king by artists like Holbein and the iconography of the Great Bible.[105] The English translation of Foxe's *De vera differentia* opened with the royal arms and an imperial crown.[106] John Oswen, the king's printer in the marches of Wales, deployed imperial iconography, with a representation of Edward enthroned, and the biblical verse 'Feare God. Honour the Kynge' (1 Peter 2:17), to reinforce *An Homelye to be read in the tyme of pestylence* by John Hooper (see Fig. 2).[107] During the rebellions of 1549, Day and his partner William Seres printed *A Copye of a Letter contayning certayne newes, and the Articles or requestes of the Devonshyre & Cornyshe rebelles*. The book bears an elaborate representation of the king's arms crowned, supported by angels, over which are the rose, the flower de luce, and the pomegranate; beneath the arms are the Beaufort portcullis, a feather, and a castle, and the royal motto 'Dieu et Mon Droyt'.[108] It was printed from an old block which in all likelihood predated Henry VIII's break with Rome (the pomegranate was the symbol of Catherine of Aragon), borrowed by Day from Richard Grafton, who had himself used it in 1547 (see below, Fig. 5, p. 120). But John Day was not content merely to borrow. From 1549 he included in his Bible his own contribution to Edwardian and Elizabethan iconography: a single sheet representing the imperial crown with the royal arms and Garter, reinforced by the motto 'O Lord for thy mercyes sake, save the Kyng. Feare God, and honour

---

[103] Guy, 'Thomas Cromwell', pp. 170–1.
[104] Hooper, *Godly and most necessary Annotations*, sigs. B2v–B3r. His texts came from Matthew 17:24–7 and 22:15–22 and Romans 13:1–7.
[105] See, for example, Aston, *King's bedpost*, pp. 28, 154–5, 157.
[106] Edward Foxe, *The true dyfferens betwen the regall power and the Ecclesiasticall power Translated out of latyn by Henry lord Stafforde* (London, 1548; *STC* 11220).
[107] John Hooper, *An Homelye to be read in the tyme of pestylence, and a moste presente remedye for thesame* (Worcester, [1553]; *STC* 13759).
[108] *STC* 15109.3, sig. A1v. For a full text and bibliographical description of *A Copye of a Letter*, see Frances Rose-Troup, *The Western Rebellion of 1549: an account of the insurrections in Devonshire and Cornwall against religious innovations in the reign of Edward VI* (London, 1913), pp. 485–95.

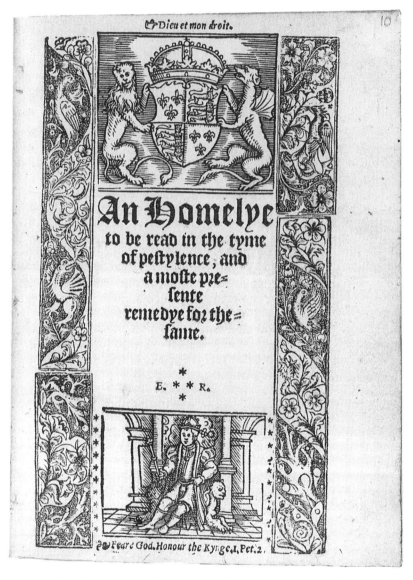

Fig. 2   The title-page of *An Homelye to be read in the tyme of pestylence* by Bishop John
Hooper, printed in Worcester by John Oswen in 1553. The verse
is 1 Peter 2:17.

the Kynge' (see below, chapter 4, Fig. 6, p. 121). It was a stylish and sophisticated presentation of Edward's claims of empire and supremacy with strong evangelical overtones, and later used by Day in his first edition of John Foxe's *Acts and Monuments*.

Edwardian political and religious culture adapted the royal supremacy of Henry VIII to suit its own theological needs. Edward Foxe's *De vera differentia* (1534), a book written to present the case for England's jurisdictional separation from the see of Rome, and issued in an elegant italic typeface, was translated and printed in 1548 in a more popular vernacular English blackletter edition. The preface to this Edwardian text, *The true dyfferens betwen the regall power and the Ecclesiasticall*, explained how David had begun the temple of God at Jerusalem, and Solomon had finished it; similarly, 'many kindes of supersticion wer abolished by the sayd good Kyng' and 'no fewer' were left to be reformed by his son.[109] Edwardians emphasized the providential continuities of 1547. Broadsheet verse explained how Henry VIII had 'extincted' blindness, error, superstition, blasphemy, false religion, and 'divilysh doctrine'.[110] The prosperity of the realm depended on the continuation by a 'noble young kyng' of the reforms of his father.[111]

This was an extremely powerful model of monarchy, and also one to which Edward was committed. He was profoundly aware of Antichrist and of his own kingly role in the destruction of the bishop of Rome. This sort of evangelical Reformation helped to define Edward's kingship and vice versa – an important notion discussed in detail in chapter 4. More prosaic was a written discussion of 'The governance of this realm', in which Edward divided the polity into its temporal and ecclesiastical parts. The ecclesiastical came first in Edward's analysis: it involved preaching the Word of God, 'continuing' the people in prayer, and maintaining the discipline of the faith.[112] He argued that bishops were a crucial part of the godly strategy. But this was not random reform. It was carefully directed from the centre of power, underpinned by kingly authority: 'i wold wish no authorite geven generally to all bishops, but that commission be geven, to those that be of the best sorte of them, to exercise it in their diocesis.'[113] Bishops very clearly held their office from him. The godly responsibilities of office also influenced Edward's notes on the reform of

---

[109] Foxe, *True dyfferens*, sig. A2v.
[110] John Turke, *A lamentation of the death of the moost victorious Prynce henry the eyght late Kynge of thys noble royalme of Englande* (London, [1547]; *STC* 13089), v. 6.
[111] Turke, *Lamentation*, v. 14.
[112] British Library, Cotton MS Nero C 10 fo. 113v (Jordan, ed., *Chronicle*, p. 160).
[113] British Library, Cotton MS Nero C 10 fo. 113v (Jordan, ed., *Chronicle*, p. 160).

the Order of the Garter, the draft statutes of which were given strong reformed and commonwealth dimensions.[114] Since the origin of the Order's foundation, Edward explained, the pleasure of God 'to have unitee and concorde in his defence that all Christians might be bounde together with the bounde of charitee' had been subverted by Eden's serpent, who had 'darkened with doutfulnes and contrarienes perverted with supersticiousnes and Idolatrie, and finally almost destroied it with bringing in of poperi and naughtines'.[115] For Edward, the sovereign was the focus of the Order, operating at the heart of its chapter meetings, and the first part of Edward's draft Garter oath committed knights to the protection of the king and his commonwealth. The second and third parts complemented the first: knights promised to 'refuse the bishopes of Romes auctorite' and to fight in their country's cause 'against him and his erronious and pestilent heresies'. Equally, they committed themselves to extinguishing 'al mens traditions against the scripture'.[116] Facing biblical texts that condemned idolatry, St George lost his place. And to distance the Order from the saint and his feast day of 23 April, Edward timetabled the major assembly of the Garter for 30 November and 1 December, with knights bound by a commitment to the Book of Common Prayer and the reception of 'the supper of our lord'.[117]

All this appears to represent a rather neat exposition of kingship. Edward VI was, even during childhood, an emperor, supreme head of the Church on earth next under God; but, even more than this, Edward was a king ordained by providence to reform his kingdom, and counselled by godly men. It is difficult to think of a more effective counter to the argument that Edward was merely a boy, incomplete in his monarchical power. But did these notions hold water? One of the great triumphs of the reign may have been the depiction of Edward as a king of Old Testament stature, personally engaged in a Reformation ordained by God. But was presentation underpinned by substance? It is certainly important to recognize the essential fragility of the regime's position, both intellectually and practically. These were claims about the governance of the kingdom during royal minority. And this was not a sedentary minority of peaceful preservation – it was a period of controversial theology, of iconoclasm,

---

[114] British Library, Cotton MS Nero C 10 fos. 98r–101r; 101r–107r. Edward's drafts probably date from 1550: British Library, Cotton MS Nero C 10 fo. 102r; John Anstis, *The register of the most noble Order of the Garter*, 2 vols. (London, 1724), II, p. 447. For a recent exploration of Edward's drafts, see MacCulloch, *Tudor church militant*, pp. 30–6.

[115] British Library, Cotton MS Nero C 10 fo. 102r.

[116] British Library, Cotton MS Nero C 10 fo. 103v.

[117] British Library, Cotton MS Nero C 10 fos. 104v–105r.

and of upheaval in the lives of the king's subjects. In promoting evangelical Reformation the regime exposed itself to profound scrutiny. In May 1547 Bishop Stephen Gardiner of Winchester reminded Edward Seymour that his primary responsibility as protector was to preserve, not to innovate. Gardiner believed that Protector Somerset's duty was to deliver to an eighteen-year-old Edward a realm unaltered in its religion.[118] Once again, Reformation threw into sharp focus the relationship between king and counsellors.

Stephen Gardiner constructed a persuasive and damaging case against the Edwardian regime, persistently testing its limits and weaknesses. His benchmark of loyalty and theology was the 'King's Book' of 1543, *A necessary doctrine and erudition for any Christian man* – the conservative doctrinal reaction to the evangelical impulses of the 1530s. This text informed his response to the Edwardian iconoclasm and reinforced his opposition to the Homilies of 1547. For Gardiner, the King's Book was the model of kingly reformation: debated, defined in parliament, and promoted by statute. It was the key, in other words, to the bishop's 'constitutional' critique of a regime that appeared willing to abandon the kingly authority of Henry VIII and the principles of common law by which (in Gardiner's reading of the 1530s and 1540s) he had governed. Stephen Gardiner's critique of the Edwardian regime was dangerous because, unlike Reginald Pole, he had accepted the Henrician royal supremacy; he even appeared to acknowledge Edward's and his protector's powers during minority. Gardiner presented himself as a mark against which to measure Edward's godly Reformation. He created for himself the role of an external counsellor to the Edwardian regime, a man who had operated at the very highest levels of politics and diplomacy for nearly twenty years; a man, too, who had established a working relationship with Henry VIII built on a foundation of mutual respect; and a bishop with a profound responsibility both to his diocese and to the kingdom.[119]

Above all, Gardiner wrote as the experienced councillor who had helped to construct the Tudor supremacy and understood its nature and texture. In 1547 he questioned the legality of the royal Injunctions and defended the Henrician Act for the Advancement of True Religion (1543).[120] He recounted conversations he had had years before with Lord Chancellor Thomas Audley and Thomas Cromwell on the relationship between law and royal power. Edward was bound by parliamentary

---

[118] James Arthur Muller, ed., *The letters of Stephen Gardiner* (Cambridge, 1933), p. 278 (21 May 1547).
[119] Glyn Redworth, *In defence of the Church Catholic: the life of Stephen Gardiner* (Oxford, 1990), pp. 248–81.
[120] Muller, ed., *Letters of Stephen Gardiner*, pp. 373–4 (Gardiner to John Mason, 30 Aug. 1547).

statute – or rather his father's parliamentary statute, concerning True Religion.[121] Gardiner claimed an exemption from the royal visitation of his diocese because of the statutory standing of the King's Book – and his contention, crucially, that the Injunctions of 31 July were unlawful.[122] Gardiner recounted Thomas Audley's pronouncement that 'he never knew or red of any act of Parliament in this realme broken till the same had ben by like authoritie of Parliament repe[a]lled': in other words, the settlement of 1543 was valid and secure.[123] Consequently, Gardiner suggested that the royal visitors operating in the king's name were in danger of exposing themselves to the charge of *praemunire*, the crime of acknowledging a foreign (usually papal) jurisdiction in England. The stunningly simple contention was that Homilies and Injunctions underpinned by the authority of Edward as supreme head of the Church were no match for an act of parliament – until they were themselves enshrined in statute.[124]

Stephen Gardiner's critique of the Edwardian Reformation was deeply subversive. Although Gardiner's stubborn stand on the principles of common law and king-in-parliament was radically different to the elegance of his defence of the Henrician supremacy in *De vera obedientia*, the arguments of 1547 and 1548 were marked by an intellectual clarity of their own.[125] Put simply, Gardiner deployed the counter-thesis of king-in-parliament against the thesis of unassailable Protestant imperial monarchy. His arguments had a resonance that helped to distinguish Gardiner from Edmund Bonner – who answered the charge that he failed to deliver a sermon acceptable to the regime on the grounds that he had found the subject too confusing – and even Reginald Pole. Bonner was lazy and incompetent; Pole had refused to accept the Henrician royal supremacy. The great benefit of Gardiner's position was that he could endorse the continued rejection of papal authority and Edward VI's royal supremacy but still point out the dangers of doctrinal innovation. 'Many common welthes have continued without the bishop of Romes jurisdiction', he wrote to Protector Somerset in May 1547, 'but without the true religion . . . no estate hath continued in the circuit of the world to us knowen since Christ came.'[126] The break with Rome was justified; but combining it with innovation in religion made it look like a pretence.

[121] Muller, ed., *Letters of Stephen Gardiner*, pp. 369–71 (Gardiner to the Privy Council, [30 Aug. 1547]).
[122] Muller, ed., *Letters of Stephen Gardiner*, pp. 370–1, 373–4.
[123] Muller, ed., *Letters of Stephen Gardiner*, pp. 369–70.
[124] Muller, ed., *Letters of Stephen Gardiner*, p. 370.   [125] Redworth, *Church Catholic*, pp. 66–70.
[126] Muller, ed., *Letters of Stephen Gardiner*, p. 279.

Stephen Gardiner was a master of ambiguity. He at once defended Reformation and condemned it. On St Peter's Day in 1548, before the king and the court, Gardiner preached a sermon which became a defining moment in the life of the regime. One of the great features of the surviving texts of this sermon is the subtlety of its account of a decade of Henrician and Edwardian reform in church and state. Gardiner referred to the books he had written in defence of the break with Rome, and recounted the royal renunciation of papal authority and his own support for the dissolution of the monasteries. Gardiner even appeared, initially, to endorse fully the supremacy of Edward. But the open criticisms he made of the kingdom's Reformation – the unacceptability for Gardiner of clerical marriage, the destruction of images, and the toleration of preaching against the mass – were underpinned by a rather more subtle critique. At Whitehall, in 1548, Gardiner accepted only a very limited reformation. Using Augustine and Jerome, he defended ceremonies used to serve God but distinguished this from their abuse, when 'man maketh him self servant to them & not them to serve him'.[127] On the same principle he defended clerical chastity. This, in turn, rather cleverly allowed him to condemn 'monkery, nonry, friery, of a wondrous nomber'; to endorse the removal of 'there houses and garments'; to defend Henry VIII's reservation of clerical obedience 'to him selfe'; and to emphasize the late king's commitment to the clerical vow of chastity. Gardiner appeared to take a hard line on the 'fancy of Idolatry and supersticion' into which people had fallen because of pilgrimages – but, once again, he condemned only the abuse of images. Some things, even abused, could not be removed from the Church: they had to be reformed 'and brought to the right use agayne'. So Gardiner defended the 'liberty' of rulers to reform or remove abuses in the Church but, simultaneously, condemned those who had stripped the altars.[128] He appeared to support the action of kings in principle but damned the evangelical Reformation being carried out in Edward's name.

These were not issues of abstruse theology or limited academic interest. Stephen Gardiner presented to the court and Council principled objections to the regime that were echoed more popularly (and more violently) in the rebellions of Devon and Cornwall in 1549. At the trial of Gardiner, in 1550, William Cecil testified to the royal commissioners that the bishop had been ordered to preach as a response to 'greate inconveniences rysen amonges the people, for an evyll opinion of the kynges

---

[127] Foxe, *Actes and Monuments*, p. 774.   [128] Foxe, *Actes and Monuments*, p. 775.

autoritye in hys yonge yeares'. The contention of these people was 'that the commaundements of the kyng were of no force duryng his yong yeares, otherwyse then they did agree with his fathers procedinges'.[129] At stake was the integrity of Edward's kingship.

The regime responded to the rebellions of 1549 in two ways: with military force and in print. *A message sent by the kynges Majestie* and *A Copye of a Letter contayning certayne newes* (both printed by the king's printer Richard Grafton) and, less officially, John Cheke's *The hurt of sedicion howe greveous it is to a Commune welth* (produced by John Day and William Seres) exhorted subjects to obey their governors. But their authors also engaged the rebels in a limited political dialogue. Writers and readers had to think seriously about the proper agent of Reformation in the commonwealth and the nature of the kingdom's governance. The regime pointed out that it was not the role of subjects to dictate to those in authority and that rebellion was a fundamental challenge to the natural order of things. But this order, in Edward's reign, was *godly* order. Archbishop Cranmer saw at the root of their demands the issue of the authority of the Antichristian bishop of Rome. 1549 became part of a long scriptural and historical tradition of rebellions orchestrated in order to restore idolatry, organized against the people's leaders chosen by God.[130] Thomas Smith argued a similar point in his notes for the sermon Edmund Bonner so conspicuously failed to preach in August 1549.[131] The English rebels of 1549 were likened to Corah and Dathan (Numbers 16), punished because they challenged the authority of Moses and offended God with idolatrous sacrifices.[132] Obedience became obedience to *godly* authority.

The events of 1549 compelled the regime to explain itself, its dynamics, and the nature of its authority to reform. It was possible to argue that Edward, even during his minority, had full kingly powers. In 1549 Edward asked the rebels to consider some important questions. 'Be we of lesse aucthorite, for our age? Bee wee not your kyng now, as wee shalbe? Or shall ye bee subjectes hereafter, and nowe are ye not?'[133] As a

[129] Foxe, *Actes and Monuments*, p. 805.
[130] Corpus Christi College Cambridge, Parker MS 102 fos. 529, 533; Jenkyns, ed., *Cranmer*, II, pp. 245, 247.
[131] SP 10/8 fos. 64v, 65r (2 Aug. 1549).
[132] Jenkyns, ed., *Cranmer*, II, p. 247; cf. 'An exhortacion, concernyng good ordre and obedience, to rulers and magistrates', in *Certayne Sermons, or Homelies* (London, 1547; *STC* 13640), sig. s2r.
[133] *A message sent by the kynges Majestie, to certain of his people, assembled in Devonshire* (London, 1549; *STC* 7506), sig. B4v. For a discussion of the legal theory and its implications, see F.W. Maitland, 'The crown as corporation', in H.A.L. Fisher, ed., *The collected papers of Frederic William Maitland*, 3 vols. (Cambridge, 1911), III, pp. 244–51; and Ernst H. Kantorowicz, *The king's two bodies: a study in mediaeval political theology* (Princeton, 1957), pp. 24–41.

'naturall man' and creature of God, the text explained, Edward had youth; but as a king he had 'no difference of yeres, nor tyme'. Edward was his subjects' rightful king, liege lord, king anointed, king crowned, and the sovereign king of England, 'not by our age, but by Gods ordinaunce', at the age of ten or twenty-one.[134] And yet as a defence of Edward's *practical* kingship – his powers of command and governance – the notion of the king's two bodies was a difficult one. After all, Edward's natural, physical body – the body that thought, talked, and acted – was still the body of a boy. The regime could declare with force that Edward was as kingly as a king could be, but it could not very easily counter the obvious physical fact that these kingly powers were trapped in a boy's body. Although the coherence of the regime's presentation of Edward's supremacy over the course of the reign was impressive, godly Josiah was not enough. The Edwardian regime learned, as all regimes probably do in the end, that merely stating a case often enough does not necessarily convince people of its essential rightness. Stephen Gardiner and the rebels of 1549 exposed a critical weakness in the Edwardian model of kingship – the weakness was Edward himself.

A better defence of Edward's kingship in these circumstances was that it was collaborative, formally and properly supported by the subjects of the crown. Once again, the defence of Reformation was indistinguishable from the defence of the power and authority to govern. During the summer of rebellion in 1549 John Cheke explained that the primitive Church of the apostles had been recovered because 'the greatest learned men of this realme hath drawen, the hole consent of the parliament hath confirmed, the kynges Mayestie hath set forth'.[135] In the same month Cheke's friend, Thomas Smith, wrote of 'the godly order' of Reformation prescribed by the king's majesty with the consent and agreement of the whole parliament.[136] By June 1549 Protector Somerset had felt confident enough to explain to Reginald Pole that the kingdom's Reformation had been properly and authoritatively constructed and maturely debated by men of learning, some of whom had been bishops and others 'equaly and indifferently chosen of Judgment'. These men reached a common agreement, which was put to the whole parliament. All were heard and all were admitted to the debate.[137] The proceedings

---

[134] *Message sent by the kynges Majestie*, sig. B5r. Cf. an identical reading of Henry VI's authority offered in 1427: S.B. Chrimes, *English constitutional ideas in the fifteenth century* (Cambridge, 1936), p. 36.
[135] John Cheke, *The hurt of sedicion howe greveous it is to a Commune welth* (London, 1549; *STC* 5109), sig. A6r.
[136] SP 10/8 fo. 79r (16 Aug. 1549; Knighton 340).   [137] SP 10/7 fo. 76r.

were 'by one hole consent of thupper and nether house of the parliament finally concluded and aproved'. So the 'forme and rite of Service [and] a trade and doctryne of Relligion' were established by the authority of king-in-parliament, published by act and statute.[138]

So Reformation was collaborative, the act of a king supported by his subjects. In *The hurt of sedicion* Cheke explained that it was the 'kinges majestie *etc*' who had 'godli reformed an uncleane parte of religion' and returned the realm to the values of the apostolic Church.[139] The king, his counsellors, and subjects in parliament, offering their advice and consent, had together legitimized the settlement of religion and the governance of the kingdom. It was a fundamentally unequal arrangement, because the king, as principal partner, was an emperor and Christ's vicar on earth. But it was still a partnership. Edward was 'a king enoincted that ruleth by counsell and kepeth his Realme in defence and quyetnes'.[140] Reform was the responsibility of parliament, whether it was the correction of problems within the commonwealth or the construction of new laws. If something needed to be altered, parliament was 'nere at hand, a place and tyme where men ought and ever hitherto have ben wounte to common [i.e., commune]'. Parliament was where the 'wise heades and the three estates of the Realme' gathered to consider and to debate 'what lawes or statutes are to be made or revoked'.[141] *A message sent by the kynges Majestie* (1549) emphasized that the Book of Common Prayer had been 'set furthe by the free consent of our whole Parliament'.[142] The draft of a letter to England's sheriffs in June 1549 explained the rebellion of some subjects 'concernyng the boke set furth by our authorite in full parlament of the rite and ceremonies to be used in our churche of England and Ireland and all our domynions'.[143]

Reformation and governance by king-in-parliament did not necessarily contradict the regime's presentation of Edward as godly emperor and supreme head but, given the basic facts of Edward's minority, it did represent a hairline crack in the Edwardian model of kingship. Henry VIII had certainly not believed that his authority to break with Rome had been given to him by the Reformation Parliament – a position rather similar to the notion of Edward as God's vicar, a 'king enoincted that

---

[138] SP 10/7 fo. 76v.   [139] Cheke, *Hurt of sedicion*, sig. F3r.
[140] SP 10/8 fo. 17r; Rose-Troup, *Western rebellion*, p. 433.
[141] SP 10/8 fo. 17r, with some punctuation added; printed in Rose-Troup, *Western rebellion*, p. 434.
[142] *Message sent by the kynges Majestie*, sig. A5r.
[143] SP 10/7 fos. 94r–95v, printed in Pocock, ed., *Troubles*, pp. 4–5 (Knighton 282). Cf. Thomas Smith's draft of a letter to the bishops (16 Aug. 1549), SP 10/8 fo. 79r. For a similar statement, see Cheke, *Hurt of sedicion*, sig. A6r.

ruleth by counsell'. In a sense, the regime had played Stephen Gardiner at his own game. For Gardiner England's (conservative) settlement of religion had been established by Henry VIII-in-parliament. By 1549 the regime could claim that its godly Reformation had been promoted by Edward VI-in-parliament. But there was still something slightly uncomfortable in this presentation of monarchical authority, perfectly expressed by Cheke's 'kinges majestie *etc*'. This was one of the great irreconcilable features of the kingship of Edward VI. All of the classic defences of Edward's authority to reform and govern were flawed: Edward as godly king, rehearsals of the ageless quality of the public power that resided within his natural body, Reformation by king-in-parliament. It took just one Catholic, convinced of the incompleteness of royal power during minority and profoundly suspicious of the quality of counsel offered to the king, for the grand edifice of Edwardian kingship to collapse like a palace of marble built on sand. At the heart of this kingship was a fascinating tension. The six years between 1547 and 1553 represented a defining period in the construction of sixteenth-century English Protestant imperial monarchy, and even prepared the foundations for the 'resistance theories' of the 1550s (discussed below, chapter 6, pp. 177–84). But it was, nevertheless, a fragile, delicate, even flawed creature.

The king's minority was the weakness, but it was, ironically enough, a weakness capable of resolving itself over time. Royal ignorance, stupidity, madness, and gender could subvert or distort the governance of the realm, and there was only so much subjects could do to offset their effects. But there is good evidence to suggest that, by 1551 or 1552, the men around Edward were conscious of the imminence of royal majority. The polity began increasingly to mould itself around an intelligent and engaged young king (see below, chapter 5, pp. 157–68). One of the great features of the reign is the seriousness with which kingship was taken by Edwardians, and the extent to which conventional notions of kingly power were communicated to Edward by preachers at court and his tutors in the Privy Chamber. Kingly power, and kingly responsibility, underpinned a political culture of coherence and sophistication. But if the nature of monarchical power was explored in detail by men like Hugh Latimer, its exercise during the reign of Edward was more problematic.

Counsel was fundamentally unsuited to the political conditions of minority – or at least counsel in its proper form. For royal governance to work properly there had to be no distinction between the location of sovereign power and its proper exercise. An adult could achieve this but a boy, however precocious, could not. The complex key to the English 'constitution' of the sixteenth century lay in definitive royal action balanced by agreement and consensus. The participation of subjects in the exercise of political power enhanced royal authority, but this participation had to be strictly controlled and carefully defined: counsel could not be turned into compulsion. Complete monarchical authority rested on education, application, ability, and, above all, adulthood. In the early years of Edward's reign royal authority was, in effect, naked and exposed. Sovereign power was exercised by others on Edward's behalf. He was king in name and blood but in practice only collaboratively and corporately.

So Edward VI counselled is profoundly misleading. It looks like the key to the dynamics of Edwardian politics but represented instead its inherent weakness. It was not the counsel of royal majority, closely controlled by a discerning monarch exercising the authority to accept or to reject it; nor was it really the counsel of compulsion, imposed on an unwilling king by the men around him. It was rather the counsel of compensation, superficially able to fill the vacuum created by the absence of a definitive and unquestionable royal will. In this sense the dynamics of Edwardian politics bear more than a passing resemblance to the early years of the Elizabethan polity, when the political elite in the Privy Council and in parliament attempted to impose on the queen solutions to problems she refused even to acknowledge. The relationship between Edward and the men around him was less forced – the presentation of the king counselled between 1547 and 1553 looks easy and natural – but it still presented a serious challenge, both intellectually and practically. The public image of Edward as the godly young king returning his realm to the purity of worship of the early Christian Church rested on rather shaky foundations. At its most ebullient, but also at its most vulnerable, Edwardian kingship was a remarkable construction.

3

The dynamics of power 1547–1549

In July 1549 William Paget asked Edward Seymour duke of Somerset to remember that 'saving for the name of a kinge, and that youe must do all thinge in the name of an other, your grace ys durynge the kings majestes young age of imperfection to do his owne things, as yt were a kinge, and have his Majestes absolute power'.[1] Paget was a frustrated and dispirited man. He had tried to counsel the protector, but had failed. Policies in Scotland and continental Europe, on religion and the economic wellbeing of the realm, appeared to be going disastrously wrong.[2] Still, Paget's considered and brutal critique exposed a real, but often simplified, truth about the first two-and-a-half years of Edward's reign: Edward Seymour, governor of the king's person and protector of the king's realms, dominions, and subjects, exercised massive power. The aim of this chapter is to explore the nature and the dynamics of that power.

Edward Seymour's protectorate has presented a number of problems for historians. In the sixteenth century, his reputation for evangelical godliness was unmatched. For later Victorian writers like James Anthony Froude and A.F. Pollard he was a liberal hero. To some extent the debate still goes on (see above, chapter 1, pp. 20–1).[3] But in spite of this presentation of Protector Somerset as a force for moral good in the reign, historians have often had the uncomfortable feeling that he actually subverted the proper working of the Tudor constitution. For a historiography used to the certainties of Council and parliamentary statute, Seymour's style of political management – personal, dominant, often informal – can look perverse and dangerous. Penry Williams explained how the protector's 'authoritarian style of government revealed itself in

---

[1] SP 10/8 fo. 10r (7 July 1549; Knighton 301).
[2] Jennifer Loach, *Edward VI*, ed. George Bernard and Penry Williams (New Haven and London, 1999), pp. 39–88.
[3] Ethan H. Shagan, 'Protector Somerset and the 1549 rebellions: new sources and new perspectives', *English Historical Review*, 114 (1999), pp. 34–63; and the subsequent debate between Shagan, Michael Bush, and George Bernard in *English Historical Review*, 115 (2000), pp. 103–33.

his use of proclamations' – an apparent misuse of royal power.[4] Elton
was clearly unhappy that Edward Seymour had decided to tamper with
the balance and modernity of Thomas Cromwell's bureaucratic revolution, and he accused the king's uncle of trying 'to turn the protectorship
into a form of personal monarchy'. For Elton, Seymour committed three
cardinal errors: he ignored the Privy Council, issued too many proclamations, and attempted to dominate government and law through his
private household.[5]

Are these fair assessments of Edward Seymour and his regime?
Exploring the nature of the protectorate is not the same as defending the
protector: Seymour undoubtedly made political mistakes, and his contemporaries pointed to a personality that exhibited in equal measure a
sharp arrogance and an indecisive weakness. The purpose of this chapter
is not to rehabilitate Protector Somerset's political reputation or defend
his moral character. Rather it tries to ask – and seeks to answer, at least in
part – some important questions. How did Seymour and his colleagues
understand the demands and responsibilities of governance? What precisely were the political dynamics and arrangements of the protectorate?
Who, or what, made the polity tick between 1547 and 1549? Why did
Edward Seymour's colleagues decide in October 1549 to withdraw their
support for a man to whom they had delegated quasi-monarchical powers of governance? The politics of the protectorate – of its formation,
of its mature years, and of its failure – are too subtle and complex to
be explained purely on the grounds of personal jealousies or faction in
Council or at court, and even its inadequacies deserve to be measured
against standards of governance and political behaviour that would have
been understandable to the king's principal subjects. And the most fundamental standard was set down in February and March 1547 in the first
statements of Edward Seymour's power as governor of the king's person
and the protector of his realms.

PROTECTOR, KING, AND COUNSEL

In one of the most familiar passages of political correspondence from
Edward's reign, William Paget revealed in 1549 that he had talked to

---

[4] Penry Williams, *The later Tudors: England 1547–1603* (Oxford, 1995), p. 38. Cf. G.R. Elton, 'The
good duke', *Historical Journal*, 12 (1969), p. 705; G.R. Elton, 'Government by edict?', *Historical
Journal*, 8 (1965), pp. 266–71; and M.L. Bush, *The government policy of Protector Somerset* (London,
1975), pp. 130–1, 140–1, 146–59.
[5] G.R. Elton, *Reform and reformation: England 1509–1558* (London, 1987 edn), p. 338.

Edward Seymour about political life after Henry VIII 'in the galerye at Westmynster, before the breathe was owt of the body of the king that dead ys'. In planning the protectorate, Seymour had agreed to follow the advice of Paget 'more than any other mans'.[6] By letter, the two men co-ordinated the gradual release of information during Seymour's journey, with Anthony Browne of the Privy Chamber, to meet Edward Tudor in Hertford and escort him, as king, to London. On 29 January 1547 Seymour suggested a public declaration of Henry's will in parliament on Wednesday 2 February, giving himself and Paget an opportunity 'in the mene tyme . . . to meght and agre therin as ther may be no contravarse hereafter'. The proposal for a Seymour protectorate was not, however, a complete secret. At Enfield, 'at the kinges Majesties cooming frome Hertforde' and in the privacy of a garden, Browne 'gave his franke consent after comunicacion in discourse of the state that his grace shoulde be protector'.[7]

The reason Anthony Browne gave for his support (or, rather, the explanation of the reason offered by his former servant, William Wightman, in 1549) was that a Seymour protectorate was 'bothe the surest kynde of governement and most fyt for this common welthe'.[8] According to the formal, institutional record of the proceedings of Henry VIII's executors, the principal justification for the appointment of a protector was the need for the authority of one man to act as 'a special Remembrancer' for the executors and a guardian against corporate disorder and confusion.[9] And so, doing precisely what Henry's will wanted them to do – to reinforce the honour and surety of the king their sovereign lord – the executors appointed Seymour protector because of his experience in the affairs of the realm and his 'proximitie of bludde' as Edward's uncle.[10] The king's subjects were perfectly aware of precedent. Royal uncles had often played a part in the governance of the kingdom during royal minorities (see above, chapter 2, pp. 49–50; and below, pp. 94–5). So when Edward recorded in his journal that Seymour was chosen to be 'protectour of the realm and gouvernor of the kinges person during his minorite to wich al the gentlemen and Lordes did agre becaus he was the kinges oncle on his mothers side' it was perhaps more a genuine statement of fact and circumstance than a reflection of nine-year-old naivety.[11]

---

[6] E.W. Ives, 'Henry VIII's will – a forensic conundrum', *Historical Journal*, 35 (1992), p. 793.
[7] SP 10/7 fo. 33r (William Wightman to William Cecil, 10 May 1549; Knighton 220).
[8] SP 10/7 fo. 33r.
[9] *APC 1547–50*, p. 5 (31 Jan. 1547).   [10] *APC 1547–50*, p. 5; also p. 68 (21 Mar. 1547).
[11] British Library, Cotton MS Nero C 10 fo. 12r; W.K. Jordan, ed., *The chronicle and political papers of King Edward VI* (Ithaca, NY, 1966), p. 4.

The timing of the executors' grants of land, money, and promotion appears to suggest that William Paget used the list of gifts inherited from the final weeks of Henry's reign to secure support for a Seymour protectorate, and commentators since the seventeenth century have assumed that Seymour himself secretly extracted from the king the later confirmation of his powers.[12] But was this really the case? There was a basic stability and coherence to the transition of January 1547. Formally at least, the establishment of a protectorate was the unanimous decision of the men entrusted by Henry with the care of his son and the realm. It was a smooth operation, principally secured by William Paget and his successful negotiation of broad support for Edward Seymour, and conducted mainly in private – but the delicacies of royal death and kingly accession demanded secrecy and unanimity at the best of times.[13] Henry VIII helped from beyond the grave. Stephen Gardiner and Thomas Howard duke of Norfolk were probably excluded from the chosen corporate group because they would have disturbed its coherence.[14] Outside the regime Gardiner was a powerful, articulate, and stubborn critic; inside it he could have been equally persuasive (see above, chapter 2, pp. 57–60; and below, pp. 83–5). What is clear is that the establishment of the protectorate was more complex than some commentators have acknowledged, and there was certainly more to it than financial or social reward. Ralph Houlbrooke has written of the importance of individual attitudes, 'governed by a range of hopes, fears, scruples, loyalties, considerations of personal advantage, and differing estimates' of Edward Seymour's fitness.[15] One should also add notions of political authority, and what must have been, after near forty years of intensely personal monarchy, an instinctive belief in the need for a man of recognized pre-eminence.

So coherence and unanimity do appear to have played an important part in the formation of the protectorate. Seymour's powers as protector were only enhanced after January 1547. He was formally nominated by the executors of Henry's will on 31 January, and they presented the arrangement to the king a day later.[16] Within six weeks they felt that his authority was too limited.[17] In March, Seymour's colleagues consented

[12] R.A. Houlbrooke, 'Henry VIII's wills: a comment', *Historical Journal*, 37 (1994), pp. 896–8; Helen Miller, 'Henry VIII's unwritten will: grants of lands and honours in 1547', in E.W. Ives, R.J. Knecht, and J.J. Scarisbrick, eds., *Wealth and power in Tudor England* (London, 1978), pp. 87–105.
[13] S.J. Gunn, 'The accession of Henry VIII', *Historical Research*, 64 (1991), pp. 278–88.
[14] Houlbrooke, 'Henry VIII's wills', p. 892.   [15] Houlbrooke, 'Henry VIII's wills', p. 895.
[16] *APC 1547–50*, pp. 7–8.   [17] Ives, 'Forensic conundrum', p. 803.

to the appointment of Seymour as 'governor of the king's person and protector of his realms and dominions and people of the same', supported by a powerful restatement of the protector's powers and letters patent.[18] Although these declarations survive in the rather sanitized institutional record of the Privy Council, they do appear to reflect a broad acceptance of Somerset's position. It is a significant comment on the coherence of the protectorate, and its ability to secure conformity, that Thomas Seymour's effort in 1548 to discredit his brother's office ran into a brick wall (see below, pp. 91–7). William Paget reminded the younger Seymour that he had assented and agreed 'with his owne hand' to his brother's powers as protector and governor.[19]

If Protector Somerset did not foist himself on the Edwardian polity, what did his colleagues expect him to do? And how did they understand their own responsibilities? The experience of minority was, of course, new to them. In January, as executors of Henry VIII's will, they found themselves empowered to govern the person of the king and order the affairs of his realms, dominions, and countries.[20] By the middle of March 1547 the executors were able to secure royal assent to their request for recognition and confirmation as the king's councillors, although they had described themselves as 'of the pryvey Counsaile' in early February.[21] In late March they explained themselves. Their aim, above all, was to secure for Edward the educational and moral upbringing appropriate and necessary for a prince of his estate.[22] So a group of men bearing corporate responsibility for the wellbeing of the king and the governance of his realm used their 'advises and counseilles' to fulfil their obligations to the wishes of the dead king.[23] Edward Seymour was granted 'full powre and autorite from tyme to tyme' as governor and protector, until the king reached the age of eighteen. He was given the authority to act for the realm in issues public or private, domestic or foreign, and discretion was his.[24] Later that year he was appointed the king's lieutenant and captain general for wars both within the realm and outside it, and was given the power to array the king's subjects, hire foreign soldiers, exercise martial law, and negotiate with foreign powers.[25] The men who had transformed themselves from executors into councillors were counsellors to the king, but Seymour was given the power to appoint men to the institutional

---

[18] *CPR 1547–48*, p. 97 (12 Mar. 1547).   [19] SP 10/6 fo. 69r (Knighton 203).
[20] *APC 1547–50*, pp. 3–4 (31 Jan. 1547).
[21] *APC 1547–50*, p. 63 (13 Mar. 1547); British Library, Cotton MS Titus B 2 fo. 34v (12 Feb. [1547]).
[22] *APC 1547–50*, p. 67 (21 Mar. 1547).
[23] For the quotation, *APC 1547–50*, p. 68 (21 Mar. 1547).
[24] *APC 1547–50*, pp. 69–70 (21 Mar. 1547).   [25] *CPR 1548–49*, p. 96 (11 Aug. 1549).

body at his discretion.[26] He was certainly accountable to his king, like all subjects, but Seymour's relationship with Edward's privy councillors was thoroughly monarchical. During Edward's minority, the protector could use his discretion to act for the king with the advice and consent 'of suche and so many of our Privey Counsaill or of our Counsaillours as he shall thincke mete to call unto him from tyme to tyme'.[27] Like a king, the protector could take counsel when, and from whom, he thought appropriate.

Historians have often questioned Edward Seymour's virtual abandonment of the institutional Privy Council. Seymour certainly isolated himself from his colleagues, but the protector's alleged contempt for the Council as an institutional body masks something more complex. In 1549, as 'thole body and estate of his majestes privie counsell consulting to gither', Edward Seymour's colleagues acted corporately to protect the person of the king and his realm.[28] This action was, as they admitted themselves (and for obvious reasons of public appearance), something that had been forced upon them.[29] But the relationship between the protector and his colleagues was profoundly ambiguous, in part because as executors in 1547 they had agreed that Edward Seymour should exercise quasi-monarchical power. In 1549 Seymour's colleagues argued that his power was conditional on their support. They won in the end, but the result was not a foregone conclusion. Similarly, the powers of governor and protector were given to Seymour on the assumption that he would govern the kingdom on behalf of the king and his people in a way that was generally acceptable. But was there really a 'contractual' foundation for Protector Somerset's authority? When William Paget wrote in 1549 that Edward Seymour was a king in all but name, able to exercise the absolute power of the monarch, the truth was that Seymour had (in theory) inherited the complete package of practical kingship. An English king had to balance sovereign power against accountability to God, and it

---

[26] *APC 1547–50*, pp. 70–1 (21 Mar. 1547).   [27] *APC 1547–50*, pp. 72–3 (21 Mar. 1547).

[28] SP 10/9 fo. 72r, printed in Nicholas Pocock, ed., *Troubles connected with the Prayer Book of 1549* (Camden Society; London, 1884), p. 113 (Knighton 411). Cf. *A Proclamacion set forth by the state and bodie of the Kynges Majest[i]es Counsayle now assembled at London, conteinyng the very trouth of the Duke of Somersets evel Government, and false and detestable procedinges* (London, 8 Oct. 1549; *STC* 7828); and *A Proclamacion, set furth by the body and state, of the Kynges Majest[y]s privey Counsayle concernyng the devisers, writers, and casters abrode, of certain vile, slaunderous, and moste trayterous letters, billes, scrowes, and papers, tendyng to the seducement of the kynges majesties good & lovyng subjectes* (London, 10 Oct. 1549; *STC* 7829).

[29] The exchanges between Protector Somerset and his colleagues in London can be reconstructed from SP 10/9 and British Library, Cotton MS Titus B 2, much of it printed in *APC 1547–50*, pp. 330–44; Pocock, ed., *Prayer Book*, pp. 74–120; and Patrick Fraser Tytler, ed., *England under the reigns of Edward VI and Mary*, 2 vols. (London, 1839), I, pp. 211–51.

was incumbent on him to take the advice of his principal subjects. Only in this way could the constitutional doublethink that lay at the heart of Tudor politics – the absolute, definitive, and sovereign power of the king governing a polity best ruled by consensus – really be reconciled. How could this possibly suit the circumstances of Edward's minority?

Edward Seymour was not a king by birth; his contemporaries recognized that, and expected him to act differently. Edward VI was the source of sovereign power in his kingdom but he could not exercise it; his uncle, as an adult, could exercise authority but not 'own' it in a monarchical sense. These were complex problems of practical governance and political thought (see also above, chapter 2, pp. 46–64; and below, chapter 5, pp. 157–68). But Edward Seymour failed in the end because he broke one of the cardinal rules of governance: in difficult political circumstances he refused to take counsel from his colleagues. William Paget told the protector that the crisis facing him in the summer of 1549 could have been averted if he had 'folowed advyse, In geving wherof as I have bene some what francke with your grace aparte, and sene lytle fruyte come of yt'.[30] Rather than using counsel to underpin and enhance his authority, Seymour pre-emptively dismissed it. When his colleagues had joined together on an issue, Paget continued, the protector worked 'to owt reason them in yt, and wrast them by reason of your aucthorytie to bowe to yt, or fyrst shewe your owne opinion in a matter, and then aske theyrs'. Seymour could excuse himself by arguing that he alone was responsible to his nephew – 'No man shall answer the kinge for these things but I' – but this was a misuse of the authority that had been delegated to him. Paget accepted that the protector would indeed have to give account because 'thaucthoritie' was in his hands; but so too would the men who had consented to give him that authority.[31] But above all, Paget argued that Seymour had failed properly to exercise the absolute power of the crown. He lacked the noble courage which was needed to put subjects in their place, and had failed to maintain justice in the realm – one of the principal responsibilities of any English king.[32] So Edward Seymour was judged for failing to live up to the expectations of the men who had countenanced the establishment of a protectorate with quasi-monarchical powers. Paget's critique depended heavily on the cultural understanding of governorship. For Paget, Seymour had failed to exercise proper, stern authority. Thomas Smith agreed. During the dark days of October 1549 Smith told William Petre that the protector

[30] SP 10/8 fo. 9r. [31] SP 10/8 fo. 9v. [32] SP 10/8 fo. 10r.

had 'as ye know rather bene to ease [easy] then cruell to others'.[33] At
the same time, Seymour was accused of arrogant contempt for the views
of his colleagues. John Dudley referred to him in the hours following his
fall from grace as 'the man that ruled all by wylffulnes'.[34]

There was an institutional dimension to this charge, because the executors of Henry VIII's will, as privy councillors, could be defined as
a group of men able to gather together to offer counsel, and, through
their involvement, strengthen the authority of the protector as *primus inter
pares*. But when the councillors in London justified their opposition to
Seymour, they referred to 'the yll gouvernement of the Lord Protectour,
who being heretofore many tymes spoken unto both in open Counsail
and *otherwise pryvately*, hath . . . refused to give eare to their advises'.[35]
Seymour's colleagues claimed that they had tried to persuade him to
govern 'by thadvise of us & the rest of your counsellors', but had found
him 'so moche given to his own will that he always refused to here
reason'.[36] As a mark of arrogance he taunted men in open Council. More
significantly, 'he began to doo thinges of most weighte & importaunce by
him self alone without calling of any of us of the counsell'.[37] Authority
per se was not the problem, but its exercise was. Edward Seymour's regime
collapsed when his colleagues questioned his capacity, politically and
morally, to exercise properly and responsibly the powers that had been
entrusted to him. As protector, the king's uncle had broken the fundamental code of good governorship.

The fact that Edward Seymour was not king undoubtedly made
political life more complex. Royal proclamations generally expressed
in entirely conventional terms the relationship between the king, the
protector, and the Privy Council. Edward acted with the advice and
consent of Seymour as his uncle and counsellor, the governor of his
person and protector of his realms, dominions, and people, supported
by the 'rest of his Majesties Counsaill'.[38] Nevertheless, a proclamation

[33] SP 10/9 fo. 41r (8 Oct. 1549; Knighton 396).
[34] Hatfield House Library, Hertfordshire, Cecil Papers 150 fo. 137r (Dudley to Edward Clinton, 15 Oct. 1549).
[35] *APC 1547–50*, p. 330 (6 Oct. 1549), with my emphasis.
[36] British Library, Cotton MS Titus B 2 fo. 36r, printed in *APC 1547–50*, p. 334 (councillors in London to Edward, 7 Oct. 1549).
[37] SP 10/9 fos. 72v–74r, printed in Pocock, ed., *Prayer Book*, pp. 114–15 (Knighton 411); quotation at fo. 74r.
[38] See, for example, *All suche Proclamacions, as have been sette furthe by the Kynges Majestie* (London, 1550; STC 7758), sigs. {b6r–v} ('advise of . . . the duke of Somerset, Governor of his moste Royall persone, and Protector of all his realmes, dominions and subjectes, and others of his counsaill', 6 Feb. 1548), c2r ('advise and counsaill, of . . . the Lorde Protector, and the rest of his Majesties

issued during the upheavals of July 1549 stated with some force that the king had 'the principall and continuall charge of the common welth & tranquilitie of this realme', and for that purpose God had 'geven to his majestie power to rule, & to all his people hath enjoyned, lowlynes to obeye'. So this divinely ordained power was exercised by an eleven-year-old boy 'by thinformacion & good advise' of his governor and protector and the Privy Council.[39] William Paget emphasized that Seymour's quasi-monarchical powers placed upon him an even greater obligation to accept advice. 'A king which shall geve men occasion of discourage to saie their opinions franckly receaveth therby great hurte and perill to his realme.' But a subject 'in great aucthoritie (as your grace ys) using suche facion' – here Paget meant 'fashion' – 'ys like to fall into great daungier and perill of his owne personne, besides that to the common wealthe'.[40] Seymour was expected to perform the delicate balancing act that was kingship in the sixteenth century: to act executively and definitively but also consensually. Protector Somerset's failure to accept advice in good part represented a dereliction of the kingly duties he exercised on behalf of his nephew – a failure thrown into sharp relief by the ambiguities and subtleties of his authority.

Like a king, Protector Somerset received written advice from subjects keen to present 'mirrors' of past experience or sententious verse on public life and its duties. 'The pleasaunt poesye of princelie practise', written by William Forrest and presented to Seymour in 1548, sat on the shelves of the duke's library at Syon House.[41] If Seymour read only the opening verses of Forrest's translation, he would have found himself cast in the role of a tutor who helped his royal pupil 'too lerne and knowe thinges after too be doon' (lines 8–11). Edward Tudor's governor was 'a man of puisaunce' (line 46), who had proved himself by 'feate and princelie entreprise' in the providential victories of the Scottish campaign of 1547 (line 51). Edward Seymour was protector, uncle, and friend (lines 64–6). He was not Richard III, 'rager of crueltee' to 'whome the fowrthe Edwarde his children beetooke' (lines 68–9). He was, rather, 'the true

Counsaill', 24 Apr. 1548), {c8v} ('advise and assent of his derest uncle, Edward duke of Somerset, Governor of his royall persone, Protector of his highnes realmes, dominions, and Subjectes, and the rest of his graces counsaill', 31 Oct. 1548).

[39] *All suche Proclamacions*, sigs. {g1v}–g2r (2 July 1549).
[40] SP 10/7 fo. 8v (8 May 1549; Knighton 217).
[41] Gordon R. Batho, 'Syon House: the first two hundred years', *Transactions of the London and Middlesex Archaeological Society*, 19 (1958), p. 8. The volume is now in the British Library (Royal MS 17 D 3), and printed in M.A. Manzalaoui, ed., *Secretum secretorum: nine English versions* (Early English Text Society, 276; Oxford, 1977), pp. 390–534.

Theseus' and the duke Epaminedon (lines 70–1). In 'thaffairs of oure noble Edwarde', Seymour offered his 'helpinge hande' (lines 79–80). 'The pleasaunt poesye' was dedicated to Edward Seymour as uncle of the king and protector 'over his moste royall person, Realmes, and Dominions'. Forrest's prologue to the king is an interesting reflection of the complexity of the protector's position. It was, above all, a verse translation in rhyme royal of the *Secretum secretorum*, a work believed in the sixteenth century to have been written by Aristotle for his pupil Alexander the Great.[42] The intention of 'The pleasaunt poesye' was thus to offer advice to the king, but in preparing his edition Forrest acknowledged that its communication to Edward was at the discretion of Seymour. Forrest presented it to the protector rather than directly to the king. This was not merely a case of circumstance: it was an expression of Seymour's tutorial care for his nephew.[43] Indeed, one of the executors' justifications for the establishment of the protectorate was the education of the king.[44] Similarly, John Cheke told Seymour that Edward's kingship depended on a blend of natural wit and experience, the 'very ground-worke of all wisdome', 'wherein his Majestie best shall be advertised by you'.[45] A preface to the sermons of Bernardino Ochino, dedicated to Seymour, explained the origin of kings and governors in human society, men who represented to their subjects 'the divine majeste of God'.[46] England could be joyful because its religion had been reformed 'through the studye of suche a Prynce as walketh in all the waies of God in goodnes and fayth, ledde by a Gouvernour that moost parfectly hath trayned hym to the same'.[47] Although, as a counterweight to the insecurities of royal minority, the notion of godly Edward supported by his Christian governor and protector had its weaknesses, it was, nevertheless, an extremely significant expression of the nature of Edwardian kingship (see above, chapter 2, pp. 50–6; and below, chapter 4, pp. 115–16).

King and subject fused in the person of Edward Seymour. Consequently, it was at times difficult to distinguish between the exercise of

---

[42] Manzalaoui, ed., *Secretum secretorum*, pp. ix–xlvi.

[43] Manzalaoui, ed., *Secretum secretorum*, p. 394 (lines 99–105).

[44] *APC 1547–50*, p. 67 (21 Mar. 1547).

[45] John Harington, *Nugae Antiquae: being a miscellaneous collection of original papers, in prose and verse; written during the reigns of Henry VIII, Edward VI, Queen Mary, Elizabeth, and King James*, ed. Thomas Park, 2 vols. (London, 1804), I, p. 43.

[46] Bernardino Ochino, *Sermons of the ryght famous and excellent clerke Master Bernardine Ochine* (Ipswich, 1548; *STC* 18765), sig. A2r–{A2}v; quotation at sig. {A2v}.

[47] Ochino, *Sermons*, sig. A3r.

royal power and the influence of Seymour as protector. English kingship in the sixteenth century rested in part on semi-mystical notions of the monarch as a direct representative of God on earth and, more prosaically, on the king as governor, ruling the kingdom from his court through intermediaries endowed by the monarch with royal authority. Edward Seymour could not claim divine sanction, but he did assume the 'political' duties of kingship. In other words, he exercised royal power. His household became an unofficial court, and his personal servants represented both their master as protector and (by association) the king himself. This was not inherently problematic – at least handled properly – because the essential purpose of the protectorate was to govern the realm effectively. In a 'Scedule' of advice offered to Seymour as a New Year's gift in 1549, William Paget exhorted Seymour to exercise power responsibly. The protector had to deliberate maturely, to execute quickly, to do justice, to maintain ministers, to punish the disobedient, and to keep ministers uncorrupted.[48] He was, in short, expected to act like a man of authority. William Gray, a household servant, exhorted his master to act liberally, to exercise justice, and to resist flatterers.[49] At the same time, there were distinctions to be made between protector and king. Paget offered advice like 'Geve your owne to your owne, and the kinges to the kinges franckelie' or 'Take fee or rewarde of the kinge onelie'.[50]

Edward Seymour's regime was a remarkably personal operation because he relied principally on the control of personal monarchy. His nephew was closely supervised, and the royal sign manual was strictly controlled – after all, the protection of the king was one of the most important functions of the establishment set up around Edward after 1547. Seymour's household became a crucial point of contact between governor and governed, and his household men were perceived to be close enough to their master to be able to secure from him favours and benefits for suitors. When, for example, Stephen Gardiner was encouraged in 1548 to preach an acceptable sermon before the king and his court, he was spoken to by the protector's household servants both before and after being heard by the Council (see below, pp. 84–5). Informality was a keynote of the protectorate; this meant, to the distress of constitutional historians, that the boundaries between the personal

[48] Barrett L. Beer and Sybil M. Jack, eds., 'The letters of William, Lord Paget of Beaudesert, 1547–63', *Camden Miscellany XXV* (Camden Society, fourth series, 13; London, 1974), p. 20.
[49] Cambridge University Library, MS Dd.9.31 fo. 12v.   [50] Beer and Jack, eds., 'Paget', p. 20.

and the institutional were eminently flexible. In 1549, for example, clerk of the Privy Council William Honing told principal secretary Thomas Smith – both members of the royal secretariat – that 'it was his graces pleasure' that Smith and the earl of Southampton should examine the debts of crown official William Sharington. Smith, however, had not heard Seymour's decision formally.[51]

These personal dimensions of the protectorate reflected a conventional ideal of the role of a king. Seymour became a recognized focus for executive action. He made decisions and instructed his personal servants and the servants of the crown. Physical proximity to the protector was important, and it is possible to distinguish between Seymour's household as a centre of political and governmental business and the king's court as a place of education, entertainment, and physical protection for Edward. Although Seymour often moved with the royal court, his habits could be flexible. In June 1548, for example, the protector slept at the court in St James' Palace but dined separately at Whitehall.[52] A month later, Michael Stanhope, the first gentleman of the Privy Chamber and the step-brother-in-law of the protector, was attendant on the king. Stanhope asked Edward North, the chancellor of the court of augmentations, to remind Seymour of a private suit. North, in turn, sent the letter to William Cecil as a servant in the protector's household.[53] Stanhope may have already spoken to Seymour – the letter may have been nothing more than a reminder – but it does suggest that even a man physically close to the king needed to secure his interests through the protector and, by extension, the protector's household.

Edward Seymour's residences became centres of power and represented the authority he exercised on behalf of the king. After 1548, he spent £10,000 on the construction of Somerset House in London, and certainly transacted the business of governance there.[54] Seymour's house at Syon (on which he spent £5500 between 1547 and 1551) assumed the role of a royal palace.[55] On the Thames in Middlesex, and nearer to London and the royal residences than Seymour's concentration of lands

---

[51] J.E. Jackson, ed., 'Longleat papers no. 4', *Wiltshire Archaeological and Natural History Magazine*, 18 (1878–79), p. 260 (Smith to John Thynne, 29 Apr. 1549).

[52] Hatfield House Library, Hertfordshire, Cecil Papers 150 fo. 111r (John Fowler to Thomas Seymour, 26 June 1548).

[53] SP 10/4 fo. 50r (North to Cecil, 6 July 1548; Knighton 121); SP 10/4 fo. 51r (Stanhope to North, 27 June 1548; Knighton 122).

[54] H.M. Colvin, ed., *The history of the king's works, IV. 1485–1660 (Part II)* (London, 1982), pp. 252–3. In 1549, for example, Protector Somerset spoke to Bishop Nicholas Ridley of Rochester in the long gallery at Somerset House (18 May 1549; Knighton 237).

[55] Colvin, ed., *King's works*, pp. 272–3.

in Wiltshire and his ancestral home of Wolf Hall near Great Bedwyn, Syon became an operational base for the protectorate. From Syon, attended by members of his household, Seymour dispatched instructions. The Privy Council met there at least once, in June 1549.[56] Katherine Brandon duchess of Suffolk certainly stayed at Syon in the same year; and Thomas Smith, one of the king's principal secretaries, was offered a 'cabyn' there in April 1549. In declining the room, Smith clearly distinguished between residence at Syon and residence at court. His wife had 'lerned well to play the courtier', and, after an illness, he preferred her to stay at court, in London, or at Eton.[57] This was the principal reason for Smith's rejection of the offer of accommodation, and not, surprisingly, his duties near Edward as a senior member of the king's secretariat. Smith's decision was unusual, because property that put Edward Seymour's household men near to their master was competitively sought. For example, Seymour's chamberlain, Richard Whalley, secured a base in Wimbledon (a short ride from Syon and Richmond) in 1549. Whalley, conscious that William Cecil had also been interested in Wimbledon, suggested that the park and tithe of Mortlake might be available as an alternative. Whalley told Cecil that he ought to discuss Mortlake with the chancellor of the court of augmentations, Richard Sackville, during their 'next wytte talk'.[58] Michael Stanhope wrote on Cecil's behalf. So did the protector himself, who requested action because he wanted Cecil 'ney unto hyme'.[59]

The senior men of Seymour's household became key members of the protectorate. The ducal establishment appears to have had a clear coherence, partly because of its conscious godliness but also in the prominence of Seymour's principal servants.[60] The wives of the protector's household men served the duchess of Somerset. Mildred Cecil dedicated an English translation of Basil the Great to Anne Seymour as 'Your Graces in service'.[61] Thomas Smith told the steward of the household, John Thynne, that 'Yf my wief can do my Ladies grace eny service, she shall wait as hir dutie is.'[62] For John Cheke, tutor to the king, Anne Seymour's

[56] SP 10/7 fo. 110r–111v, printed in Pocock, ed., *Prayer Book*, pp. 12–13 (26 June 1549; Knighton 289).

[57] Jackson, ed., 'Longleat papers', pp. 260–1.

[58] SP 10/6 fo. 81r ([?11 Apr.] 1549; Knighton 211).

[59] SP 10/6 fo. 82r (Robert Tyrwhitt to Cecil, 12 Apr. 1549; Knighton 212).

[60] John N. King, 'Protector Somerset, patron of the English Renaissance', *Papers of the Bibliographical Society of America*, 70 (1976), pp. 307–31.

[61] British Library, Royal MS 17 B 18 fo. 2v.

[62] Jackson, ed., 'Longleat papers', p. 261 (20 Apr. 1549).

'singular Favor' had been one of his 'chefe confortes' in his 'diligent service' to Anne's nephew. In January 1549 Cheke felt compelled to apologize to the duchess for the misbehaviour of his wife.[63] The bonds of loyalty were strong. Seymour's household men stayed with him after the collapse of the protectorate, when the public coherence of the Somerset household was reflected in *A Spyrytuall and moost precyouse Pearle*. This included 'A humble peticyon to the lord, practysed in the commune prayer of the whole famylye at Shene, during the trouble of their Lord and mayster the duke of Somerset his grace' by Thomas Becon, 'Minister there'.[64] William Cecil was a household servant until his promotion to royal office in September 1550 (see below, chapter 5, pp. 139–40). In the case of John Thynne, trying to leave senior household office in 1550 was a sensitive business, and its negotiation rested on the intercession of William Cecil as a former Seymour servant. But Thynne made it clear that it was the office of steward he wanted to leave and not the household: 'and I shall be glad to serve him faithfull to the utter most of my power in any other service his grace wol appoint me dureing my lief'.[65]

John Thynne was an old hand. His uncle, William Thynne, was chief clerk of the king's kitchen in the 1520s, a master of the royal household after 1540, and an editor of Chaucer. In 1535, in his early twenties, John Thynne was listed as a salaried member of the household of Lord Vaux of Harrowden. A year later he presented his first account as steward of the household of Edward Seymour, and in October 1536 Thynne was responsible for distributing gifts at Windsor on his master's elevation to the earldom of Hertford.[66] Thynne certainly found his service profitable. In 1540 he was sold the site of Longleat priory, and when other parts of Longleat and Hinton in Wiltshire were granted by the crown to Edward Seymour, Seymour transferred them to Thynne in 1541.[67] Seymour was prepared to intervene personally in Thynne's relationship with the elite of London, and in August 1547 sent 'one M[aster] Cycell' with letters to the common council of the city, insisting that Thynne should be given the packership of strangers' goods. The office had been filled, so a day

[63] British Library, Lansdowne MS 2 fo. 85r, printed in John Gough Nichols, ed., 'Some additions to the biographies of Sir John Cheke and Sir Thomas Smith', *Archaeologia*, 38 (1860), p. 115.
[64] *STC* 25255, sig. O1r.
[65] SP 10/10 fo. 68r (Thynne to Cecil, 14 Sept. 1550; Knighton 464).
[66] S.T. Bindoff, ed., *The House of Commons 1509–1558*, 3 vols. (History of Parliament; London, 1982), III, p. 463; cf. also Michael L. Bush, 'The rise to power of Edward Seymour, Protector Somerset, 1500–1547', PhD dissertation, University of Cambridge (1965), pp. 194–206.
[67] *Letters and papers, foreign and domestic, of the reign of Henry VIII*, ed. J.S. Brewer, J. Gairdner, R.H. Brodie *et al.*, 21 vols. and *Addenda* (London, 1862–1932), XVI no. 947 (57).

later Thynne became a freeman of the city as a member of the Mercers' Company. In 1549 he cemented his links with the London establishment by marrying Christian, the daughter of Richard Gresham, a former mayor of London associated with the Mercers.[68] In the tense summer of that year, Edward Seymour entrusted Thynne with the recruitment and command of a group of footmen to protect the king.[69] He was closely associated with protector and protectorate, as he found to his cost in November 1549.[70]

Thynne, like other principal members of the household, served in a number of county offices. In 1548 he was a commissioner for chantries in Wiltshire and Salisbury, and between 1548 and 1549 served as sheriff in Somerset and Dorset. He was a commissioner for inquisitions *post mortem* in 1548, again for Wiltshire and Salisbury. Richard Whalley, the protector's chamberlain, was a JP for the North Riding of Yorkshire and a chantry commissioner for Yorkshire, York, and Hull. Thomas Fisher and Seymour servant John Hales were chantry commissioners for Leicestershire, Warwickshire, and Coventry. Hales was also a JP.[71] These men were not imposed on counties, and their appointments tended to reflect their own areas of territorial interest and influence. William Cecil, Seymour's master of requests, and Lawrence Eresby (Cecil's brother-in-law) were two of the commissioners for Lincolnshire and Lincoln.[72] Richard Fulmerston, the comptroller of Seymour's household, was responsible for Norfolk, Suffolk, and Norwich – understandable, because Fulmerston owned some of the property confiscated from Thomas Howard duke of Norfolk.[73] But the performance of local duties and offices was enhanced by association with the protector. When Edward Seymour wrote to William Cecil as surveyor of Lincolnshire in the court

[68] Bindoff, ed., *Commons 1509–1558*, III, p. 464.
[69] Longleat House Library, Wiltshire, Seymour Papers 4 fo. 12r (Seymour to Thynne, 18 July 1549).
[70] 'Thaunswer of Sir John Thynne knight unto certayn Interogatories deliverid to him', 28 Nov. 1549: *Calendar of the manuscripts of the marquis of Bath preserved at Longleat, Wiltshire*, 4 vols. (Royal Commission on Historical Manuscripts; London, 1904–68), IV, p. 112; Longleat House Library, Wiltshire, Seymour Papers 4 fos. 127r–128r.
[71] For Thynne, see Bindoff, ed., *Commons 1509–1558*, III, p. 463. JPs in 1547: John Hales (Middlesex and Warwickshire: *CPR 1547–48*, pp. 86, 90); and Richard Whalley (Yorkshire, North Riding: *CPR 1547–48*, p. 92). Chantry commissioners in 1548: Thomas Fisher (Leicestershire, Warwickshire, and Coventry: *CPR 1548–49*, p. 135); Richard Fulmerston (Norfolk, Suffolk, and Norwich: *CPR 1548–49*, p. 136); John Hales (Leicestershire, Warwickshire, and Coventry: *CPR 1548–49*, p. 135); John Thynne (Wiltshire and Salisbury: *CPR 1548–59*, p. 135); and Richard Whalley (Yorkshire, York, and Hull: *CPR 1548–49*, p. 136).
[72] For the reference to Eresby, a commissioner for chantries in 1548 (*CPR 1548–49*, p. 136), see SP 10/10 fos. 94r–95v (William Rede to William Cecil, 12 Oct. 1550; Knighton 482).
[73] *CPR 1547–48*, pp. 129–30, 211.

of augmentations, in 1548, in a letter requesting action on manors and lands in the county, Cecil was addressed as 'our Loving servaunte'.[74]

William Cecil was the brightest star of Edward Seymour's household. Richard Whalley, one of Cecil's friends, was in his late forties and had worked his way through the households of Thomas Lovell (in the 1520s) and Thomas Manners earl of Rutland (1540–41) before his appointment as Seymour's chamberlain at the beginning of Edward's reign. Cecil, by contrast, was twenty-seven years old in 1547, and he was promoted with remarkable speed. Precisely when and how Cecil joined the protector is unclear. Cambridge may have been one route. His university friend, Thomas Smith, joined Seymour's household in 1547 with money he had saved from his university lectureship in civil law, his chancellorship to the bishop of Ely, and a benefice.[75] But Smith, unlike Cecil, had spent the 1540s in academic life. Cecil had left Cambridge in 1540 without taking a degree, and entered Gray's Inn, following in the footsteps of future Edwardian lawyers like Richard Goodrich and Nicholas Bacon, and Thomas Wroth, servant to Edward as prince of Wales. Four years after the death of his first wife, Mary Cheke, in 1541, he had married Mildred Cooke, entering a family clearly associated with Catherine Parr and the reformers gathered around her.[76] Cecil's father, Richard, was also a point of contact with the royal court. He had been yeoman of the robes to Henry VIII and received New Year's gifts from Edward in the same office in 1548 and 1549.[77] Another link with court was John Cheke, Cecil's brother-in-law, whose duties as tutor to Edward as prince of Wales and king may have allowed Cecil a degree of access and contact, complemented by the influence of Anthony Cooke. There is some evidence to suggest that by 1547 at the latest, and probably between 1545 and 1547, Cecil had made some useful connections with the Parrs and with Katherine Brandon, the evangelical duchess of Suffolk (see below, chapter 4, pp. 123–4).

Beyond speculation is the fact that William Cecil was 'with my lord protectores grace' in July 1547.[78] His role may have been fairly informal

[74] British Library, Lansdowne MS 2 fo. 49r–v (15 Oct. 1548).
[75] Nichols, ed., 'Sir John Cheke and Sir Thomas Smith', p. 123.
[76] James Kelsey McConica, *English humanists and Reformation politics under Henry VIII and Edward VI* (Oxford, 1968 edn), pp. 200–34; Maria Dowling, *Humanism in the age of Henry VIII* (London and Dover, New Hampshire, 1986), pp. 211–14; Maria Dowling, 'The gospel and the court: Reformation under Henry VIII', in Peter Lake and Maria Dowling, eds., *Protestantism and the national church in sixteenth century England* (London, 1987), pp. 60–71.
[77] John Gough Nichols, ed., *The literary remains of King Edward VI*, 2 vols. (London, 1857), I, p. cccxii.
[78] SP 10/2 fo. 10v (Lord De La Warr to Cecil, 25 July 1547; Knighton 48).

and perhaps initially unpaid.[79] Robert Goche referred to him in 1547 as 'agent for my lorde protectores grace'.[80] There were contemporary rumours that Cecil had been used to ease Thomas Smith out of the office of master of requests to the protector, and the suggestion, from Smith, that Cecil had taken full advantage of the benefits of his new position in partnership with his servant and kinsman Lawrence Eresby.[81] Smith, piqued by criticism of his personal and professional lives, may have overstated the case. But Cecil and Eresby certainly purchased property in the summer of 1549.[82] It is equally clear Cecil was acting as 'Master of the requestes' to Edward Seymour by July 1548.[83] He appears also to have worked as the protector's secretary, perhaps complementing, rather than replacing, Thomas Fisher.[84]

Physical proximity to the protector had its benefits. Correspondents relied on Cecil's ability to communicate personally with his master. Elizabeth Browne, the wife of Anthony Browne of the Privy Chamber, asked Cecil to recommend her brother to Seymour 'to goo into scotlande to serve the kings majestie there'.[85] John Cheke acknowledged the part Cecil had played in a 'sute to mi lordes grace', successful because of 'mi lordes goodnes, and your frendship'.[86] Cecil's position undoubtedly reflected the dynamics of the maturing protectorate. John Dudley earl of Warwick regularly sued for property and office. Within a month of the establishment of the protectorate he wrote to William Paget in an

---

[79] Cecil's name does not appear in the book of household wages prepared by John Thynne for 31 July–31 Dec. 1547: Longleat House Library, Wiltshire, Seymour Papers 10 fos. 167r–170r.

[80] SP 10/4 fo. 10v (Knighton 6).

[81] Nichols, ed., 'Sir John Cheke and Sir Thomas Smith', p. 124. For Smith's and Cecil's careers as masters of requests, see Michael L. Bush, 'Protector Somerset and requests', *Historical Journal*, 17 (1974), pp. 451–64.

[82] *CPR 1549–51*, p. 59 (6 July 1549).

[83] SP 10/4 fo. 56v (Anthony St Leger to Cecil, 13 July 1548; Knighton 124). William Patten suggested that Cecil was 'master of Requestes, with my lorde Protectours grace' in Jan. 1548: *The Expedicion into Scotlande* (London, 1548; *STC* 19479), sig. {P4v}. Correspondents like Robert Goche and John Dudley did not commit themselves: SP 10/4 fo. 10v (Goche to Cecil, 14 Apr. 1548; Knighton 101); SP 10/4 fo. 27v (Dudley to Cecil, 4 June 1548; Knighton 106).

[84] SP 10/4 fo. 58v (Edward North *et al.* to Cecil, 13 July 1548; Knighton 125).

[85] SP 10/2 fo. 7r (Browne to Cecil, 25 July 1547; Knighton 47).

[86] SP 10/4 fo. 49r (4 July 1548). The suit may well have concerned the suppressed College of St John Baptist at Stoke-by-Clare (Suffolk), which was granted to Cheke and Walter Moyle of Kent on 21 Oct. 1548 (*CPR 1547–48*, pp. 284–5). Matthew Parker had been dean of the college between 1535 and its suppression, and Cheke played an important part in securing Parker a pension of £40 per year as compensation for the loss of income: James Goodwin, ed., *The Gospel according to Saint Matthew and part of the first chapter of the Gospel according to Saint Mark translated into English from the Greek, with original notes, by Sir John Cheke, knight* (London and Cambridge, 1843), p. 113 (Cheke to Parker, 7 June [1547]); *A history of Suffolk*, ed. William Page, 2 vols. (Victoria History of the Counties of England; London, 1907–11), II, p. 149.

attempt to secure for himself the castle, meadows, and park of Warwick.[87] He asked Paget to use his 'frendship, to move the Rest of my Lordes to this affect'.[88] Dudley eventually fell into the habit of working directly through the protector's household servants. Cecil and John Thynne became useful and regular correspondents.[89]

Cecil's role must be kept in perspective. He was one man in a complex network of personal and political influence; a network that extended out from the protector to his family and household and the king's Privy Chamber. Although suitors and household servants could hope to influence, success was not inevitable. In 1549, for example, Thomas Smith tried to persuade Edward Seymour to help John Thynne, who had lost money in his dealings with William Sharington. Smith emphasized that Thynne had been wronged but the protector refused to help. Smith had even prepared a warrant but 'in no wyse' could he secure Seymour's signature.[90] But collaborative efforts did sometimes pay off. In July 1548 Smith wrote a letter to William Cecil on behalf of one Edward Gascoigne, a former pupil at Queens' College, Cambridge. Smith recommended Gascoigne for the deanery of Peterborough, was prepared to vouch for his former student's 'wit and judgement', and proposed a meeting between Gascoigne and Cecil. Smith hoped Cecil would 'so forther hym as miche as ye can, and as ye wold have me do for one of yowrs'. If Cecil agreed to help, Smith proposed to ask the protector's wife to intercede on Gascoigne's behalf.[91] A year later, Cecil had done enough for Gascoigne to warrant Smith's thanks for his 'gentlenes'.[92]

Even gentlemen of the king's Privy Chamber made similar demands. The suit by Michael Stanhope from July 1548 was of course communicated to the protector through William Cecil (see above, p. 76). A letter from Anthony St Leger, one of Stanhope's colleagues in the Privy Chamber (but recently returned from Ireland), demanded even more active intercession and intervention by Cecil. St Leger asked him to speak to Protector Somerset on behalf of St Leger's brother and in a personal suit for land in Ireland. St Leger would do his best to return the favour: 'although I be not hable to requiet your gentlenes towardes

---

[87] SP 10/1 fo. 104r–v ([24] March 1547; Knighton 28).   [88] SP 10/1 fo. 104r.
[89] For example, Longleat House Library, Wiltshire, Thynne Papers 1 fos. 11r–18v (John Dudley to Thynne, Mar.–Apr. 1549).
[90] Jackson, ed., 'Longleat papers', p. 260 (Smith to Thynne, 29 Apr. 1549).
[91] SP 10/4 fo. 59r (25 July 1548; Knighton 127).
[92] SP 10/8 fo. 58r (Thomas Smith to Cecil, 19 July 1549; Knighton 330). In Oct. 1552 Gascoigne was granted a canonry and prebend at Winchester Cathedral: *CPR 1550–53*, p. 271.

me yet shall I labour to do the same'. But as a small token of his gratitude he sent Cecil two dozen marten skins 'but for a remembraunce till bettere comme'.[93] This was not, strictly speaking, political influence. There is no evidence to suggest that Cecil played a part in the policy-making of the protectorate. But he could, and did, establish contacts and connections with some extremely influential men and women, people who, in turn, depended on his physical proximity to Edward Seymour: the formula 'Master Cecil with my lord protector's grace' became a key element in the Cecil correspondence between 1547 and 1550. Cecil's contacts also helped him to negotiate the difficulties of the autumn of 1549. His relationship with John Dudley, the petitioning earl of Warwick, involved a substantial correspondence. This was the context of Cecil's promotion by Dudley to the Marshalsea Court during the Scottish campaign of 1547.[94] It also reinforced his view of Cecil as 'A ffaiethfull servant and by that Terme most wytte Cowncelor' after the collapse of the protectorate (see below, chapter 5, pp. 139–40).

Cecil's service during the protectorate was emphatically personal. In August 1549, at a time of real instability for the regime, Cecil and principal secretaries William Petre and Thomas Smith were given the authority to examine all books in English about to be printed. Cecil was personally and solely responsible for the supervision of John Mardeley. Mardeley could only print with the licence of 'my Lord Protectour and the rest of the Kinges Majestes Counsaile' and his works had 'to be first subscribed with the hand of William Cicill, esquier'.[95] Just as personal – and certainly more politically sensitive – was the part Cecil played as the protector's emissary to Stephen Gardiner, the bishop of Winchester, in 1548. The regime claimed that, in his preaching in 1547 and 1548, Gardiner had ignored a royal command to avoid the controversial subject of the mass, resulting in contempt for the king and a disturbance of the common quiet and the unity of the realm.[96] Gardiner and his views were sensitive subjects. He had been a Henrician councillor of authority, and the regime believed that the bishop's opinions were dangerous in the context of violence in Cornwall (discussed above, chapter 2, pp. 57–60). The aim of Cecil's mission of June 1548 was to encourage Gardiner to 'teache the people the truthe in that matter', and to present this truth publicly in a sermon at court on St Peter's Day (29 June).[97]

[93] SP 10/4 fo. 55r (13 July 1548; Knighton 124).   [94] Patten, *Expedicion into Scotlande*, sig. {P4v}.
[95] *APC 1547–50*, p. 312 (13 Aug. 1549).
[96] John Foxe, *Actes and Monuments of these latter and perillous dayes* (London, 1563; *STC* 11222), p. 777.
[97] Foxe, *Actes and Monuments*, p. 805.

Cecil visited Gardiner in Southwark.[98] According to Gardiner's chaplain, Thomas Watson, 'in opening to the sayd byshop the Dukes pleasure' Cecil told him 'that the sayd byshop should preach before the kynges majesty, and write his sermon'. Cecil emphasized that Edward Seymour had shown Gardiner favour 'and not doone extremity'. Both Gardiner and Watson found the tone and content of the message insulting, and Watson was sent by the bishop to complain to the protector about Cecil's behaviour. Watson, like his master, had assumed that Cecil had 'misused his graces message'. He had not. In the king's garden at Whitehall, the protector heard Watson's complaint and called Cecil into their presence. When Cecil began to relate what he had said to Gardiner, Watson realized that Cecil had only spoken 'accordingly as the sayd Dukes grace had commaunded him to do'. Watson was asked to tell his master not to 'suspect the sayd Dukes trustye servauntes, whome he used to sende unto hym'.[99]

The attempt to persuade Stephen Gardiner to preach an acceptable sermon in June 1548 offers a fascinating insight into the operation of the regime. Gardiner's refusal to cooperate meant that Seymour instructed Cecil 'to make a letter unto him, from the lord Protector in the kinges majesties name', ordering him not to discuss the mass. Seymour signed the prepared letter at Syon, and it was sent by special messenger to the bishop.[100] Gardiner himself described how Cecil personally carried articles to him, 'which the said master Cicil woulde have had the said bishop to reherse in his sermon woorde by woorde, lyke a lesson made for a childe to learn, whiche the sayde bishop refused to do'.[101] This was a persistent and personal campaign of persuasion. When Gardiner visited Seymour, he spoke to Thomas Smith and discussed the articles in the protector's 'privye chamber'.[102] Smith and Cecil were sent 'divers tymes' to 'travayle with hym, to agree to certayne of the kynges majestyes procedynges'. On the orders of the Council, Smith and Cecil wrote articles and discussed them with Gardiner during a number of visits. Gardiner refused to give way, so he was sent for by the lords of the Council to a chamber in the garden at Whitehall. During the meeting, William

---

[98] From 'A longe matter proposed by the bishop of Winchester' (8 Jan. 1551): Foxe, *Actes and Monuments*, p. 784.
[99] Foxe, *Actes and Monuments*, p. 809.
[100] From Cecil's deposition: Foxe, *Actes and Monuments*, pp. 805–6.
[101] From 'A longe matter proposed by the bishop of Winchester': Foxe, *Actes and Monuments*, p. 785.
[102] Foxe, *Actes and Monuments*, p. 785.

Paulet earl of Wiltshire was given the responsibility of bringing Gardiner to a 'full agreemente, to settefoorth the sayde artycles'. Paulet and Smith were sent to 'wayte on hym' and 'to take his fynall resolution'.[103]

The protectorate failed to coerce Stephen Gardiner. Nevertheless, these accounts do offer a snapshot of the regime in 1548. The men who gave written depositions at Gardiner's trial in 1550 revealed interesting and significant details – the importance of characters like Cecil and Smith, for example, or the responsibilities of men near to the king but just outside the inner circle of power. Cecil heard Gardiner's sermon and tested it against his own copy of the articles presented to the bishop. He thought that some subjects were handled in 'suche doutfull sorte' that they should have been left unspoken, 'namely of the kinges supremacy, & of the byshoppe of Romes auctority'.[104] The king's tutors were able to hear and to judge the sermon. John Cheke listened to Gardiner 'standing beside the kinges majestyes person, where he might and dyd perfectly heare the sayd byshop'.[105] Richard Cox had been given a copy of the articles for the sermon by Thomas Smith's clerk.[106] Thomas Wroth, a gentleman of the Privy Chamber, also heard the sermon; Nicholas Throckmorton, however, probably still in the household of Catherine Parr, 'stoode so farre of, and in suche a thrust of the people, as he could not well heare at all tymes what was sayde by the sayde byshoppe in the tyme of hys sayde Sermon'.[107]

Strong hints of a relationship with the Parrs connect William Cecil to another Seymour servant, and former Cambridge colleague, Thomas Smith. Cecil wrote the preface to Catherine Parr's *The lamentacion of a sinner*, printed in November 1547 'at the instant desire' of one of Cecil's close personal friends, Katherine Brandon duchess of Suffolk, and the 'earnest request' of Queen Catherine's brother William, the marquess of Northampton.[108] Catherine Parr's death in 1548 appears to have given Thomas Smith an opportunity to buy a substantial piece of property in Somerset. The transaction was suggested to him by John Thynne of the protector's household, and countenanced by William Parr.[109] Indeed, Smith probably owed his Marlborough seat in the parliament of 1547 to a combination of Parr and Seymour influence in Wiltshire.[110] This new,

[103] Foxe, *Actes and Monuments*, p. 808.   [104] Foxe, *Actes and Monuments*, p. 805.
[105] Foxe, *Actes and Monuments*, p. 807.   [106] Foxe, *Actes and Monuments*, p. 808.
[107] Foxe, *Actes and Monuments*, pp. 776–7.
[108] *STC* 4827 (unpaginated); *STC* 4828 (28 Mar. 1548), sigs. A2r–{A7r}.
[109] Nichols, ed., 'Sir John Cheke and Sir Thomas Smith', p. 123.
[110] Bindoff, ed., *Commons 1509–1558*, III, p. 338.

political phase of Smith's career was consciously and carefully planned. Smith himself separated his Cambridge career, broadly defined to cover his lectureship in civil law and his office as chancellor to the bishop of Ely, from his arrival at court. He entered the protector's service quickly, with the intention of spending the money he had saved from his lectureship, his chancellorship, and the benefice of Leverington in Cambridgeshire on a number of strategic purchases suitable for a courtier. Thynne's advice gave him land in Somerset. But Smith also bought two London houses: the first in Cannon Row, Westminster (which he let to William Paget); and the second, purchased with the help of his younger brother George, in Philpot Lane.[111]

George Smith had merchant connections in London and also the primary responsibility for looking after his brother's savings. Thomas Smith consolidated his own London connections in April 1548 when he married Elizabeth Carkeke, the daughter of printer William; there may well have been a link between Elizabeth's dowry of a thousand marks and Smith's lease of the house in Cannon Row a month later. But Smith's base in London also reflected the security of his position within the regime. He worked as Seymour's master of requests, his secretary, an informal clerk of the Privy Council, and, from April 1548, principal secretary to the king. Elton disapproved of the part Smith and Cecil played, as personal servants to the protector, in subverting Thomas Cromwell's 'bureacratic foundations of the reformed administration' during Seymour's protectorate.[112] But the fact is that clear distinctions between the formal mechanics of government (principally the Council) and the informal (the protector's household) were blurred in the extreme. Cecil, still a household servant rather than a servant of the king, helped principal secretaries Smith and Petre to censor books in 1549. Between March 1547 and April 1548 Smith acted as unofficial clerk of the Privy Council.[113] Smith, like Cecil, was approached by suitors, even in his 'formal' role as principal secretary. In May 1549 Mary Fitz Roy duchess of Richmond asked 'master secrytary smythe' to secure from the protector preaching licences for the 'honest and godly' John Hontyngeton, Thomas Some, and Dr Henry Kynge. She also thanked Smith for his help in enabling her 'cossyn' William Farmer to secure property in Norfolk and Suffolk, purchased with Richard Fulmerston, the comptroller of the protector's

---

[111] Nichols, ed., 'Sir John Cheke and Sir Thomas Smith', p. 122.
[112] Elton, *Reform and reformation*, p. 338.
[113] D.E. Hoak, *The King's Council in the reign of Edward VI* (Cambridge, 1976), p. 271.

household.[114] Smith certainly replied, and he must have done so extremely quickly. He questioned the duchess of Richmond's choice of candidates. Within a day of her first letter, Fitz Roy wanted Smith to withdraw his 'evell opynyon' of Hontyngeton, and asked him once again 'to soles[i]te thes my seute to my lordes grace' so that she would 'have juste caus to render to you my harty thankes'.[115]

CONTROL AND OPPOSITION

So power in the protectorate rested with Edward Seymour, and between 1547 and 1549 Seymour governed the kingdom, through intermediaries, from his household. In turn, the household and its men represented a powerful nexus of interest and patronage. But the polity was a personal monarchy, in which the king was a natural focus of attention and concern. His court was still an important point of contact between monarch and subjects. Although, physically, the influence of the ducal household reflected Protector Somerset's exercise of sovereign power on behalf of his nephew, the establishment set up around the king was exceptionally important. This may explain why Edward Seymour strongly influenced the choice of men entrusted with the care of the king. One list of salaried court officers 'nuely placed in ordinary of the chamber' suggests that the king's chaplains and the clerk of the closet (the king's chapel), his surgeons, the yeomen of the chamber, the groom porter, and even a page were nominated by the protector.[116] Edward's transformation from prince to king meant that some of the gentlemen who had served him as prince found themselves 'unplaced' in the early months of 1547. Edward inherited his father's royal secretariat; this meant that his former secretary, Thomas Eynns, found himself unemployed, along with a whole team of salaried and unsalaried gentleman waiters – men like Philip Gerrard, a groom of Edward's chamber in 1545, a yeoman by 1547, and a minor but published author.[117]

---

[114] SP 10/7 fo. 1r–v (Fitz Roy to Smith, 4 May 1549; Knighton 213). Less than a fortnight later, Farmer and his partner in the transaction, the protector's household comptroller Richard Fulmerston, were granted properties in Norfolk and Suffolk in return for over £2000 paid by them into the court of augmentations: *CPR 1548–49*, p. 241 (17 May 1549).

[115] SP 10/7 fo. 5r (Fitz Roy to Smith, 5 May 1549; Knighton 215).

[116] British Library, Royal MS 7 C 16 fo. 96r–v.

[117] British Library, Royal MS 7 C 16 fo. 94r–v (Eynns and Gerrard); Desiderius Erasmus, *A very pleasaunt & fruitful Diologe called the Epicure, made by that famous clerke Erasmus of Roterodame*, trans. Philip Gerrard (London, 1545; *STC* 10460), sig. B3r; Philip Gerrard, *A godly invective in the defence of the Gospell* (London, 1547; *STC* 11797), sig. {a6v}.

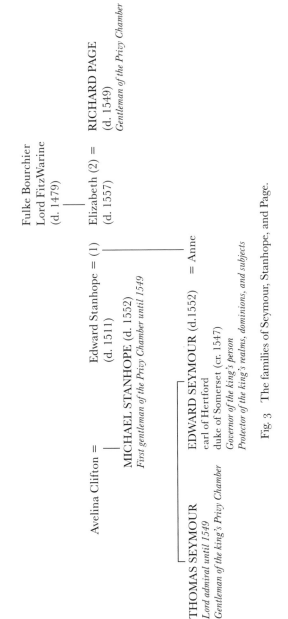

Fig. 3   The families of Seymour, Stanhope, and Page.

And yet some members of Edward's household as prince of Wales did represent a strong element of continuity in the court establishment. Richard Cox, who had served as the prince's almoner, continued to serve as tutor and almoner after 1547. Other members of Cox's establishment, including cupbearer Henry Sidney, were 'to remayn and have their enterteinment as they had before'.[118] Sidney went on to serve as a gentleman of the king's Privy Chamber after 1551 (see below, chapter 5, pp. 155–6). Dr Thomas Bill, Edward's physician in 1544 and the brother of William Bill of St John's College, Cambridge, was still in post in 1547.[119] John Cheke continued to share with Richard Cox responsibility for the king's education. John Ryther, the cofferer of Edward's princely household since 1541, was still cofferer over ten years later.[120] Thomas Wroth served in the private rooms of Edward as prince and as king (see below, chapter 5, pp. 155–6). But the most important link between Edward's princely past and his kingly entourage was Richard Page, a rather elusive character whose name does not appear in the list of the men of the 'privie chamber & certen of the counsell at large' from 1548.[121] He was, nevertheless, an ideal guardian for the king. In Page continuity of royal service and allegiance to Seymour dovetailed. He was the second husband of Elizabeth Stanhope, the daughter of Fulke Bourchier Lord FitzWarine. Elizabeth's first marriage had been to Edward Stanhope; their daughter Anne married Edward Seymour (see Fig. 3). But Edward Stanhope had been married before, and his son from this first marriage was Michael Stanhope, the other major figure, along with Richard Page, in Edward VI's Privy Chamber. So, through the two families of Elizabeth Bourchier, Page, Stanhope, and Anne and Edward Seymour were all closely related.

Richard Page – like William Bill, John Cheke, Richard Cox, and John Ryther – represented continuity. During the 1520s he had served in the household of the duke of Richmond; in the late 1530s and early 1540s Page was lieutenant of the gentleman pensioners. But in July 1544 he was appointed chamberlain to Edward as prince of Wales. By 1548 he shared with Michael Stanhope the supervision and governance of the king. Stanhope was responsible for the physical security of Edward in 1547 and 1548, and slept in or near the king's private apartments. It

---

[118] British Library, Royal MS 7 C 16 fo. 96r.
[119] *Letters and papers*, ed. Brewer, Gairdner, Brodie *et al.*, XIX:1, no. 864 (July 1544); British Library, Royal MS 7 C 16 fo. 96v.
[120] *Letters and papers*, ed. Brewer, Gairdner, Brodie *et al.*, XVI, no. 1488 (4) (Dec. 1541); Knighton 234, 285, 421; 666, 667, 682.
[121] SP 10/5 fo. 55r–v (Knighton 137).

is possible that Stanhope's appearance as 'first gentleman' of the Privy Chamber (a title he held from August 1548) coincided with Richard Page's retirement. But Stanhope, unlike Page, had no clear claim to the governorship of the king, beyond the fact that he was the step-brother of the protector's wife and was personally close to Edward Seymour. During the late 1530s and early 1540s, Stanhope was the keeper of royal parks in Nottinghamshire, Suffolk, and Surrey. There is a strong northern theme to his accumulation of property and his office-holding. Stanhope bought land in Yorkshire. He served as a justice of the peace and as a commissioner for chantries in Yorkshire, and was lieutenant of Hull between 1542 and his death. His career had begun in the household of Thomas Manners earl of Rutland, and he became, after two years in the royal stables, an esquire of the body in 1540.[122]

Michael Stanhope's Henrician career had not developed with the speed and fluency of, say, Thomas Darcy, a contemporary of Stanhope and another gentleman of the Edwardian Privy Chamber. But Stanhope was, nevertheless, a key link between the protector and the king's entourage. He was responsible for co-ordinating entertainment for the king, and on at least one occasion wrote to Thomas Cawarden, the master of the revels, with instructions from the protector.[123] Even more significant was Stanhope's effective control of the finances of the Privy Chamber. Edward Seymour held the keys to the supplies of royal cash, but as groom of the stole Stanhope was responsible for the royal purse.[124] Similarly, a report on the king's secret rooms at Whitehall Palace revealed how, in 1547 and 1548, items had been taken to the chambers and houses of Edward and Anne Seymour by Stanhope and John Thynne. It is Thynne's position, rather than Stanhope's, that should probably raise eyebrows: in 1548 the steward of the protector's household carried the keys to the king's silk house.[125]

The coherence and the stability of Edward Seymour's regime rested on an establishment of men at once loyal to the king and trusted by the protector. Opposition to Seymour's power, and the methods he used to enhance and protect it, rarely made political waves. His dominance of the governing establishment reflected the quasi-monarchical powers he exercised. The protectorate only collapsed when Edward Seymour

[122] Bindoff, ed., *Commons 1509–1558*, III, pp. 368–9.
[123] Albert Feuillerat, ed., *Documents relating to the revels at court in the time of King Edward VI and Queen Mary* (Louvain, 1914), p. 33.
[124] Dale Hoak, 'The secret history of the Tudor court: the king's coffers and the king's purse, 1542–1553', *Journal of British Studies*, 26 (1987), pp. 218–20.
[125] SP 10/6 fos. 72r–73v (Knighton 204).

abused the authority that had been entrusted to him, and that abuse silhouetted itself against the policy failures and miscalculations of 1549. But there was one major challenge to Protector Somerset's authority. It was crushed, quickly and brutally, at the end of 1548 and the beginning of 1549. And yet although this was not political opposition in the conventional sense – it came from within the Seymour family, in the person of Edward's younger brother Thomas – it nevertheless exposed the nature of the establishment set up around the king and tested the durability of Protector Somerset's regime.

In 1549 the Privy Council contended that Thomas Seymour had attempted to secure the king's person and to take 'the same into his order and disposicion'. Also, they contended, Lord Thomas had tried to persuade the king, without the advice or knowledge of the protector or the Council, to write letters 'of his devising' to parliament.[126] In order to do this, he had attempted to bribe men in the Privy Chamber, 'and of the nerest about his Majesties persone', and had plotted with noblemen. According to the Council, Thomas Seymour had also worked for a marriage to Elizabeth Tudor, the second in the line of succession.[127] Fraternal jealousy was one cause of Thomas Seymour's dissatisfaction. A household servant, William Wightman, later recalled that Nicholas Throckmorton – a cousin of Thomas Seymour's wife Catherine Parr – told him once in conversation that 'the desyr of A kingdome knoweth no kynred'.[128] But there was a purpose to Thomas Seymour's attempt to secure a position of prominence in the regime that belied his indiscretion and incompetence. The fact that Edward Seymour had a brother, and yet claimed the office of protector of the king's realms and power as governor of Edward's person, became an issue that challenged the structure and nature of the regime. Even Thomas Seymour knew his English history well enough by 1548 to realize that, during the minority of a king, there was precedent for dividing power more equally between the principal men of the realm.[129]

Thomas Seymour pursued a conscious and consistent plan of attack. He wanted a formal recognition of his importance and his nearness to the king in blood. This, he knew, was impossible – at least through his brother. So what Lord Thomas planned, with some precision, was a parliamentary endorsement of a separation of the offices of protector and

---

[126] *APC 1547–50*, p. 237 (17 Jan. 1549). [127] *APC 1547–50*, pp. 238–9 (17 Jan. 1549).
[128] Hatfield House Library, Hertfordshire, Cecil Papers 150 fo. 44v (20 Jan. 1549).
[129] Hatfield House Library, Hertfordshire, Cecil Papers 150 fo. 54r (from an interview with Thomas Seymour's servant John Harington, 25 Jan. 1549).

governor. According to the Privy Council, in 1549, Thomas Seymour's model was the reign of Henry VI, when Humphrey duke of Gloucester was appointed protector, John duke of Bedford regent of France, and the duke of Exeter and bishop of Winchester 'Governors of the kinges parsonne'.[130] To remodel the political establishment in 1548 Seymour needed the support of the king and, ideally, the power of the king's signature. These, in turn, rested on physical proximity to Edward, and Seymour's ability to establish a number of positive relationships with the men around the king. His status as a gentleman of the king's Privy Chamber certainly helped. He regularly talked to at least three grooms of the chamber – John Fowler, John Philpot, and Robert Maddox – and Fowler in particular became an important contact, able to brief Seymour on the king's daily routine and the itinerary of the protector. Seymour also used Fowler to 'put the King in remembraunce of him' at Greenwich, Westminster, and Hampton Court, palaces which were visited, in 1548, in January, February, and June. Two men of more senior social rank, and in positions of particular trust, were John Cheke and Thomas Wroth. Seymour spoke at least once to Wroth in the 'ynner gallery' of St James' Palace, and appears to have asked Wroth to intercede with the king on his behalf.[131] Cheke received £20 from Seymour, paid indirectly through Fowler.[132] He was also asked to 'breke with the King' on subjects of conversation raised by Seymour.[133]

Seymour challenged the integrity, and the security, of Edward's Privy Chamber, and he did very little to mask the fact. During a walk in the privy garden with Henry fitz Alan earl of Arundel, the two men were unable to open a gate. Fitz Alan asked Seymour about his keys, and reminded him that 'yow have a doble key, for so it is in the bok'. Seymour innocently replied that he could not 'tell whither I have or not but if I have eny it is in my casket' at his house in Bromham.[134] On one occasion, at St James' Palace, Seymour commented that a determined individual could seize the king: he had walked through the court unchallenged, and found that there were more men in his retinue than the 'whole house'. The king's outward and inward chambers were effectively left unguarded.[135] At the same time, the royal establishment does seem to

---

[130] SP 10/6 fo. 69r (Knighton 203; 24 Feb. 1549).
[131] Nichols, ed., *Literary remains*, I, p. cxvi; SP 10/6 fo. 24v.
[132] Nichols, ed., *Literary remains*, I, p. cxix.
[133] Nichols, ed. *Literary remains*, I, p. cxvi.
[134] Hatfield House Library, Hertfordshire, Cecil Papers 150 fo. 101v (Thomas Smith's holograph notes of an interview with Seymour, 18 Feb. 1549).
[135] SP 10/6 fos. 24r–28v (Knighton 185).

have been aware of the physical threat to its supervision of Edward. In 1548 John Fowler told Thomas Seymour that Michael Stanhope had 'over about half a yere past & at ij or iij other sondry tymes' issued a 'Commaundment that if eny man shuld knock at the dore after that he was a bed thei shuld call hym up & waken hym before thei did open the dore'.[136]

Seizing the physical person of the king had to be complemented by at least two other strategies. The first was the removal of Edward from reliance on the establishment set up to control and to supervise him. The second was the building of a relationship of trust – and, importantly, of equal reliance – between the king and Lord Thomas. Here, the protectorate was remarkably effective in shielding the king: even for a gentleman of the king's Privy Chamber, an officer of state, and Edward's second uncle, the establishment maintained by Michael Stanhope and Richard Page was a frustrating and irritating nut to crack. Both men had the king under close and constant supervision. Thomas Seymour admitted in February 1549 that he would have been 'contented that he shoulde have the governaunce of him [the king] as Master Stannop hade'.[137] Page had also presented a problem. William Sharington told his interrogators that during Edward Seymour's time in Scotland, in 1547, Lord Thomas had told him that 'he misliked that my said lord Protector had not apointed him to have the government of the king before so dronken a sole as Sir Richerd Page was'.[138] In April 1548 ('aboute Easter tyde') Thomas Seymour told John Fowler that if he could have 'the kinge in his custodie as Master Page had he wolde be gladde'.[139]

Thomas Seymour did his best to subvert the protectorate's close supervision of the king, and, in particular, Michael Stanhope's control of the royal purse. Although Edward later denied it, he appears initially to have accepted Lord Thomas' contention that he was a 'beggarly' king with no money to play with or to give away.[140] John Fowler began to receive money from the lord admiral shortly after Edward's coronation in February 1547, and the gifts continued for another year, sent to Hampton Court, Westminster, St James', and Greenwich. According to Fowler, Lord Thomas spent £200 on gifts for the king and his household servants. His intention was to establish a good relationship with his nephew

[136] Hatfield House Library, Hertfordshire, Cecil Papers 150 fo. 101r (Smith's holograph notes of an interview with Seymour, 18 Feb. 1549).
[137] SP 10/6 fo. 70r; Knighton 203 (Seymour's answers, 24 Feb. 1549).
[138] SP 10/6 fo. 35r (Knighton 188).   [139] SP 10/6 fo. 69r (24 Feb. 1549; Knighton 203).
[140] G.W. Bernard, 'The downfall of Sir Thomas Seymour', in G.W. Bernard, ed., *The Tudor nobility* (Manchester and New York, 1992), p. 220.

and the men around the king, but Edward's written recognition of his uncle's kindness was just as important. This was Thomas Seymour's most significant – and, for his brother, most dangerous – achievement. On at least three separate occasions Lord Thomas received papers signed by the king, short notes of thanks, greeting, or recommendation passed to Thomas Seymour by Fowler, and seen (but probably not handled) by John Cheke.[141]

The implications of this sort of written communication between Edward and Thomas Seymour were profound. Cheke later explained how, during the first parliament of the reign, Lord Thomas had approached him 'with a pece of paper in his hand, declaring unto me that he had a Sute to the Lordes of the Parliament house, and that the k[ing's].m[ajesty]. was wel contented to write unto them for him'. The bill was, in effect, a blank cheque. Cheke remembered that the paper had read 'Mi Lordes I prai yow favor mi L[ord] Adm[iral] mine uncles sute, which he wil make unto yow.' The sentence was written in Thomas Seymour's own hand. Cheke had been given a formal order that the king should add his sign manual to nothing that had not been first signed by the protector – an important insight into the nature of Protector Somerset's governance and the 'political' responsibilities of the king's tutor. Thomas Seymour countered that Cheke could deliver the paper and have Edward sign it because the king 'had promised him'. Cheke nevertheless refused.[142]

Thomas Seymour's strategy had a definite shape. He attempted to secure a parliamentary endorsement of his seniority within the regime, or, as Edward Lord Clinton put it, 'it was essy [i.e., easy] to parseve he ment to get som auctoryte that waye whyche he thought otherwyse he could not attayne'.[143] Lord Thomas was conscious of the nature of the king's minority. He admitted to the Privy Council that he had once talked to the earl of Rutland about Edward's 'towardnes', whom he thought 'wold be a man iij yeres before onny chyld levyng'. Seymour told Rutland that within two or three years the king would desire more liberty and the honour of his own things. He was willing to inform the protector and the Council of this if the king asked him to do so. But Seymour denied the suggestion that he had questioned his brother's position as the 'cheff derecter of his graces afferres' or the 'alterashion' of any of the

---

[141] Hatfield House Library, Hertfordshire, Cecil Papers 150 fo. 111 r–v (John Fowler to Lord Thomas Seymour, with a short holograph introduction by Edward, 26 June 1548); Knighton 129 (John Fowler to Lord Thomas Seymour, with two notes of commendation from the king, 19 July 1548; Knighton 130 and 131).

[142] SP 10/6 fo. 68r (20 Feb. 1549; Knighton 202).   [143] SP 10/6 fo. 30v (Knighton 186).

king's councillors.[144] Seymour's servant, John Harington, denied that he had talked privately to his master 'concernyng an ordre to be taken for the governement of the kyngs Majestie & thordre of his Cownsell'. But Seymour apparently did tell others that it was unprecedented during 'the mynoritie of a kyng, when ther hath bene two brethern, that thone brother shuld have all rule, & thother none, but that thone were protector thother shuld be governor'.[145]

During the reign of Richard II a parliamentary statute had established that the governance of the king's person and of his realm was committed to a salaried council of nine.[146] But the model that appealed most to Thomas Seymour dated from the beginning of the fifteenth century, and the constitutional arrangements planned for Henry VI. In 1422 Henry V had divided responsibility for his son and the kingdom between Humphrey duke of Gloucester as protector and other personal guardians of the king's person.[147] Lord Thomas knew this. His brother, of course, bore responsibility as both governor and protector – and that was an issue of public record. According to the Privy Council, in February 1549, Thomas Seymour had 'harde and uppon that soughte oute certeine precedentes that there was In Englande at one time oone Protector & an other Regent of ffraunce and the Duke of Exeter and the Busshop of Wynchester Governors of the kinges parsonne'. And so Thomas Seymour 'hadd thoughte to have made sute to the parliament house for that purpose'.[148] He had attempted to bypass the authority of his brother by building up a constituency of noble support in the House of Lords. Or, as the institutional record of the Privy Council chose to put it, 'he hadde the names of all the Lordes and tottid them whome he thoughte he mighte have to his purpose to labor them'.[149] He canvassed the marquesses of Dorset and Northampton, Edward Lord Clinton, and Lord Francis Russell, but in conversations so critical of his brother that he must have alienated – rather than inspired – these noblemen.[150] Thomas Seymour's plan was not without merit; its execution, however, was flawed.

[144] Hatfield House Library, Hertfordshire, Cecil Papers 150 fo. 64r (25 Jan. 1549).
[145] Hatfield House Library, Hertfordshire, Cecil Papers 150 fo. 54r (25 Jan. 1549).
[146] J.S. Roskell, 'The office and dignity of protector of England, with special reference to its origins', *English Historical Review*, 68 (1953), p. 211; cf. Hatfield House Library, Hertfordshire, Cecil Papers 150 fo. 32r.
[147] Roskell, 'Protector of England', p. 201.   [148] SP 10/6 fo. 69r (24 Feb. 1549; Knighton 203).
[149] SP 10/6 fo. 69r (24 Feb. 1549; Knighton 203).
[150] The evidence does of course come from the depositions of men keen to distance themselves from Seymour: Bernard, 'Thomas Seymour', p. 220.

There was something classically baronial about this campaign to build up support in and around parliament. Thomas Seymour was conscious of the power of land and, in particular, of landed nobility. He offered advice to Henry Grey and William Parr on the subjects of households and estates. He presented a competitive notion of local landed power.[151] Lord Thomas advised Henry Grey to keep his house in Warwickshire 'chiefly to match with my lorde of Warwike, so as he should not be hable to matche with me there'.[152] Henry Manners, earl of Rutland, later reported a conversation with Thomas Seymour in which the admiral had asked him about Rutland's standing in his country. Seymour thought Manners 'friended' enough to match the earl of Shrewsbury. 'I said I could not tell', replied Manners, 'howbeit I thought my lord woold do me no wronge.'[153] Thomas Seymour nevertheless advised Manners to befriend sympathetic local yeoman and gentlemen.[154] He told his brother-in-law, William Parr, to set up house in the north where his lands lay so that, being loved by his tenants and friends, he would be stronger to serve the king.[155] And William Sharington, Seymour's principal financial agent, claimed that the admiral had often shown him a map of England and explained how strong he was in terms of both land and men. His boast had been that as many gentlemen loved him as any nobleman in the kingdom – and more than the protector.[156]

Noble marriage, as well as landed power, was one of the keys to Thomas Seymour's strategy. The death of Catherine Parr in September 1548 probably accelerated his campaign for acceptance and support. Henry Manners told Thomas Seymour that the queen dowager's death had diminished his power; Lord Thomas is not reported to have disagreed. The lord admiral told Rutland that the Council had never feared him as much as they did at that point.[157] The attention Lord Thomas paid to Elizabeth Tudor is one of the major themes of writing on his fall from power, and it formed one of the articles against him in February 1549. Elizabeth, as one of Edward's heirs, would have been an important match. But, typically, Seymour was also interested in her estate, and he questioned Elizabeth's cofferer, Thomas Parry, about her servants, houses, and lands.[158] More indirectly, Seymour proposed Jane Grey, the daughter of the marquess of Dorset, as a wife for the king – an important

[151] Bernard, 'Thomas Seymour', p. 222.
[152] SP 10/6 fos. 18r–21v (Knighton 182); Bernard, 'Thomas Seymour', p. 222.
[153] SP 10/6 fo. 33r (Knighton 187).   [154] Knighton 187.   [155] Knighton 189.
[156] Knighton 188; Bernard, 'Thomas Seymour', pp. 222–3.   [157] Knighton 187.
[158] Bernard, 'Thomas Seymour', pp. 216–17.

strategy in itself, but a useful way of cementing his own relationship with Henry Grey, to whom Seymour also lent money.[159] Thomas Seymour failed spectacularly. The depositions of the king, Princess Elizabeth, the marquess of Dorset, John Fowler, Lord Clinton, the earl of Rutland, William Sharington, the marquess of Northampton, the earl of Southampton, Lord Russell, Thomas Parry, and others revealed the scale of his campaign and offered damning (and generally consistent) proof of his guilt. These answers were turned into formal articles with remarkable speed. On 24 February 1549 the Council secured the king's permission for action against his uncle. The next day, a bill was introduced into the House of Lords, and this was passed on 5 March. A fortnight later, on 19 March, Seymour was executed.[160] If the case against Thomas Seymour does not appear to have been fabricated, it does, as John Guy has argued, smack of overkill.[161] But why is the Seymour affair so significant? And what does it have to tell us about the nature of Edward Seymour's protectorate? The destruction of Thomas Seymour by his brother has always fascinated commentators. Structurally, and morally, it has often underpinned accounts of the reign. The execution of Seymour has been used to explore the emotional response of the king – at best guarded, at worst cold – and to explain the political ambitions of John Dudley earl of Warwick (see above, chapter 1, pp. 9, 25). Thomas Seymour challenged the physical and political integrity of his brother's protectorate. Denied the governorship of the king's person, and effectively marginalized in the corporate group responsible for exercising sovereignty on behalf of Edward, Lord Thomas worked with what he had: occasional contact with the king, access to the private apartments at court, some historical knowledge, and an instinctive faith in the power of land and its owners.

So was Thomas Seymour a wronged man? Were the political arrangements of the years between 1547 and 1549 – the powers of Edward Seymour as protector, the prominence of his household servants in the business of royal governance, the protective structures of the royal court – expressive, or indicative, of a dominant, manipulative, and arrogant regime? In 1953 the medieval historian J.S. Roskell argued that, in their Edwardian form, the powers of the office of protector 'had put on weight'. Edward Seymour was, on paper, a more powerful protector than his medieval predecessors.[162] Protector Somerset certainly dominated the

---

[159] Bernard, 'Thomas Seymour', pp. 223–4.   [160] *APC 1547–50*, pp. 261–3.
[161] John Guy, *Tudor England* (Oxford and New York, 1988), p. 201.
[162] Roskell, 'Protector of England', p. 229.

Edwardian political scene between 1547 and 1549, but the power he exercised reflected the intellectual and practical complexities of royal minority. The presentation of Edward Seymour as the godly and Christian protector acting in the best interests of his nephew may look forced and rather fragile; and yet, quite apart from the fact that this model became an important element in the presentation of Edward VI's kingship (see below, chapter 4, pp. 115–16), it does match some of the cultural expectations of Seymour's role as governor of the king's person and the protector of his realms. Tutor, governor, the definitive representative of royal power during the king's minority: these were important components in the complex machinery of the protectorate. The later Edwardian polity worked rather differently – but Edward was older, and the arrangements at court and in the Privy Council had to respond to the implications of a gradually emerging king (see below, chapter 5, pp. 157–68).

Even the more practical – and powerful – dimensions of the protectorate reflect the complexities of politics between January 1547 and October 1549. The constitutional 'irregularities' that have so often offended the historians of Edward's reign mask a more sophisticated and adaptive political culture. Governance was governance, whether transmitted through the king's officers or communicated by members of Protector Somerset's household – or both. Concentrating on the men who represented royal power, and mapping the dynamics of the protectorate, is arguably more important than measuring it against a constitutional model. But even here it is worth emphasizing that 1547–49 did not necessarily represent a perversion of the Tudor 'ideal'. It was, rather, one response to the practical issue of governing the kingdom during royal minority. Even Bishop Stephen Gardiner of Winchester accepted the need for a protectorate and endorsed the authority of Edward Seymour as protector, the acknowledged representative of royal power.[163] In 1548 Gardiner and Thomas Watson objected to William Cecil's message because they believed that Cecil had exceeded his instructions; there is no evidence to suggest that, once Watson had heard Cecil supported by his master, they openly questioned the political authority of Protector Somerset. Other men appear to have accommodated themselves to the practical arrangements of the protectorate: for men like John Dudley earl of Warwick, navigating channels of communication was rather more important than subverting them.

[163] James Arthur Muller, ed., *The letters of Stephen Gardiner* (Cambridge, 1933), p. 278 (21 May [1547]).

The protectorate was not marked by the dominance of an isolated elite operating at the centre of power, determined to protect its position. There were too many continuities, too many familiar faces around the king, and too many traditions of service. Edward VI was guarded, monitored, taught, and governed every hour of his life. His uncle exercised the absolute power of the Tudor imperial crown. But this was, after all, the purpose of the protectorate, the reason that made the unreason of royal minority intellectually and practically bearable – or so the subjects of the crown hoped. Policy, of course, was a different matter, and it was here that Edward Seymour failed. Failure, in turn, exposed Seymour to the complexities of the office of protector. He clearly lacked the character and personality appropriate and necessary for the office he held. But the collapse of the protectorate in October 1549 was, strangely enough, the great mark of its success over the two years of its existence. It demonstrated that Edward Seymour's authority as protector – the strange hybrid of king and subject, in October 1549 so fragile and ambiguous – really did depend on the consent of the men who had agreed to his elevation as *primus inter pares*. Only when this consent was withdrawn – and when, more importantly, Seymour failed properly to discharge his ministry – was the protector left truly isolated. In October 1549 even physical possession of the king, the stamps of his sign manual, and the presence of William Paget and Archbishop Cranmer at Hampton Court could not protect the protector from his colleagues. The protectorate had not failed, but Edward Seymour had.

4

Reforming the kingdom

At the heart of Edwardian kingship was the notion of a reforming king, a second Josiah, supreme head of the Churches of England and Ireland on earth next under God, but a king counselled, profoundly conscious of his duty of care to God and to His subjects. Edward VI was very personally associated with the kingly, and definitively and distinctively Tudor, Reformation of 1547–53. This Reformation was a complex creature, a challenging set of claims and notions of power and authority designed in part to compensate for the restrictions or weaknesses of royal minority; but it was also strongly, and more positively, associated with the governance of England as a 'Christian commonwealth' and the return of the kingdom's worship to the form of the 'primitive' Church of Christ's apostles.

Reformation defined Edward's kingship, and vice versa. The relationship between the two was a complex one. Edwardian preachers and writers regularly presented their king as the godly son of a godly father, personally and valiantly moving to a natural second stage of the Reformation begun by Henry VIII. This presentation had as much to say about the nature of middle Tudor kingship as it did about Edwardian theology. At the king's coronation Archbishop Cranmer had sketched a model of absolute royal power and linked it explicitly to Edward's role as a second Josiah.[1] During the course of his reign Edward embraced the projection of himself as the principal agent in the rescue of his realm from the corruption of Roman Catholicism. He wrote on the destruction of idolatry and on the removal of 'the bishopes of Romes auctorite . . . and his erronious and pestilent heresies' from the Order of the Garter (*c.* 1550).[2] In a written exercise supervised by his tutor in French, Jean

---

[1] Diarmaid MacCulloch, *Thomas Cranmer* (New Haven and London, 1996), pp. 364–5; Henry Jenkyns, ed., *The remains of Thomas Cranmer*, 4 vols. (Oxford, 1833), II, pp. 118–20.
[2] British Library, Cotton MS Nero C 10 fo. 103v; Diarmaid MacCulloch, *Tudor church militant: Edward VI and the Protestant Reformation* (London, 1999), pp. 30–6.

Belmaine, Edward presented the bishop of Rome as 'the true son of the devil, a bad man, an Antichrist and abominable tyrant'.[3] The Edwardian Reformation was the king's Reformation, defined and promoted by royal authority. But even supremacy was underpinned by duty and royal obligation. In 1549 the London publisher and entrepreneur Walter Lynne produced John Ponet's translation of Bernardino Ochino's *A tragoedie or Dialogue of the unjust usurped primacie of the Bishop of Rome*, a book that related in fascinating detail the great battle between Christ and Antichrist, in which the godly and reforming kingship of Edward was presented as the resolution of a long historical fight for the souls of Christian subjects. This was kingly duty in its purest form, a bold but in many ways natural extension of the conventional relationship between monarch and people; a kingship, in other words, unashamedly providential in its presentation. Both Edward and John Dudley duke of Northumberland owned copies of *A tragoedie or Dialogue*, and so one of the aims of the first part of this chapter is to present an account of the thesis of a book that represented a magisterial 'mirror' the king could hold up to himself and the Reformation carried out in the king's name.[4]

DEPOSING ANTICHRIST

Antichrist was no stranger to Tudor evangelicals. In *The obedience of a Christian man* (1528) William Tyndale had identified the pope with Antichrist.[5] So did William Marshall who, in his translation of Marsilius of Padua's *Defensor pacis* (1535), identified as the major threat to the peace of the commonwealth 'the great dragon, and olde serpente antychryste of Rome'.[6] A year later, in February 1536, Thomas Cranmer preached along the same lines.[7] This became a familiar theme for Cranmer, godfather to Edward and a man closely connected to Walter Lynne, John Ponet, and Bernardino Ochino. In a response to the articles

---

[3] MacCulloch, *Tudor church militant*, pp. 26–31; quotation at p. 26.

[4] MacCulloch, *Tudor church militant*, pp. 52–3. *A tragoedie or Dialogue of the unjuste usurped primacie of the Bishop of Rome, and of all the just abolishyng of the same, made by master Barnardine Ochine an Italian, & translated out of Latine into Englishe by Master John Ponet Doctor of Divinitie, never printed before in any language* (London, 1549; *STC* 18770) [hereafter *TD*]. The variant edition is *STC* 18771.

[5] John Guy, 'The Henrician age', in J.G.A. Pocock, ed., *The varieties of British political thought, 1500–1800* (Cambridge, 1993), p. 33; MacCulloch, *Cranmer*, p. 150. There were at least three Edwardian editions of *The obedience of a Christian man*: *STC* 24448, by William Hill (1548); *STC* 24450, by Thomas Raynold and William Hill (sold by Richard Jugge, c. 1548); and *STC* 24451, by William Copland (c. 1548).

[6] Shelley Lockwood, 'Marsilius of Padua and the case for the royal ecclesiastical supremacy', *Transactions of the Royal Historical Society*, sixth series, 1 (1991), p. 92.

[7] MacCulloch, *Cranmer*, p. 150.

of the western rebels of 1549, for example, Cranmer presented a coherent account of his opposition to papal authority. He argued that the holy laws and decrees of the Catholic Church meant the effective exemption of the clergy from temporal control and the submission of princes to the bishops and the decrees of the Church.[8] So when the rebels demanded a return to the religion of their forefathers they wanted

> no thynge elles but a clere subversion of the hole state & lawes of this realme, & to make this realme to be holly governed by Romyshe lawes, & to crowne the idol & Antichrist of Rome kynge of this realme, & to make our most undouted & natural kynge his vile subje[c]t & slave.[9]

For Cranmer, the papal subversion of princes was one element in a providential conflict between Christ and Antichrist. Antichrist had established his superstitions in the name of holiness so that, like the Devil (who sought also to draw people from Christ), Christians would 'take hym in the stede of Christ, and byleve that we have by him, such thynges as we have only by Christ, that is to say, spiritual fode, remission of our synnes and salvation'.[10] Before the king and his court, in 1550, John Ponet denounced the 'Antichristian Bushope of Rome' as the 'chefe & arche capitayn tread worde', who, during mass, trod the Bible under his feet as a symbol of papal authority over scripture.[11] Any man who believed that the Roman Catholic Church could not err was challenged by the scriptures, 'which geve justly and truelye unto the kinges Majesty hys tytle of the supreme hed of the church'. That man was, quite simply, a heretic and a traitor (see also above, chapter 2, pp. 36–7).[12]

Ponet's sermon was published and distributed by Walter Lynne, the naturalized Dutchman who had been selling books in London since 1540. Ponet's denunciation of claims for papal authority, and Cranmer's unmasking of Antichrist a year earlier, represented the conceptual foundation for *A tragoedie or Dialoge*, and for the volume that neatly predated (indeed almost prefaced) it, Lynne's *The beginning and endynge of all popery*.[13] Diarmaid MacCulloch puts Cranmer at the centre of both volumes: the archbishop certainly worked through Lynne to print his Catechism of

---

[8] Corpus Christi College Cambridge, Parker MS 102 fo. 348.
[9] Corpus Christi College Cambridge, Parker MS 102 fo. 350.
[10] Corpus Christi College Cambridge, Parker MS 102 fo. 373.
[11] John Ponet, *A notable Sermon concerninge the ryght use of the lordes supper and other thynges very profitable for all men to knowe* (London, 1550; *STC* 20177), sigs. {E4v}–{E5r}.
[12] Ponet, *Notable Sermon*, sig. {F6r–v}.
[13] Walter Lynne, *The beginning and endynge of all popery, or popishe kyngedome* (London, 1548; *STC* 17115) [hereafter *BE*].

1548, a volume which, in its own way, contributed iconographically to a Reformation so heavily dependent on visual statements of the imperial power of the crown promoting fundamental religious change. The title-page introduced the characters of Victoria, Justitia, and Prudentia, complemented by the royal arms bearing the motto 'Dieu et mon droyt' topped by an imperial crown, and supported on either side by a dragon and a lion crowned imperially. Inside the book, the reader found Edward handing the Bible to his subjects in a woodcut reinforced by important scriptural texts on kingship (see above, chapter 2, Fig. 1, p. 42). In the same year Lynne produced *A treatyse of the ryght honourynge and wourshyppyng of our saviour Jesus Christe*, by one Richard Bonner, and dedicated to Cranmer. The character of Bonner was fictional. MacCulloch believes him to have been one of Cranmer's 'fleet of chaplains', used to introduce Martin Bucer's 'eucharistic ideas to the English reading public'.[14] It was an elaborate ruse, and Lynne was involved in it.

Walter Lynne's historical critique of papal power was sponsored at the highest level. In December 1547 he was granted a licence under the great seal to print a 'book wich is callyd in our vulgare tonge the begynnyng and endyng of all poperey or popishe kyngdom, and all other maner of bokes consonant to godliness'. Other printers were prohibited from producing *The beginning and endynge of all popery* for a period of seven years, on pain of forfeiting £100: half payable to the king and half to Lynne and the accuser.[15] So Lynne was able to negotiate support for his explicitly anti-papal text and secure targeted protection for the final published volume. The regime certainly had an interest in promoting a book like *The beginning and endynge of all popery*, because it was, like *A tragoedie or Dialoge*, a work of historical explanation and exploration, the key to understanding the Reformation of the kingdom. Knowledge was critical. For John Ponet, preaching before the king and his court in March 1550, it was not enough to believe 'as the churche of the electes and chosen of god doth beleve, oneles ye know and feele in your hertes what thynge it is that the churche beleveth'. The faith of an individual had to be grounded solely on Christ, and this had to be a faith based on understanding. The individual believer had to have eyes of his own in order to distinguish the true Church from the false, good doctrine from bad, the spiritual preacher from the carnal, Christian learning from papistry, and Christ from Antichrist.[16] This is precisely what Lynne, Bernardino Ochino, and Ponet himself attempted to do in print.

[14] MacCulloch, *Cranmer*, pp. 402–3; quotation at p. 403.   [15] *CPR 1547–48*, p. 61.
[16] Ponet, *Notable Sermon*, sig. {F7r–v}.

The beginning and endynge of all popery was a translation of *Practica der Pfaffen* (*c.* 1535), attributed to Joachim de Fiore (*c.* 1135–1202).[17] Lynne introduced the volume as a 'little boke wherin is declared what maner of thinges the bishops of Rome were at the first, what was their estate and condicion, and what was their office or deutye', and he structured it around a series of fifteen anti-papal woodcuts taken from *Practica der Pfaffen*.[18] These illustrations were presented as the keys to unlock the concerns of 'the fathers of auncient tyme' who 'sawe in the papacie, the thinge that they durst not utter, eyther by wordes or writinge'. For Lynne, they were symbolic representations in painting and portraiture, figures of an apocalypse, or revelation, rather than the products of human invention.[19] The truth they presented was that Satan had played a central role in the establishment of the Roman Church, instructing successive popes to interpret falsely the supposed authority for papal primacy, 'Thou art Peter, and uppon this stone or rocke I will buyld my churche' (Matthew 16:18).[20] Lynne likened the Church to a beautiful building, supported by learning and scholarship, an institution that had successfully convinced princes of their duty to labour for the pope. Rome became recognized throughout Christendom as 'the fountaine and well of all mercie', the sole authority to offer the remission and forgiveness of sin.[21] The book explained how the bishops of Rome left Christ and sought the 'secular power', and it examined this power in the context of the Tudor experience.[22] It celebrated the part Henry VIII had played – and Edward VI would play – in leading England out of darkness.

Lynne explained that there had been 'but bishoppes untill the time of Constantine', and these men had done exactly what Edwardian preachers exhorted their own bishops to do: study the scriptures, teach the people, and live soberly.[23] The first woodcut of the book shows the pope surrounded by bears, who represented the worldly powers, offered money by the bishop of Rome. In this way lords, dukes, emperors, kings, lands, and people had been 'made subject unto them'.[24] The pope is

---

[17] John N. King, *Tudor royal iconography: literature and art in the age of religious crisis* (Princeton, 1989), p. 166.

[18] *BE*, sig. A3r; King, *Tudor royal iconography*, p. 167 and n. 64.

[19] *BE*, sig. A3r{v}; quotation at sig. A3r.   [20] *BE*, sig. {A2r–v}.   [21] *BE*, sig. {A2v}.

[22] *BE*, sig. A3r.

[23] *BE*, sig. {B4r}. Cf. Hugh Latimer, *The seconde Sermon of Maister Hughe Latimer, whych he preached before the Kynges majestie, with in his graces Palayce at Westminster the .xv. day of Marche. M.ccccc.xlix* (London, 1549; *STC* 15274.7), sig. D1r–{v}; and Thomas Becon, *The Fortresse of the faythfull agaynst the cruel assautes of povertie and honger newlye made for the comforte of poore nedye Christians, by Thomas Becon* (London, 1550; *STC* 1721), sig. {A6r}.

[24] *BE*, sig. {C4r–v}.

rebuked by God, but a fox 'doth counsell the contrarye'. The foxes are the 'Cardinalles, Notaries, and other of that see' who fear that, in following the example of St Peter and St Paul, they would become poor. They counsel the pope to reject the true nature of 'the apostolicall function' in favour of wealth and worldly power.[25] The pope has the eagle by the throat but also holds down other birds with his three-forked sceptre. Temporal governance is thus overthrown. The popes used to be servants of the emperor as prince and governor of the empire, but now the relationship has been reversed: the temporal ruler must kiss the feet of his subject, a humiliation for which the papacy claims scriptural support.[26] The pope receives his commandments from the Devil, a prince of this world.[27] This is an unholy and subtle alliance. The pope's claim of temporal power is supported by the Devil because the Devil 'is the father, and the pope the sonne'. So it is the Devil who has given him the keys, the rod, and the sword – the three instruments that are used to secure papal authority. If people disobey the power of the keys, the pope can admonish them with the rod or even kill them with a charge of heresy.[28] The relationship is absolutely conspiratorial: the papacy has helped to extend the power of the Devil, which in turn has meant that the pope can exercise full spiritual and temporal authority.[29] He bears the sword, which should belong 'to the highe powers havinge landes and people, for the wealth of the good, and punishment of the evill'. He also rules the consciences of men, 'And soche as heare hym not, he punysheth with the blody sword.'[30]

In *A tragoedie or Dialoge* the papacy similarly represents two separable but combined evils: the usurped power it has taken from princes and other governors to exercise the temporal sword; and the corrupting and idolatrous spiritual power it exercises over the consciences of men. Both *The beginning and endynge of all popery* and *A tragoedie or Dialoge* examine the historical roots of papal power, and both books map its final collapse. Lynne, limited in the main part of his text to the work of Joachim of Fiore, concludes with representations of the fall of the pope – the keys of absolution removed by angels, the pope beset by bears and a unicorn knocking the papal crown from his head – reinforced by the prophecies of Hildegard of Bingen.[31] *A tragoedie or Dialoge* sets the Edwardian Reformation in the broadest context possible, balancing speeches by Archbishop Cranmer, Henry VIII, Edward VI, and Protector Somerset against the

---

[25] *BE*, sigs. D2r–{D3r}.   [26] *BE*, sigs. {D3r}–{D4r}.   [27] *BE*, sigs. {D4v}–E1 r.
[28] *BE*, sig. {E3r}.   [29] *BE*, sigs. {E3v}–{E4r}.   [30] *BE*, sig. F1 r.   [31] *BE*, sig. F1 v–{H4r}.

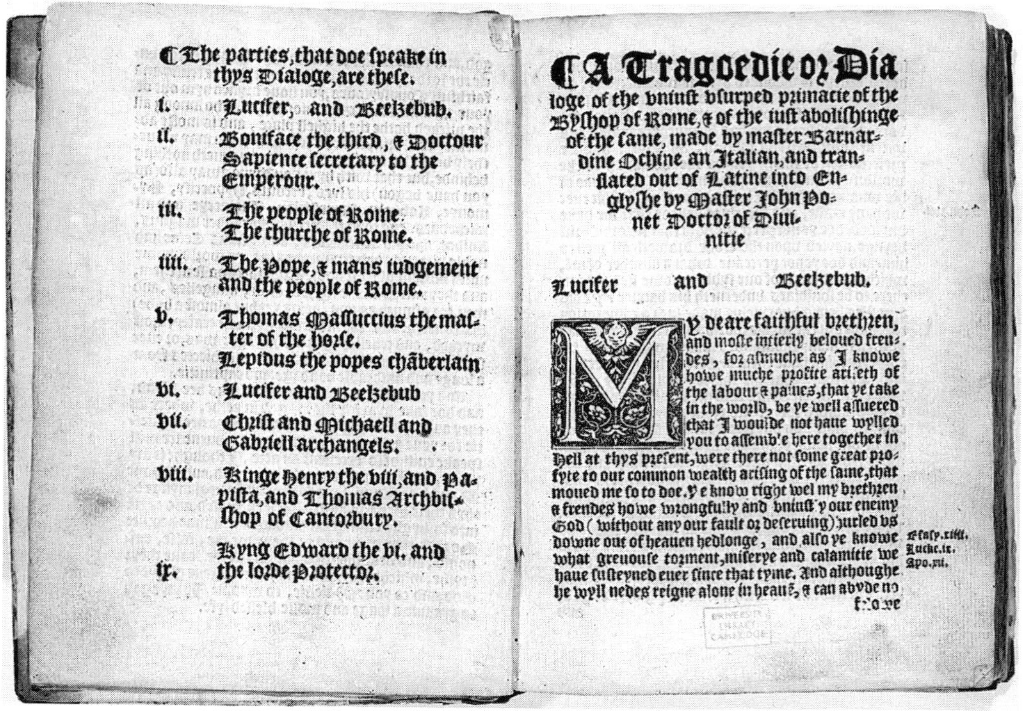

¶ The parties, that doe speake in thys Dialoge, are these.

i. Lucifer, and Beelzebub.

ii. Boniface the third, & Doctour Sapience secretary to the Emperour.

iii. The people of Rome. The churche of Rome.

iiii. The Pope, & mans iudgement and the people of Rome.

v. Thomas Massuccius the master of the horse. Lepidus the popes châberlain

vi. Lucifer and Beelzebub

vii. Christ and Michaell and Gabriell archangels.

viii. Kinge Henry the viii, and Papista, and Thomas Archbishop of Cantorbury.

ix. Kyng Edward the vi. and the lorde Protector.

¶ A Tragoedie or Dialoge of the vniust vsurped primacie of the Byshop of Rome, & of the iust abolishinge of the same, made by master Barnardine Ochine an Italian, and translated out of Latine into Englyshe by Master John Ponet Doctor of Diuinitie

Lucifer and Beelzebub.

My deare faithful brethren, and moste intierly beloued frendes, for asmuche as I knowe howe muche profite ariseth of the labour & paines, that ye take in the world, be ye well assuered that I woulde not haue wylled you to assemble here together in Hell at thys present, were there not some great profyte to our common wealth arising of the same, that moued me so to doe. Ye know right wel my brethren & frendes howe wrongfully and vniustly our enemy God (without any our fault or deseruing) hurled vs downe out of heauen hedlonge, and also ye knowe what greuouse torment, miserye and calamitie we haue susteyned euer since that tyme. And althoughe he wyll nedes reigne alone in heauē, & can abyde no Esay.xiiii. Luke.x. Apo.xii.

felowe

Fig. 4 The contents page of the first edition of *A tragoedie or Dialoge of the unjuste usurped primacie of the Bishop of Rome* (1549) showing the ninth dialogue between 'Kyng Edward the vi. and the lorde Protector'. The later variant had 'Kyng Edwarde the .vi. and the Counseil'.

contributions of agents of the pope, eastern ambassadors, Christ, the archangels Michael and Gabriel, Lucifer, and Beelzebub (see Fig. 4).

A tragoedie or Dialoge begins with a discussion between Lucifer and his companion Beelzebub which establishes, very literally, Ochino's preoccupation with the papacy as the creation of the Devil. Determined to undermine the kingdom of Christ, but conscious that persecution only strengthens Christians, Lucifer explains his plan to destroy the Church 'by arte, policie, diligence, crafte, subteltie, gyle, and prodition'. Practising his politic arts, he plans to establish an institution built on idolatry, superstition, ignorance, and corruption – something Christians will consider a 'spirituall kingdome most holy, and most godly'.[32] Rome was the natural target, 'the heade citie of the worlde', and it would not be hard 'to persuade menne that the bishop therof is the head of all christian menne'.[33] And the pope, Boniface III, was a man of ambition happy to oblige Lucifer.[34]

'O immortall God', Boniface declares, 'howe sweete and pleasaunte a thing is the glory of the world, trewly it is more to be estemed, then all worldlye treasures or pleasure.' Boniface is the patriarch of Rome, the governor of an unlimited number of people, with money and pleasures at his commandment. He wants more: worldwide dominion over other bishops and worship as a god.[35] In conversation with Boniface, Doctor Sapience, the emperor's secretary, is unimpressed by the bishop's 'rolling rhetorical vanitie of wordes' – Boniface's public motives are Christian charity and zeal, to end factions, sects, contentions, and heresies in the Church – but he nevertheless dissimulates and agrees to further Boniface's cause.[36] He plays the part of the persuasive courtier and counsellor to perfection. He walks with his emperor, Phocas, who shares with him 'certayne secret counselles, wherby he thought to increase his ryches, & to cause hys whole dignitie roiall to be the more estemed'. Sapience explains that this could be done, but builds up to the subject of Boniface slowly and carefully. He tells the emperor that subduing the dominions of other princes is dangerous and difficult.[37] He explains how the Church of Christ is divided, and tells Phocas that the cause is the lack of 'one

---

[32] *TD*, sig. {A4r–v}; quotation at sig. {A4v}.   [33] *TD*, sig. b3r.
[34] *TD*, sigs. C2r–{v}, E2r, {z4v}; *BE*, sig. C1r–{v}. William Thomas, in print in September 1549, similarly mentioned in his 'Abbridgement of the lives of the Romaine Bishoppes' that 'Boniface the .iii. obteined a privilege of the emperour, that he and his successours from thensefoorth shoulde be taken for Primates and chiefe of all Christian bishops.' *The historie of Italie, a boke excedyng profitable to be redde: Because it intreateth of the astate of many and divers common weales, how thei have ben, & now be governed* (London, 1549; *STC* 24018), sig. {L4v}.
[35] *TD*, sig. {C2v}.   [36] *TD*, sig. D1r.   [37] *TD*, sig. {D3v}.

supreme spiritual, and unyversall heade in earthe'. This supreme head could use 'the thunder boltes of excomunicacion', which would be 'terrible to all nacions, so that in shorte space it shoulde injoye a fyrme & a perfecte Dominion'. What is more, Doctor Sapience explains, there were clear imperial interests in having a universal head of the Church who was a subject of the emperor, and who would 'hang all together upon the Emperors will and pleasure'. Boniface is recommended as the candidate.[38]

So the origin of the papal supremacy of Rome is seen to rest on the political arts and moral and personal weaknesses of three men: the ambition of Boniface, countenanced by Sapience as a counsellor perfectly aware of the motives of the bishop of Rome but determined to indulge him and promote his cause; and the weakness of the emperor, Phocas, seduced both by the persuasive abilities of his secretary and by the prospect of power. In addition, importantly, Ochino emphasized in several places that the pope received his power from the emperor: Boniface recognizes the benefits of harnessing the royal authority of the emperor, 'agaynst whose wyll and pleasure as I dare attempte nothynge'.[39] The dialogue is marked by ambition, the desire for worldly power, dissimulation, and manipulation; but it is also an issue of language, of (in the words of Doctor Sapience) 'craftie glosynge and deceytfull wordes'.[40]

In the third dialogue, the character of the People of Rome explores the implications of the emperor's decision to grant Boniface universal headship and supremacy. The character argues that a time will come when the emperor 'if he will have hys crowne he shall aske it & receyve it (if it please him to geve it) at our bishops handes'.[41] The People of Rome touches a raw nerve in sixteenth-century Protestant culture. Like *The beginning and endynge of all popery*, with its representation of the Holy Roman Emperor being held by the throat, forced to kiss the feet of the pope, the character of the People of Rome argues that the emperor will become a suitor and 'kysse his fete, and he (in the name of God) a very holy byshoppe shall trede with hys fote upon the Emperours throte'.[42] In his *Acts and Monuments* of 1563 and 1570, John Foxe used woodcuts of German emperors submitting to the pope, with representations of Frederick Barbarossa being humiliated by Pope Alexander III.[43] Christopher Marlowe inherited this tradition when, in *Doctor Faustus*,

[38] *TD*, sig. {D4r}.   [39] *TD*, sig. {C4r}.   [40] *TD*, sig. {E1v}.   [41] *TD*, sig. E2r.
[42] *BE*, sigs. {D3r}–{D4r}; *TD*, sig. E2r–{v}.
[43] Margaret Aston, *The king's bedpost: reformation and iconography in a Tudor group portrait* (Cambridge, 1993), pp. 150–3.

Pope Adrian uses the example of Alexander and Frederick to emphasize his authority over temporal rulers. 'Is not all power on earth bestowed on us?', he asks; 'And therefore, though we would, we cannot err.'[44] Papal infallibility is a central theme of the dialogue between the People of Rome and the Church of Rome, who has just walked out of the Church of St John Lateran to declare that she is the mother of all churches, upon whom the health of the whole world depends.[45] She is now blameless; she can no longer err.[46] To test these claims, the People of Rome questions the Church of Rome on the hypothetical issue of obedience to a heretical pope. Although the Church admits that a general council can judge and condemn the pope as a heretic, and even depose him from office, it argues that his authority is above that of the council. So Ochino exposed an uncomfortable ambiguity for the Roman Church: the constitutional tension between the actions of a lawfully assembled council and a man who was believed to be 'above them and more indewed with supernaturall light then they be'.[47]

The People of Rome argues one point which becomes crucial to the critique of papal power: that Christ is the head of the Church, who has governed it, and will govern it, until the day of judgement. So the emperor has appointed a second head, and this was something monstrous.[48] One element of Ochino's technique is to condemn and discredit an argument for papal power in one dialogue and then encourage the pope or his agents to deploy it later in the book. In the fourth chapter, a member of the pope's 'pryvye counsell', Man's Judgement, advises Boniface that the best defence of his position is a claim of ordination by Christ: that the primacy of Rome is an ordinance of God rather than of man, and that Christ ordained the bishop of Rome as supreme head of the Church, 'and that with a whole fulnes of power'.[49] Man's Judgement constructs this argument as a defence against the eastern ambassadors arriving to challenge the claim of Rome to primacy, but it is presented as a principle that would also allow the pope to do other things. The pope could distance himself from the emperor, and challenge the removal of papal power from Rome. Equally, the pope's office as Christ's Vicar would enable him to extend papal authority beyond the territorial limits of the Empire.[50]

---

[44] Christopher Marlowe, *Doctor Faustus* (B-Text), III:1:136–45, 151–2.   [45] *TD*, sig. {E2v}.
[46] *TD*, sig. E3r.   [47] *TD*, sigs. {F4r}–G2r; quotation at sig. G1r.
[48] *TD*, sigs. {F2v}–F3r. Cf. *Here begynneth a boke, called the faule of the Romyshe churche* ([London, 1548]; *STC* 21305.3), sig. {c6r}.
[49] *TD*, sig. G3r.   [50] *TD*, sig. {G3v}.

The arguments for the primacy of Rome and papal authority are cleverly constructed but inevitably flawed. The notion of direct ordination
by Christ is comprehensively challenged; the counter-position is that
papal power is territorially limited and depends on the authority of the
emperor. It is, more dangerously, transferable: Man's Judgement works
on the assumption that the emperor can take back the authority he has
given to his bishop. Just as corrosive is the fact that Man's Judgement consciously fabricates on ancient paper 'certayne epistles' from early Roman
Christians 'wherin there is oft mencion made of Peter as thoughe he had
bene at Rome, and not onely Byshop of thys citie, but also Pope, and
universall head of all the churche militant'.[51] These arguments are put to
the test in the book's most structured and challenging critique of papal
power, the report of the debate at the imperial court of Rome on the
subject of the 'highe power of the Pope'.[52] The reporter was Lepidus,
the pope's chamberlain, who heard the disputation between the papal
representatives and ambassadors 'which came from sundrye coastes of
the world'. The commentator was Thomas Massuccius, master of the
horse.[53]

From the beginning of his report, Lepidus makes a structurally significant admission. He refers to the tension between the claim of papal
prerogative derived directly from Christ and the fact that the disputation
was held 'in the presence of Cesar'. So to avoid the charge that the debate was being held under imperial jurisdiction, Lepidus records that the
pope did not speak directly: the defence of his power was conducted by
papal representatives.[54] In opening the disputation, the ambassador of
Constantinople argued that Christ was the true and only head of his
Church 'in thys militant exile', just as he was the head of the trium-
phant Church of the heavenly Jerusalem.[55] For the pope, Master
Falsidicus replied with the conventional scriptural reference to Peter
receiving from Christ the keys to bind and loose.[56] The ambassador
countered with the arguments for Christ's headship. Massuccius comments that the papal position assumes that Christ governed the Church
during his time on earth, but, after his ascension, 'tyred with rulynge and
laboringe', left Peter and his papal successors in his place.[57]

One major theme of the disputation is the nature of temporal authority
and the relationship between earthly governors and the pope, a subject
that had exercised writers since the eleventh century, grounded in the

---

[51] *TD*, sig. {G4v}; cf. Thomas, *Historie of Italie*, sig. L2r.   [52] *TD*, sig. I3r.   [53] *TD*, sig. I2v.
[54] *TD*, sigs. {I3v}–{I4r}.   [55] *TD*, sig. {I4v}.   [56] *TD*, sig. K1r; Matthew 16:19.
[57] *TD*, sigs. K1r–{K2v}; quotation at sig. {K2v}.

work of the Church fathers, medieval theologians, and canon and civil lawyers.[58] Edwardian court preachers consistently argued that a king was absolute in his own kingdom. They denied absolutely that a foreign institution or individual could exercise jurisdiction in England. The principle was that the king, as king, exercised absolute temporal jurisdiction over all his subjects, both lay and spiritual (see above, chapter 2, pp. 41–3). The papal position in *A tragoedie or Dialoge* is of course quite different, but it nevertheless rested on centuries of biblical commentary and pro-papal writing – texts and traditions Ochino and Ponet were able to manipulate really quite effectively. When Master Falsidicus deployed the example of the disciples providing for themselves two swords before Christ's prayer on the Mount of Olives (Luke 22:38) – and from this argued that the pope had 'two swordes, and the highest power upon both sydes, the one spiritual, the other temporall' – the papal representative was travelling a well-beaten path.[59] Thomas Massuccius dismisses this argument as the product of 'a fyne dialecticall witte', and wonders why St Peter has not been represented with keys hanging from his belt and two swords in his hands. Christ, argued the ambassadors, told Peter to put away his sword, because the kingdom of Christ was heavenly and spiritual. Christ was sent to minister and to serve.[60] He did not give swords to his apostles, and so it followed that they did not have the supreme power and authority, spiritual and temporal, which is 'shadowed' by the two swords. This point marks the end of this part of the debate because, Ochino has Lepidus tell Massuccius, the pope commanded Master Falsidicus to stop, 'fearinge leste thys hatefull dysputacyon of bothe swordes should offend themperour'.[61]

The ambassador from Alexandria presents the final, compelling argument against papal authority. The primacy of the pope is neither godly nor of God. It must, therefore, be a creation of man or of Devil. But it is not of man, and for a number of reasons. The emperor cannot give to the bishop of Rome spiritual power. Spiritual power is given by Christ; so, like all other bishops, the bishop of Rome must acknowledge that Christ is the supreme head. Furthermore, the emperor can only exercise and

---

[58] Antony Black, *Political thought in Europe 1250–1450* (Cambridge, 1992), pp. 42–84; J.H. Burns, *Lordship, kingship, and empire: the idea of monarchy, 1400–1525* (Oxford, 1992), pp. 97–123; Joseph Canning, *A history of medieval political thought 300–1450* (London, 1996), pp. 135–61, 174–84; J.A. Watt, 'Spiritual and temporal powers', in J.H. Burns, ed., *The Cambridge history of medieval political thought c. 350–c. 1450* (Cambridge, 1988), pp. 367–423.

[59] *TD*, sig. {M3v}. For the medieval reading of the significance of the disciples' swords, close to the interpretation presented by Lepidus, see Watt, 'Spiritual and temporal powers', pp. 370–2.

[60] *TD*, sig. {M3v}.   [61] *TD*, sig. {M4v}.

delegate temporal power in the countries under his governance. What, then, was the position of Africa and Asia? So it follows that the emperor could not make the bishop of Rome superior to the other bishops. He could not offer the bishop of Rome primacy, unless he wanted to surrender his empire and put the bishop in his own place.[62] The papal line is that the bishop of Rome is Christ's Vicar, his representative on earth. But a vicar of Christ, argues the Alexandrian representative, would follow Christ. And because Christ told his apostles that they should serve rather than bear temporal rule, his vicar would not have built for himself this sort of power. During his time on earth Christ refused temporal power but concentrated solely on saving souls and preaching the gospel. So the primacy of the pope derives neither from God nor from man; instead it comes from the Devil.[63] And this was the account of the nature of papal power Edward's subjects would have heard in their parish churches. 'An exhortacion, concernyng good ordre and obedience' maintained that the usurped power of the bishop of Rome, from which he claimed to be the successor of Christ and Peter, did not have a sufficient basis in scripture or in doctrine. Both Christ and Peter taught obedience to kings as the chief and supreme rulers in the world next under God; the bishop of Rome taught immunities, exemptions, and disobedience. This was why he should be called Antichrist rather than Christ's Vicar or St Peter's successor.[64]

Tudor monarchs claimed for themselves the supreme headship of the churches of England and Ireland next under God on earth (see also above, chapter 2, pp. 50–6). This notion underpinned the Edwardian assault on papal authority: indeed, it positively demanded it. The denunciation of the Antichristian bishop of Rome was only partly negative. The deposition of Lucifer and Antichrist also involved the acknowledgement of Christ and the English king in their proper authority. Promoting Edward as a godly king, and associating his kingly powers with the destruction of Antichrist and his blasphemies, became a critical element in Edwardian culture. Here the royal supremacy and godly Reformation fused. Just as central was the notion that Edward was continuing the work of his father. In his draft response to the articles of the rebels of 1549, Cranmer described how Henry VIII, 'pityinge to see his subjectes many yeares so brought up in darkenes & ignorance of god, by the erronious

---

[62] *TD*, sig. {R3v}.   [63] *TD*, sigs. {R3v}–{R4r}.

[64] *Certayne Sermons, or Homelies, appoynted by the kynges Majestie, to be declared and redde, by all persones, Vicars, or Curates, every Sondaye in their churches, where they have Cure* (London, 1547; *STC* 13640), sigs. {S2v}–S3r.

doctrine & traditions of the busshope of Rome', led them from that darkness into the light and knowledge of God's word. Edward had succeeded
him in this 'godly intent' and had 'with no lesse care & diligence studied
to performe his fatheres godly intent & purpose'.[65]

So, formally and publicly, 1547 formed a natural bridge between two
reigns. Edward Foxe's *De vera differentia* (1534), written to present the case
for England's jurisdictional separation from the see of Rome, was translated into English and printed in 1548. The preface to this Edwardian
incarnation, *The true dyfferens betwen the regall power and the Ecclesiasticall*,
explained how David had begun the temple of God at Jerusalem, and
Solomon had finished it; similarly, 'many kindes of supersticion wer abolished by the sayd good Kyng' and 'no fewer' were left to be reformed
by his son.[66] Less challenging than *The true dyfferens* was *A lamentation* on
the death of Henry VIII, printed by John Day and William Seres for
John Turke. Turke openly welcomed the new evangelical possibilities
of the reign. Henry had already extinguished blindness, error, superstition, idolatry, blasphemy, 'divilysh doctrine, and Romyshe papry'. He
had funded students and colleges in Cambridge and Oxford, supported
preachers in their efforts to advance the truth, and helped the poor.
Edward would continue to advance the work of his father.[67]

This was the operation of providence, and not a historical accident.
With its roots in the discussions between Lucifer and Beelzebub and in
the history of the papacy, *A tragoedie or Dialoge* set the reigns of Henry and
Edward in this providential – even cosmic – scheme. After the long and
complex discussions of papal power by Pope Boniface, Doctor Sapience,
the People of Rome, the Church of Rome, Man's Judgement, Thomas
Massuccius, Lepidus, and the eastern ambassadors, Lucifer congratu-
lates himself and Beelzebub on the birth of Antichrist and the creation
of a powerful and corrupt Church.[68] One dialogue later, Christ explains
how a man claiming to be the universal head of His Church has defiled
and infected it, but he outlines to the archangels Michael and Gabriel
a plan for its recovery.[69] Henry VIII would 'deliver hys dominions from
the tiranny of thys mischievous robber'. But he would not completely
cleanse it from idolatry and superstition, 'whose rotes be further enteryd
in to the heartes of menne, then that they can be pulled out agayne at

[65] Corpus Christi College Cambridge, Parker MS 102 fo. 367.
[66] Edward Foxe, *The true dyfferens betwen the regall power and the Ecclesiasticall power Translated out of latyn by Henry lord Stafforde* (London, 1548; STC 11220), sig. {A2v}; cf. MacCulloch, *Tudor church militant*, p. 15.
[67] STC 13089. [68] *TD*, sigs. S2r–{X2v}. [69] *TD*, sig. X3r.

the first plucke'.[70] That task would fall to Henry's son Edward, a king endowed with godly gifts, who, following in the steps of his father, 'shall pourge all hys kyngdomes, and dominions from all the supersticion and ydolatry of Antichrist'. Edward would have the support of both Christ and 'a Christian protectour', a friend of 'right religion' responsible for the instruction of the king in a life of war against those things which displeased God.[71]

The final dialogues of the book play out this providential drama. In asking for counsel from a 'papist' and his archbishop of Canterbury, Henry VIII allows Cranmer to construct a compelling case against the pope. Working from scripture and the Church fathers, he outlines the prophecies and realities of Antichrist.[72] Cranmer traces the origins of the power of the Roman bishop back to the fifth century, and, in order to reinforce the coherence of the book, explains the subtlety and ambition of Boniface III and the violence, fraud, and treason of the emperor, Phocas.[73] He rehearses some of the classic arguments against papal power: the poverty and spirituality of Christ, the usurpation of Christ as head of the Church, and the false premise of the Roman Church – that Christ's sacrifice had been inadequate, corrupted by the papal ordination of 'the sacryfice of the masse, and other offeringes, and meritoriouse workes'.[74] Henry willingly accepts that the pope is Antichrist and sets out to prove that the king has 'more full authoritie in oure owne dominions, and kingdomes then he hath'. The Catholic counters that the king will lose his title of Defender of the Faith. 'Nay', replies Henry, 'we wil be called the destroyers of the false faythe of Antichriste, and maynteners of the trewe fayth of Christe.'[75]

The character of Edward liberates his realm from the power of Antichrist, and he does this as a fundamental expression of kingly duty. It was vital to continue the work of Henry VIII, who had been prevented by death from achieving its 'perfect end, as hys mynd was at the fyrste attemptinge therof'. It was the intention of Edward 'to plucke up by the rootes, and utterlye bannishe out of our kingdome the name of Antichrist and his Jurisdiction'.[76] Temporal authority was only half the story, because Edward's powers extended to the minds and consciences of his subjects. The king was God's instrument, a David striking off the head of Goliath with the sword of the Word of God. Some emperors of the past had already tried to destroy the power of the pope, but they

---

[70] *TD*, sig. {x4v}.   [71] *TD*, sig. yɪr.   [72] *TD*, sigs. {zɪv}–{z3v}.   [73] *TD*, sigs. {z3v}–{z4v}.
[74] *TD*, sig. Aa2r.   [75] *TD*, sig. Bb4r.   [76] *TD*, sig. ccɪr.

had failed because 'he reygned in the myndes of men'. People accepted the pope as their god on earth, afraid of his powers of excommunication and damnation.[77] Edward argues that the only effective way to counter the pope is to 'dryve him out of the heartes of menne'. Once he loses his spiritual kingdom in the consciences of men, his power will soon collapse. The weapon was the Word of God.[78] The fundamental assumption of the dialogue is that it was the king's right – even his duty – to exercise this sort of spiritual supremacy and guidance. The temporal authority of the crown only enhanced the king's power to provide for the religious needs of his kingdom. 'Counsel' argues that God had endowed subjects 'with a certayne naturall feare towardes their leage lordes, that they may reverently obey them'. This was certainly the case when 'he offereth matters unto them, that be juste and godlye'.[79] Ochino cast Edward in two connected roles. The first was providential agent sent by God to free his subjects from the corrupt and damaging spiritual spell of the papacy. The second was royal physician, ministering to a sick body full of corrupt humours, offering to his patients 'the wholesome medecine of the gospell'.[80]

A tragoedie or Dialoge presented the conventional evangelical assault on the papal Antichrist as an exploration of the kingship of Edward VI. Like printed court sermons or scriptural commentaries, the book presented the godliness of the king as a natural extension of his traditional monarchical duties. All kings protected their subjects and dispensed royal justice; Edward, using the Word of God, also attended to their hearts and consciences. *A tragoedie or Dialoge* presented Edward's kingship in its broadest possible context. History and providence unlocked the origins of the great papal lie and underpinned the ordered progress of Tudor Reformation – a Reformation in which godliness and supremacy were indistinguishable. These representations of the Henrician and Edwardian Reformations underpinned the presentation of Tudor kingship after 1547. *A tragoedie or Dialoge* was a remarkably effective expression of Edwardian monarchy at its most confident and godly.

PROMOTING THE GODLY COMMONWEALTH

Because Ponet's translation of Ochino appeared in October 1549, and collided with the collapse of Edward Seymour's protectorate, Walter Lynne had to produce a second, more politically acceptable edition of the

---

[77] *TD*, sig. cc2r.   [78] *TD*, sig. {cc2v}.   [79] *TD*, sig. {cc3v}.   [80] *TD*, sig. cc4r.

book. Edward VI's 'Christian protectour' became 'a christian Counsell'. The four lines of text describing Protector Somerset as 'a very valiant manne both in noblenes, and in upryghtnes of mynde, and a singuler lover and frende of right religion' were cut. The man who printed the volume for Lynne, Nicholas Hill, had a spare page to play with and so he filled it with a woodcut from *The beginning and endynge of all popery*: the pope, with attendant cardinals, bishops, and friars struck by the spirit of God's mouth.[81] The final dialogue between 'Kyng Edward the vi. and the lorde Protector' became an exchange between Edward and his 'Counsel'.[82] This second edition sat on the shelves of Edward's library.[83] *A tragoedie and Dialoge* was, in this sense, a 'live' text, and Walter Lynne was certainly a live member of a fascinating printing community. Biblical translations and commentaries, sermons, books of devotion, iconographical representations of godly, reforming, and imperial kingship represent, collectively, one of the most successful and enduring achievements of the Edwardian years.[84] So who, apart from Lynne, produced these books? And was print consciously promoted by the regime?

The short answer is yes. The printing community of Edwardian London represented a close and intricate network of association and co-operation. In 1550, for example, Walter Lynne printed Peter Martyr Vermigli's *Epistle* to Protector Somerset.[85] The volume had been translated into English by Thomas Norton, the step-son of the printer Edward Whitchurch, and Norton helped also to produce Whitchurch's edition of the *Paraphrases* of Erasmus, one of the major printing projects of Edward's reign (see below, pp. 122–3). The Dutchman Steven Mierdman printed for Lynne. Mierdman also produced books for Richard Jugge, printer of the work of Matthew Parker and the English New Testament, and later royal printer to Elizabeth I. Mierdman may have worked with another of Lynne's contacts: the ubiquitous and immensely productive John Day, a man closely linked to senior members of the Edwardian political establishment. During the reign of Edward, Day borrowed woodcuts from the king's printer Richard Grafton; and Grafton had worked closely

[81] *STC* 18771, sig. {Y1v}; Aston, *King's bedpost*, p. 139; MacCulloch, *Tudor church militant*, p. 28.
[82] *TD*, sig. {A2v}; *STC* 18771, sig. {A2v}.
[83] The copy from Edward's library, signed by Lynne, is now British Library, shelf-mark C.37.e.23; MacCulloch, *Tudor church militant*, pp. 27, 226 n. 42.
[84] For a discussion of 'Print, patronage, and propaganda', see John N. King, *English Reformation literature: the Tudor origins of the Protestant tradition* (Princeton, 1982), pp. 76–121.
[85] *An epistle unto the right honorable and christian prince, the Duke of Somerset written unto him in Latin, awhile after hys deliveraunce out of trouble, by the famous clearke Doctour Peter Martyr, and translated into Englyshe by Thomas Norton* (London, 1550; *STC* 24666).

with Edward Whitchurch in the 1540s. Walter Lynne's name exposes a spidery network of authors, translators, and printers.

The Edwardian regime was certainly conscious of the potential of print. In 1549 and 1551 the Privy Council endorsed direct intervention in the print trade, something that was certainly not unprecedented but still critically significant in a period of doctrinal change and Reformation.[86] In August 1549 William Cecil, as a servant in the household of Protector Somerset, became responsible for vetting the books and ballads of John Mardeley, a clerk of the Southwark mint, and, with principal secretaries William Petre and Thomas Smith, of examining all works in English before their publication.[87] In 1551 English books were expected to pass the signature of the king or six of his privy councillors.[88] How all this worked in practice is difficult to measure, but perhaps the important issue here is to try to separate the mechanics of conventional regulation from ideological intent. Was there, in other words, a relationship between the regime's supervision of print and the promotion of 'godliness' in the Edwardian works produced and distributed by printers and booksellers?

Royal privileges for printing had been granted during the reign of Henry VIII for the support of named texts for a limited number of years, the works of an individual author, or whole classes of books. But by the late 1540s and early 1550s the evangelical buzzword 'godliness' had become a key term in explaining royal favour and support for authors and printers. In January 1549 John Oswen of Worcester was granted the licence of royal printer for Wales and the Marches 'for the godlye edifieng and ease' of the king's subjects. He was given the right to print and sell the books 'set forth by the king' for worship, and other volumes 'conteyning any storye or exposycion of Goddes Holie Scripture or of any parte thereof'.[89] Like John Day, William Seres, Richard Jugge, and Thomas Raynald, Oswen printed the work of Bishop John Hooper of Worcester and Gloucester.[90] He ran, in other words, a privileged provincial operation. But metropolitan printers more regularly benefited from privileges granted by the regime. Richard Grafton, for example, was printer to the

---

[86] Peter Blayney, 'William Cecil and the Stationers', in Robin Myers and Michael Harris, eds., *The Stationers' Company and the book trade 1550–1990* (Winchester and New Castle, DE, 1997), pp. 11–34.
[87] *APC 1547–50*, pp. 312–13 (13 Aug. 1549).   [88] Blayney, 'William Cecil', p. 12.
[89] E. Gordon Duff, *The English provincial printers, stationers and bookbinders to 1557* (Cambridge, 1912), pp. 111–16; *CPR 1547–48*, p. 269.
[90] John Hooper, *Godly and most necessary Annotations in the .xiii. Chapyter too the Romaynes: Set furthe by the right vigilant Pastor, Jhon Hoper, by gods calling, Busshop of Gloucestre* (Worcester, 1551; *STC* 13756); John Hooper, *An Homelye to be read in the tyme of the pestylence, and a moste presente remedye for thesame* (Worcester, [1553]; *STC* 13759).

king proper, appointed in 1547 after a distinguished and prolific Henrician career. He shared with Edward Whitchurch the privilege exclusively to print books of divine service, sermons, and exhortations used in the Churches of England and Ireland.[91] From at least 1545 Grafton had been printer to Edward as prince of Wales, an office that had allowed him to construct a device representing the crown, the prince of Wales' feathers, and the motto 'Ich Dien'.[92] Grafton was given New Year gifts by the king in 1548 and 1549. So was the 'stacioner' Reynold Wolf, the king's printer for Latin, Greek, and Hebrew.[93] In 1551 Wolf was supported by the Privy Council in the publication and sale 'under the Kinges Majesties priviledge' of 'the booke lately by hym enprinted and set owt by the Archebysshop of Cauntorbury against Doctour Gardiners booke'.[94] Targeted royal favour also supported the London stationer Richard Jugge in January 1550 when he was granted a licence under the great seal to print the New Testament in English in large and small volumes.[95] The text – Tyndale's, 'Faythfully translated out of the Greke' – was printed in Jugge's workshop in Paul's Churchyard 'at the signe of the Byble, with the kynge his moost gratious lycence' in 1552. On the title-page was an impressive and sophisticated portrait of Edward, the evangelical king.[96]

John Day was one London printer and stationer who appears not to have enjoyed this form of privilege, at least formally. Day was, nevertheless, ubiquitous: it would be easier to list the books and the authors he did *not* print, rather than his texts of the sermons of Thomas Becon, Robert Crowley, John Hooper, Hugh Latimer, and Thomas Lever, all in fairly inexpensive English blackletter editions. Although Day printed some of these volumes alone, it was more usual for him to work with his business partner William Seres. In 1548 both men worked in a print shop in St Sepulchre's parish at the sign of the Resurrection near Holborn Conduit. A year later, Day was in Aldersgate and Seres in Peter College near

91 *CPR 1547–48*, p. 100 (22 Apr. 1547).
92 For example, *A very pleasaunt & fruitful Diologe called the Epicure, made by that famous clerke Erasmus of Roterodame, newly translated*, trans. Philip Gerrard (London, 1545; *STC* 10460), sig. {f6v}; Thomas Langley, ed., *An Abridgement of the notable worke of Polidore Vergile* (London, 1546; *STC* 24657), sig. {A1r}.
93 Blayney, 'William Cecil', p. 4.
94 *An answer of the Most Reverend Father in God Thomas Archebyshop of Canterburye, primate of all Englande and metropolitane unto a crafty and sophisticall cavillation devised by Stephen Gardiner doctour of law, late byshop of Winchester* (London, 1551; *STC* 5991).
95 *CPR 1549–51*, p. 227 (15 Jan. 1550).
96 *The newe Testament of our Saviour Jesu Christe. Faythfully translated out of the Greke* (London, 1552; *STC* 2867); King, *Tudor royal iconography*, pp. 95, 96.

St Paul's. From here, selling the books they produced at Day's 'newe shop by the lytle Conduyte' in Cheapside, they produced editions of Calvin as well as Becon, Hooper, Latimer, and Lever.[97] Perhaps their most impressive achievement was the Bible they printed after 1549, a volume regularly complemented by the Day colophon of Edward VI's crown imperial, the royal arms, the Garter, and the motto 'Vivat Rex' (see Figs. 5 and 6). Day and Seres effectively recast the personal device of Emperor Charles V as a 'patriotic emblem' for Protestant Tudor imperialism.[98]

John Day appears to have been the dominant partner. Books printed by both men often carried his motto of 'Arise, for it is Day', and the Corinthian columns of the Day–Seres colophon had at their bases Day's initials. But William Seres was an important printer in his own right. In March 1553 he was given the privilege and licence to print primers, 'private prayers' compatible with the Book of Common Prayer, which had to be approved either by the Privy Council or by the lord chancellor and by any two of the king's ordinary chaplains, and sold at a price set by the regime.[99] According to Seres' son, William Cecil was responsible for securing this patent for his father.[100] Cecil's support for Seres does make sense, because he was a servant in the Cecil household, close to Cecil's wife Mildred. In an account of the liveries made out 'of the best pece of clothe' and bearing 'badges of the beste' for members of the household (*c.* 1553), Seres' name appears fourteenth in the list 'by the commandemente of my Ladie'.[101] But the relationship between Seres and the Cecils can be traced to an earlier point in Edward's reign, when, in March 1549, Cecil leased some London property to Seres. So when it was revealed in the books printed by John Day and William Seres that Seres was based in Peter College, he tacitly acknowledged the support of a master who began Edward's reign as a senior member of Protector Somerset's household and ended it as a principal secretary to the king.[102]

Seres, the servant of a leading member of the regimes of Edward Seymour and John Dudley, co-produced Day's imperial colophon. Equally, it is just possible that business and personal obligation met in the production of *The hurt of sedicion* (1549) by John Cheke, partly printed

---

[97] Becon (*STC* 1712, 1721); Hooper (*STC* 13763); Latimer (*STC* 15270.7); Lever (*STC* 15543, 15547).
[98] Dale Hoak, 'The iconography of the crown imperial', in Dale Hoak, ed., *Tudor political culture* (Cambridge, 1995), p. 90.
[99] *CPR 1553*, pp. 50–1.
[100] Richard C. Barnett, *Place, profit, and power: a study of the servants of William Cecil, Elizabethan statesman* (Chapel Hill, NC, 1969), p. 117.
[101] Hatfield House Library, Hertfordshire, Cecil Papers 151 fo. 122r.
[102] Blayney, 'William Cecil', pp. 13–14.

Fig. 5   The representation of the imperial arms in *A Copye of a Letter contayning certayne newes, and the Articles or requestes of the Devonshyre & Cornyshe rebelles*, printed by John Day and William Seres in 1549. Day borrowed the block from the king's printer Richard Grafton, who had used it in 1547 in James Henrisoun's *Exhortation to the Scotts*. The block appears to predate the break from Rome (it features Catherine of Aragon's symbol of the pomegranate), and it may have encouraged Day to produce his own, more sophisticated representation of Edward's imperial kingship in 1549.

Fig. 6 John Day's and William Seres' imperial colophon of 1549 with the verse from 1 Peter 2:17. Day and Seres inserted this single sheet into their editions of the Bible. The '.E. .R.' of 'Edwardus Rex' conveniently suited the initials of his sister Elizabeth, so in 1563 Day voided '1549' and 'Vivat Rex' and reproduced the woodcut in John Foxe's first English edition of *Acts and Monuments*.

in property leased to Seres by Cheke's brother-in-law. In 1549 Seres
worked with Anthony Scoloker, a printer who had moved to London
from Ipswich.[103] Scoloker's provincial operation had produced the *Sermons of the ryght famous and excellent clerke Master Bernardine Ochine*, translated
by the local schoolmaster Richard Argentine.[104] Two years later, Seres
co-printed with Day Ochino's sermons on predestination, translated by
Cecil's sister-in-law Anne Cooke.[105] So Seres and Cecil operated at the
heart of Edwardian godliness. It is possible that these relationships – even
Seres' membership of the Cecil household – had at their root a common
association with Katherine Brandon, the evangelical duchess of Suffolk.
The duchess' arms appeared in volumes printed by Day and Seres in
1548, and Cecil was closely connected to Katherine Brandon as a friend
and neighbour in Lincolnshire.[106] Katherine, in turn, closely followed
Cecil's career, and regularly used him as an intermediary both before
and after the collapse of the protectorate in 1549 (see below, chapter 5,
p. 140).

Katherine Brandon leads very naturally to Catherine Parr, whom
she had served as a lady in waiting; Catherine Parr, in turn, to the
court reformers of the 1540s.[107] Perhaps the best example of Edwardian
Parr patronage is the first volume of Erasmus' *Paraphrases*, printed by
Edward Whitchurch in 1548. The *Paraphrases* helped to define the early
Edwardian Reformation: Erasmus' commentary on the New Testament
was actively promoted in the royal Injunctions of 1547, complementing the abolition of the jurisdiction of Rome, the establishment of the
king's supremacy, and the destruction of images, relics, miracles, and
pilgrimages.[108] The broad sweep of the Edwardian edition of the *Paraphrases* was clear from Nicholas Udall's letter of dedication to the king.
This established a standard for understanding Edward and explaining
the distinctive challenges – and opportunities – of his minority. Udall
praised the king's 'towardnes' of virtue and godly zeal, the 'lively sparkes
of vertue & Christian regiment', which confirmed that England was 'the

[103] Duff, *English provincial printers*, pp. 106–7.

[104] *Sermons of the ryght famous and excellent clerke Master Bernardine Ochine* (Ipswich, 1548; *STC* 18765).

[105] *Fouretene Sermons of Barnardine Ochyne, concernyng the predestinacion and eleccion of god: very expediente to
the settynge forth of hys glorye among hys creatures. Translated out of Italian in to oure natyve tounge by A.C*
(London, 1551; *STC* 18767).

[106] New Testament (*STC* 2791a, 2853); Pierre Viret (*STC* 24784); Hugh Latimer (*STC* 15291);
William Tyndale (*STC* 24441a).

[107] Maria Dowling, 'The gospel and the court: Reformation under Henry VIII', in Peter Lake and
Maria Dowling, eds., *Protestantism and the national church in sixteenth century England* (London, 1987),
pp. 60–71.

[108] *Injunccions geven by the moste excellente Prince, Edwarde the VI. . . . To all and singuler hys Lovinge Subjectes,
aswel of the Clergie, as off the Laietie* (London, 1547; *STC* 10088), sig. {a4v}; cf. sigs. {a2v}–a3r.

most fortunate Royalme that ever was, to whom God hath geven suche a Kyng, as in his minoritye of tendre babehood, learneth to have mynde on his funccion, and to considre whose ministre he is'.[109] Edward's childhood was marked by perfect grace, godly zeal, desire of literature, gravity, prudence, justice, and magnanimity. For Udall, the continuities of the reigns of Edward and his father were clear. Henry VIII had plainly seen that 'no waye there was to a reformacyon, but by thys only meane yf the auctoritie and usurped supremitie of the See of Rome were extirped, abolyshed, and clene extincte'. Henry had defeated the 'Romyshe Hydra', with its 'moste monstuous heades' of idolatry, pilgrimages, superstitions, counterfeit religions, 'and innumerable abuses moe'.[110]

This was the presentation of Edward's godly kingship at its most public and accessible. Nicholas Udall's epistle to Edward is important because his volume of the *Paraphrases* became a document to which the king's subjects were encouraged 'moste commodiously [to] resorte . . . & reade' in their parish churches.[111] It represented, for Udall, a lifelong interest in Erasmus.[112] But it also clearly reflected Parr patronage. The title-page of the *Paraphrases* bears the coat of arms of Catherine Parr, and the volume begins with a letter of dedication to the queen dowager as well as the epistle to the king and a preface to the reader. Catherine was lauded as the individual 'by whose good meanes & procurement this present worke hath been by sondry mennes labours turned into our vulgare toung'.[113] This was not a random or isolated dedication. A year after the publication of the *Paraphrases*, Udall translated into English Peter Martyr Vermigli's debate with Oxford conservatives, and he dedicated it to Catherine Parr's brother William, the marquess of Northampton.[114] It was Udall who, in June 1548, preserved a text of Stephen Gardiner's controversial St Peter's Day sermon on Edward's kingly Reformation (see above, chapter 2, pp. 57–60). Udall recorded the sermon at the behest of a 'noble personage': this may well have been Catherine Parr, who was at Whitehall to hear Gardiner preach.[115]

---

[109] *The first tome or volume of the Paraphrases of Erasmus upon the newe testament* (London, 1551; *STC* 2866), sig. (2)r.

[110] *Paraphrases of Erasmus*, sigs. {(3)v}–{(4)r}.   [111] *Injunccions*, sig. {a4v}.

[112] Udall's copy of Erasmus' *Epistolae . . . ad diversos* (Basle, 1521), annotated probably since his student days in Cambridge, was bought by John Maynard Keynes in 1903: King's College Library, Cambridge, shelf-mark E.12.14.

[113] *Paraphrases of Erasmus*, sig. {(:)6v}

[114] *A discourse or traictise of Petur Martyr Vermilla Florentine, the publyque reader of divinitee in the Universitee of Oxford wherin he openly declared his whole and determinate judgemente concernynge the Sacrament of the Lordes supper in the sayde Universitee* (London, 1550; *STC* 24665), sigs. *2r–{*5r}.

[115] John Foxe, *Actes and Monuments of these latter and perillous dayes* (London, 1563; *STC* 11222), pp. 771–6.

With his connections to the Parrs, Nicholas Udall was in good company. William Cecil prepared an introduction for the two editions of Catherine's *Lamentations* in November 1547 and March 1548.[116] The career of Thomas Smith in Protector Somerset's household was underpinned by the support of the Parrs (see above, chapter 3, pp. 85–6). Nicholas Throckmorton, a gentleman of the king's Privy Chamber from the spring of 1550, shared a grandmother with Catherine Parr and her brother William, and was a member of the queen dowager's household until 1548 (see below, Fig. 8, p. 152). Udall was also associated with other members of the wider Parr circle. In 1551 he asked Thomas Wilson to obtain letters of recommendation from Katherine Brandon and Charles Willoughby in order to press the suit of one John Grenberye. Grenberye wanted the post of victualler to the garrison of Calais, where Charles Willoughby's father was lord deputy. Wilson used his connections with Katharine Brandon and his responsibilities within her household as schoolmaster and servant to her son Charles.[117] Udall's short verse on rhetoric followed Walter Haddon's commendation in Wilson's *The Arte of Rhetorique* (1553).[118]

Katherine Brandon's sons, Charles and Henry, died in Cambridge in 1551, only a few months after the funeral in the town of the German reformer Martin Bucer. Katherine's private memorial to her sons was an endowment to support four poor scholars at their Cambridge college, St John's.[119] But there were other, more public memorials, to which Nicholas Udall and others contributed. Soon after the deaths of Bucer and the Brandons, commemorative and collaborative volumes were composed under the direction of four major figures of Edwardian Cambridge: John Cheke, Walter Haddon, Udall's friend Thomas Wilson, and Nicholas Carr. Richard Rex has written that these memorial volumes were an attempt, on the part of their editors, to use humanism to bolster the regime's evangelical policy, representing an alternative to the commemoration of the dead by 'traditional funeral masses and monuments, with all their

---

[116] In Catherine Parr, *The lamentacion of a sinner, made by the most vertuous Ladie, Quene Caterin, bewayling the ignoraunce of her blind life: set furth and put in print at the instaunt desire of the righte gracious ladie Catherin Duchesse of Suffolke, & the earnest requeste of the right honourable Lord, William Parre, Marquesse of North Hampton* (London, 1547; *STC* 4827), where Cecil's preface is unpaginated; cf. *STC* 4828, the second edition, sigs. A2r–{A7v}.

[117] A.W. Reed, 'Nicholas Udall and Thomas Wilson', *Review of English Studies*, 1 (1925), pp. 278–81.

[118] Thomas Wilson, *The Arte of Rhetorique, for the use of all suche as are studious of Eloquence, sette forth in English, by Thomas Wilson* (London, 1553; *STC* 25799), unpaginated.

[119] Katherine Brandon gave a farm to one Robert Colville of Much Glemham, Suffolk, who covenanted to pay to St John's the annual amount of £6 13s 4d for the exhibition of four poor scholars: *The Eagle: a magazine supported by members of St John's College*, 24 (1903), pp. 289–309.

overtones of blasphemous prayers and idolatrous sacrifice for the dead'.[120] They were also the response of an academic community in mourning. At the funeral of Bucer – the principal figure of the godly three – Matthew Parker emphasized how the life of the reformer had affected scholarship in the university and the Christian order of the town Bucer had lived and taught in since 1549.[121] The volumes were public and conscious celebrations of the regime's godly heritage, projects in which the Edwardian establishment declared its commitment to learning and Reformation. Richard Grafton, printer to the king who had shared his lessons with Charles and Henry Brandon, produced *Vita et obitus duorum fratrum Suffolciensium*, a volume of letters written by Walter Haddon and Thomas Wilson.[122] Like the book prepared by Cheke as a memorial to Martin Bucer – *De obitu doctissimi et sanctissimi theologi doctoris Martini Buceri* (printed by Reynold Wolf) – Haddon and Wilson presented set-piece letters and orations, and a series of contributions of classical verse.[123] Cheke may have been inspired by the scale of Bucer's funeral, after which, according to a later account, men proficient in Latin and Greek 'set up some Verses, as witnesses of his just and unfained sorowe, upon the walles of the church' of St Mary the Great.[124]

These memorial volumes can be used to reconstruct a fascinating network of friends, associates, and professional relationships in the universities and at court. The universities were, ideally, flagships of Reformation, and both inside the scholarly communities of Cambridge and Oxford, and outside them, the Edwardian regime tried its hardest to blur the boundaries between learning, kingly authority, and godly religion. The authors and editors of the memorial volumes of 1551 are excellent examples of these complex and sophisticated networks of association and

---

[120] Richard Rex, 'The role of English humanists in the Reformation up to 1559', in N. Scott Amos, Andrew Pettegree, and Henk van Nierop, eds., *The education of a Christian society: humanism and the Reformation in Britain and the Netherlands* (Aldershot, 1999), p. 27.

[121] Matthew Parker, *Howe we ought to take the death of the Godly, a Sermon made in Cambrydge at the buriall of the noble Clerck. D.M. Bucer* (London, [1551]; *STC* 19293), sig. E3r; Basil Hall, 'Martin Bucer in England', in D.F. Wright, ed., *Martin Bucer: reforming church and community* (Cambridge, 1994), pp. 144–60.

[122] Walter Haddon and Thomas Wilson, *Vita et obitus duorum fratrum Suffolciensium, Henrici et Caroli Brandoni prestanti virtute, et splendore nobilitatis ducum illustrissimorum, duabus epistolis explicata* (London, 1551; *STC* 25817).

[123] John Cheke, *De obitu doctissimi et sanctissimi theologi doctoris Martini Buceri, Regii in celeberrima Cantabrigiensi Academia apud Anglos publice sacrarum literarum prelectoris Epistolae duae* (London, 1551; *STC* 5108).

[124] Arthur Goldyng, trans., *A briefe treatise concerning the burnynge of Bucer and Phagius, at Cambrydge, in the tyme of Quene Mary, with theyr restitution in the time of our moste gracious soverayne lady that nowe is* (London, 1562; *STC* 3966), sig. {I6v}.

interest. Walter Haddon and Thomas Wilson, for example, were old friends. Wilson entered Haddon's Cambridge college, King's, in 1541, where he was very probably taught oratory, rhetoric, and civil law by Haddon.[125] After Wilson left Cambridge, the two men collaborated on a number of projects. Apart from the memorial volume for the Brandons, Haddon wrote a poem of introduction for Wilson's *The rule of Reason* of 1551.[126] Wilson returned the compliment in 1553, when he used as an example of rhetorical amplification the sentence 'There is no better Latine man within England, excepte Gualter Haddon the lawyer.'[127] When John Cheke fell seriously ill in 1552, and wrote to Edward VI from what he thought was his deathbed, he asked the king to consider Haddon as his replacement as provost of King's.[128] Haddon was an Etonian (*c.* 1529–33) who had moved to Henry VI's complementary foundation in Cambridge in 1533.[129] His Edwardian career was distinctively academic. He taught oratory and rhetoric, served as the vice-chancellor of the university between 1549 and 1550, and was elected regius professor of civil law in 1551. A year later Haddon was appointed master of Trinity Hall, Cambridge, but almost immediately found himself parachuted into the presidentship of Magdalen College, Oxford. Although Matthew Parker preached the sermon at the funeral of Bucer in January 1551, it was Haddon, the Latin stylist, who delivered the oration.[130]

John Cheke and Walter Haddon were exact contemporaries, but Cheke's career had developed along different lines. A Cambridge classicist rather than a lawyer, Cheke had taught Greek at St John's College in the 1530s. In 1540 he was elected to the regius chair and became the university's public orator. When Edward Tudor reached the age of six, in 1543, Cheke became one of his tutors, grounding him in classical texts and the arts of oratory and rhetoric (see above, chapter 2, pp. 44–6). In 1548 Cheke replaced Bishop George Day of Chichester as provost of King's College, Cambridge, and, on Easter Day, he swore as provost

---

[125] For three short studies of Wilson and his career, Reed, 'Nicholas Udall and Thomas Wilson', pp. 275–83; A.J. Schmidt, 'Thomas Wilson, Tudor scholar-statesman', *Huntington Library Quarterly*, 20 (1957), pp. 205–18; and A.J. Schmidt, 'Thomas Wilson and the Tudor commonwealth: an essay in civic humanism', *Huntington Library Quarterly*, 23 (1959), pp. 49–60.

[126] Thomas Wilson, *The rule of Reason, conteinyng the Arte of Logique, set forth in Englishe, by Thomas Wilson* (London, 1551; *STC* 25809), sig. {A7v}.

[127] Wilson, *Arte of Rhetorique*, sig. R4r; L.V. Ryan, 'Walter Haddon: Elizabethan Latinist', *Huntington Library Quarterly*, 17 (1954), p. 99.

[128] John Harington, *Nugae Antiquae: being a miscellaneous collection of original papers, in prose and verse; written during the reigns of Henry VIII, Edward VI, Queen Mary, Elizabeth, and King James*, ed. Thomas Park, 2 vols. (London, 1804), I, p. 21.

[129] For a short account of Haddon and his work, see Ryan, 'Haddon', pp. 99–124.

[130] Cheke, *De obitu*, sigs. {f3v}–{g2v}.

to maintain the true doctrine of the Church of England, acknowledging 'such facultye, liberte, or licence as the Kynges highnes alredy hath gyven me or herafter shall of his Kynglye power gyve me'.[131] As the provost of a royal foundation so clearly and visually associated with the power of the Tudor dynasty, Cheke became a vital point of contact between the regime and the college communities of Cambridge. In May 1549 he read the new statutes to the university's vice-chancellor and the heads of the colleges gathered together in King's College Chapel.[132] During the visitation he entertained at King's two important members of the Parr circle – the marquess of Northampton and Nicholas Throckmorton – and the royal commissioners.[133]

Cheke's academic reputation was still formidable. In 1548 Edmund Gest, a fellow of King's, dedicated *A Treatise againste the prevee Masse* to 'the righte worshipful maister Cheke, scole maister to the Kynges majestie, and provost of his worthy colledge in Cambridge'.[134] Three years later, Thomas Wilson identified Cheke and Anthony Cooke as Edward's teachers and schoolmasters 'in all good litterature'.[135] After a successful translation of Chrysostom, edited by Thomas Chaloner, Cheke was still active as a biblical translator in the 1550s.[136] He translated the gospel of Matthew and the first chapter of the gospel of Mark, work which demonstrated his continuing interest in the nature of the English language.[137] In 1550 Roger Ascham, in Augsburg with Richard Moryson, corresponded with his former teacher about classical authors and did his best to promote Cheke's pronunciation of Greek.[138] In the same year, Cheke wrote a preface to Thomas Gaultier's parallel Latin and English translation of the New Testament. This revealed two of Cheke's interests: the part

[131] King's College Archive Centre, Cambridge, Protocollum Book 1500–78, fo. 135.
[132] John Lamb, ed., *A collection of letters, statutes, and other documents, from the MS library of Corpus Christi College, illustrative of the history of the University of Cambridge, during the period of the Reformation, from AD MD, to AD MDLXXII* (London, 1838), pp. 109, 122–38; SP 10/7 fo. 39r (William Rogers to Thomas Smith, 14 May 1549).
[133] Lamb, ed., *Letters, statutes, and other documents*, pp. 114, 115.
[134] Edmund Gest, *A Treatise againste the prevee Masse in the behalfe and furtheraunce of the mooste holye communyon, made by Edmund Gest* (London, 1548; *STC* 11802).
[135] Wilson, *Rule of Reason*, sig. {A5v}. Cooke was not one of Edward's formal tutors, but it has been suggested that he taught the king during Richard Cox's absences from court: Paul S. Needham, 'Sir John Cheke at Cambridge and court', 2 vols., PhD dissertation, Harvard University (1971), I, pp. 173–4.
[136] John Cheke, *An homilie of saint John Chrysostome . . . newely made out of Greke into latin by master Cheke, and englished by Tho. Chaloner* (London, 1544; *STC* 14637).
[137] Hugh Sykes Davies, 'Sir John Cheke and the translation of the Bible', *Essays and Studies*, 5 (1952), pp. 1–12.
[138] J.A. Giles, ed., *The whole works of Roger Ascham*, 3 vols. in 4 (London, 1864–5), I:2, pp. 216–22 (18 Nov. 1550).

scripture played in the reformation of religion; and the advancement of the study of Latin and English.[139] In 1552 Cheke also put his linguistic powers to the test in a public debate on the descent of Christ into hell.[140]

Nicholas Carr was one of the other leading members of the group associated with the Bucer and Brandon volumes of 1551. His Cambridge career had begun at Christ's College but he moved to Nicholas Ridley's Pembroke Hall, and then, in 1546, became one of the first fellows of Henry VIII's Trinity College. A year later, Carr was elected as John Cheke's successor to the regius chair of Greek.[141] At twenty-eight , he was a young and clearly influential contributor to Cheke's *De obitu* and Haddon's and Wilson's *Vita et obitus*.[142] Like the other editors and contributors to the memorial volumes, Carr was conscious of the common sense of loss following the deaths of Martin Bucer and Charles and Henry Brandon. Roger Ascham offered a deeply providential reading of the impact of their deaths. In a letter written in 1552 to William Cecil, Ascham explained how he trusted that God's wrath had been 'satisfied in punishing diverse orders of the realme, for there misordre, with taking a way singuler men from them, As lernyng by Master Bucer' and 'nobilitie by the two yong dukes'. The loss to 'Counsell' was the death of Anthony Denny, the man to whom Thomas Chaloner had dedicated his edition of Cheke's translation of Chrysostom in 1544.[143] For Cheke, Haddon, Wilson, and Carr the deaths of Bucer and the Brandons were hard not to associate. Charles and Henry Brandon wrote in memory of Bucer; Bucer is mentioned frequently in the volume dedicated to the Brandons; and Denny is the subject of a poem in Cheke's *De obitu*.[144]

The memorial volumes reveal a culture of some complexity, a culture that at times transcended the exclusively theological. In 1550 Roger Ascham wrote to Cheke about a young fellow of St John's College, Cambridge, Henry Wright, who had been recommended to Ascham

---

[139] *The new Testament in Englishe after the greeke translation annexed wyth the translation of Erasmus in Latin* (London, 1550; *STC* 2821), 'J.C. unto the Christen reder'.

[140] Christopher Carlile, *A discourse, Concerning two divine Positions . . . Publiquely disputed at a Commencement in Cambridge, Anno Domini 1552* (London, 1582; *STC* 4654).

[141] Nicholas Carr, *Demosthenis, Graecorum Oratorum Principis, Olynthiacae orationes tres, & Philippicae quatuor, e Graeco in Latinum conversae, a Nicolao Carro* (London, 1571; *STC* 6577), sig. XI r–{v}.

[142] 'De obitu D. Martini Buceri' forms part of the bibliography of Carr published in his *Demosthenis*, sig. {X2v}.

[143] British Library, Lansdowne MS 3 fo. 2r (Roger Ascham to William Cecil, 12 July 1552); *An homilie of saint John Chrysostome*, sig. {AI v}.

[144] Cheke, *De obitu*, sigs. I2r (Henry and Charles Brandon), nI r–n2r (Anthony Denny); Haddon and Wilson, *Vita et obitus*, sig. LI r–{v} (Bucer).

by his friend Henry Eland. Ascham introduced Wright to Cheke as a talented and industrious student committed to his work on Aristotle, Plato, and Cicero, a young man worthy of the support of men like Cheke. The recommendation worked: a year later, Wright wrote for Cheke's volume on Bucer.[145] Robert Pember, Ascham's former tutor at St John's, presents a rather different case study. He also contributed to *De obitu*, but in no sense fitted the model of an academic in the vanguard of evangelical change. Godliness could be (and often was) associated with classical learning. This helps to explain the connection Edward VI's subjects made between the liberal sciences and godly Reformation, but it is an association that, as Richard Rex has shown us, was not inevitable.[146] Ascham's own network of friends in Edwardian Cambridge was in part evangelical but also reflected his academic interests and the nature of his college community. Similarly, there seems to have been a close Edwardian relationship between classical learning and the civil law, represented in the work of Thomas Smith as a lawyer and Greek scholar and Walter Haddon as a civilian and Latin stylist of European reputation (see below, chapter 6, pp. 199–203).

The memorial volumes of 1551 do not represent a definitive list of the godly of Edwardian Cambridge. But they do, nevertheless, suggest the presence in the town of a diverse group of individuals and communities sympathetic to Reformation. Perhaps the most striking feature of the long list of contributors to both books is their association with King's College. All colleges were communities but King's was probably even more self-contained than other institutions in Cambridge. There was a natural progression in its membership: from Eton to King's, and from scholar, three years and a day after admission, automatically to fellow. King's was an integrated and coherent community, populated by men who would have known one another from boyhood, moulded by the environment and culture of Henry VI's linked foundations at Windsor and in Cambridge. Ten fellows of King's contributed to John Cheke's *De obitu*, four of whom held teaching positions within the college, including lecturer in Hebrew and dean of theology Edmund Bovington, and the fourth most senior fellow of King's – the ubiquitous Walter Haddon.[147] It was an impressive group: a quarter of the entire fellowship, in January 1551,

---

[145] Giles, ed., *Roger Ascham*, I:1, p. 176 (Ascham to Cheke, 28 Jan. 1550).
[146] Rex, 'English humanism', pp. 19–40.
[147] John Cheke (provost), Walter Haddon, Edmund Bovington (dean of theology and lecturer in Hebrew), William Buckley, Thomas Gardiner, John Baker, William Temple, Nicholas Carvyle, John Seaman, and Thomas Lewis: King's College Archive Centre, Cambridge, Mundum Book 1550–51, unfoliated.

of forty-one. Haddon was the most senior contributor, but the general impression is one of youth. The other writers from King's were in their middle twenties. The youngest contributor was Thomas Lewis, twenty-three and from Henley, and a fellow since 1549.[148] Thomas Gardiner, one of the older contributing fellows, was only twenty-six or twenty-seven in 1551. Seven fellows of King's and one former fellow wrote verse for Haddon and Wilson.[149]

This 'King's connection', in its Cambridge context, can be reconstructed in some detail. Edmund Bovington had arrived in Cambridge from Eton in 1530. He was ordained in 1536; thirteen years later, in 1549, he was college sacrist and lecturer in Hebrew. In 1552 Bovington was rector of a college living in Kingston, Cambridgeshire, living on a stipend earned as dean of theology and a bachelor of divinity. William Buckley was seven years younger than Bovington, a mathematician who was a fellow in 1551, but with contacts at court. In April 1546 he dedicated a manuscript to Elizabeth Tudor and probably taught her brother mathematics.[150] Edward Aglionby was a former fellow of King's who, like Buckley, left Cambridge to pursue a career outside the college. He appears to have been chaplain to John Dudley Viscount Lisle, the eldest son of John earl of Warwick, and wrote at least one letter to his 'frynde' William Cecil in 1548.[151] Small groups of contemporaries wrote for Bucer: Nicholas Carvyle, William Temple, and John Baker entered King's as undergraduates on the same day in 1545 and became fellows in 1548. John Seaman and Thomas Lewis were admitted in 1546 and both were elected to their fellowships in 1549.

King's represents an important point of contact between Edwardian Cambridge and the short careers of Bucer and Charles and Henry Brandon, but its members did not contribute to the exclusion of other colleges. John Thompson, who wrote for Cheke's *De obitu*, studied at St John's during the 1530s. He was Lady Margaret Preacher in Cambridge between 1552 and 1554 and a canon of Gloucester. Charles Willoughby, the son and heir of William Baron Willoughby, was a fellow-commoner of St John's in 1549. He was a man with Brandon connections, and, through them, knew Thomas Wilson, which may explain his

---

148 King's College Archive Centre, Cambridge, Commons Books 1549–50, unfoliated.
149 John Cheke, Walter Haddon, William Buckley, William Day, William Temple, and Edward Cooper; the former fellow was Thomas Wilson: King's College Archive Centre, Cambridge, Mundum Book 1550–51, unfoliated.
150 British Library, Royal MS 12 A 25; Needham, 'Cheke', I, p. 223.
151 British Library, Lansdowne MS 2 fos. 72r, 73v (Aglionby to Cecil, 3 Dec. [1548]).

contribution to Haddon's and Wilson's *Vita*. John Goodrich was a fellow of Christ's College in 1551, but he had migrated from St John's via Jesus. Another character connected with Ascham and Edwardian St John's, and (like Goodrich) a contributor to *De obitu*, was Pietro Bizarri (or Perusinus). Bizarri was a member of Roger Ascham's extensive network of friends and associates at St John's. In 1549 Bizarri was a fellow of the college. In the same year he carried a letter from Ascham to his friend William Ireland.[152]

Students and academics in Oxford, as well as Cambridge, supported the memorial volumes, because Carr, Cheke, Wilson, and (perhaps principally) Haddon were able to recruit some important contributors from Oxford colleges. Haddon was appointed by the crown to the presidentship of Magdalen College in 1552 but his *Vita et obitus* suggests that he knew four of the college's evangelical fellows before his move from Cambridge to Oxford. Laurence Humphrey (a friend of John Foxe and later the biographer of John Jewel), John Mullens, William Overton, and Michael Reniger all contributed: Overton in Latin, Mullens in Greek, and Humphrey and Reniger in both languages.[153] Probably in the same year, three of them had complained to Cranmer and Bishop Thomas Goodrich of Ely about the 'behaviour' of their Catholic president Owen Oglethorpe. The fellows' articles described his actions against the proceedings of king and Privy Council.[154] Walter Haddon's presidentship of Magdalen was engineered by a regime closely associated with the men who had petitioned for action against Oglethorpe. William Cecil, principal secretary to the king, was fully briefed on the situation at Magdalen. In August 1551 Michael Reniger met Cecil to discuss the philosophy lectures he had been delivering at the college for over a year.[155] Cecil used him as a source on Oglethorpe and the problems at Magdalen.[156]

The Edwardian establishment was tightly bound together, both at the centre of power – in the Privy Council, the Privy Chamber, the financial courts – and in the universities and the Church. The memorial volumes

[152] Giles, ed., *Roger Ascham*, I:1, p. lvii (Ascham to Ireland, 8 July [1549]).
[153] Haddon and Wilson, *Vita et obitus*, sigs. {D4r}–E1r (Overton), {E1v}–{E3v} (Humphrey), {E3v}–{G3r} (Reniger), H1r–H3r (Mullens).
[154] For the articles, signed by Humphrey, Mullens, and Reniger, Corpus Christi College Cambridge, Parker MS 127 fo. 408; cf. Parker MS 127 fos. 411–14; cf. SP 10/13 fo. 9r (Walter Bower to William Turner, 20 Jan. 1551).
[155] Michael Reniger carried his brother Robert's letter to Cecil of 21 Aug. 1551: Hatfield House Library, Hertfordshire, Cecil Papers 151 fo. 23r.
[156] British Library, Lansdowne MS 2 fo. 116r–v (Michael Reniger to Cecil, Jan. 1551).

compiled by Carr, Cheke, Haddon, and Wilson in 1551 were more than academic exercises: they were humanist *Festschriften* expressive of culture and community. Just as importantly, they help to expose some of the sinews of the Edwardian polity, and in particular the shape of the Edwardian Church. One of Nicholas Udall's contemporaries at Oxford, Bartholomew Traheron, wrote for Cheke's *De obitu*. But there was more to Traheron than a single contribution of classical verse. In 1551 his name appeared in a list of men proposed 'to rough hewe the Cannon Lawe': Cecil, Anthony Cooke, Matthew Parker, Peter Martyr, and Cheke were also nominees (see also below, chapter 5, pp. 150–1).[157] In the same year Cheke and William Cecil secured for Traheron the deanery of Chichester. Two men from Chichester visited Traheron, and from them he 'lerned that the prebendaries there have fre election; howbeit they doubte not but that a lettre procured from the kinge wolde prevaile'.[158] Less than a month later, the wheels were turning. The Privy Council sent a letter to the prebendaries allowing the election of Traheron, 'requiring them to goo thourough with placing of hym accordingly'.[159] He resigned a year later, but the letter of resignation clearly marks Cecil and John Cheke as his supporters. 'To speake somewhat of myne awne matters', he wrote to Cecil, 'I am fully determined to resigne the deanrie of Chichester, and bicause I obtained it by your procurement and master Checkes, I wolde it shulde remain in you to appointe my successor.' Traheron's suggestion was Thomas Sampson, a fellow of Pembroke Hall, ordained a deacon by Nicholas Ridley in 1550, and described by Traheron as a London preacher 'of such integritee, as I wolde be glad to see placed there'.[160] The world of politics and religion between 1547 and 1553 was an extremely small one.

The Edwardian regime committed itself to the public promotion of kingly and godly Reformation. In turn, the printers and stationers, their books, the men and women who sponsored them, and their translators and editors formed a complex and fascinating network of connection and interest that has as much to say about the shape of the polity as the texts they produced. *A tragoedie or Dialoge of the unjust usurped primacie of the Bishop of Rome* and *The beginning and endynge of all popery* were rather different from the memorial volumes of 1551, but they shared a number of common themes and concerns. Walter Lynne, Bernardino

---

[157] *APC 1550–52*, p. 382.   [158] SP 10/13 fo. 92r (Traheron to Cecil, 19 Sept. 1551).
[159] *APC 1550–52*, p. 377 (2 Oct. 1551).   [160] SP 10/15 fo. 153r (Dec. 1552).

Ochino, and John Ponet set out to explain Edward's providential and kingly duty to administer the wholesome medicine of the evangelical gospel to the body of a commonwealth made sick by idolatry and blasphemy. This was the broad historical framework of Reformation, and *De obitu* and the *Vita* celebrated it in action. In his sermon at the funeral of Martin Bucer, Matthew Parker celebrated the life of a man who had worked for 'the hole state of the Universitie for the furderaunce of the mere learned sorte, and for the Godly instruction of the youth' and 'the body of the towne'. 'And over al that care', Parker explained, Bucer

> had also a speciall eye and desier to the politique and Christen order of the hole Townshyp, in the respect of the civyll societie and commonly order therof. In whiche policie he was so notably expert to the devyse therfore, that other whiles, I was in doubt wether I might judge hym to have bene befortyme more occupied in the studye of learnyng, or exercysed in the affayres of governaunce [of] the common wealthe.[161]

Bucer had supported the Christian commonwealth of Cambridge, but he had also, in 'De regno Christi', presented to the king as a New Year gift in 1551, constructed a model for the godly Reformation of the realm.[162] Like Lynne and Ponet, Bucer envisioned the establishment of the kingdom of Christ in England. In a modest way, he mirrored the relationship between governor and people presented in the work of Ochino, Ponet, and Lynne. 'To this caring mind', wrote Nicholas Carr of Bucer, 'came the concern about polity and civil administration of the town that everything should be administered in it for the usefulness and preservation of the whole body.'[163]

This was the broad vision of Reformation. But in the production of *A tragoedie or Dialoge* and *The beginning and endynge of all popery* (and perhaps even more obviously in *De obitu* and *Vita et obitus*) the mechanics of the promotion of Reformation reveal themselves in print. Tracing these networks of authors, translators, sponsors, printers, and (in the case of William Cecil and William Seres) servants and masters is extremely important. This chapter has scratched only the surface: there is certainly more work to be done on the professional relationships

---

[161] Parker, *Howe we ought to take the death of the Godly*, sigs. {E2v}–E3r.
[162] N. Scott Amos, '"It is fallow ground here": Martin Bucer as critic of the English Reformation', *Westminster Theological Journal*, 61 (1999), pp. 46–52.
[163] Hall, 'Bucer in England', p. 147 n. 11.

between Edwardian printers and booksellers. One dimension is the Dutch exile connection. Nicholas Hill (Nicolaes van den Berghe), Steven Mierdman, Reynold Wolf, and, of course, Walter Lynne were all natural-ized Dutchmen.[164] Mierdman printed for Richard Jugge (the graduate of King's College, Cambridge who produced Matthew Parker's funeral sermon for Bucer), Walter Lynne, and John Day. Day, Richard Grafton, and Edward Whitchurch employed in their workshops several Dutch journeymen.[165] The clearest examples of men who reflected the inter-ests of the regime are perhaps Day and William Seres. The regime, in turn, deployed Day and Seres very effectively. This was not necessarily a rigid and inflexible form of 'state-sponsored' print, because printers – even godly printers – were businessmen. Significantly, however, godly print seems to have represented good business.

Reformation is, of course, the key to all of these texts. In the royal visitation of the University of Cambridge in May and June 1549 it was clear that the royal commissioners and university and college officers sympathetic to Reformation were engaged in the trench warfare of per-suasion and exhortation, occasionally (and importantly) in the form of set-piece debates attended by prominent councillors and courtiers, but more usually in the close questioning of men who had failed properly to conform themselves. On the first day of the visitation, in King's College Chapel, Bishop Goodrich of Ely briefly declared 'the great and boun-teous Liberalitie of the kinges highnes towards the maintenaunce of lerninge' and his 'fervent zeale to setfurthe thesame' in *his* university.[166] This was a call for a 'worthy reformac[i]on as well in the universyte and colleges *as of every private person*'.[167] The Cambridge memorial volumes of 1551 demonstrated beyond doubt that their most important contrib-utors – both William Cecil and John Day, for example, contributed to Haddon's and Wilson's *Vita et obitus*[168] – believed they shared a sense of common culture and identity with the footsoldiers of Reformation in the college communities: teaching fellows, tutors, and some students. Learning, Reformation, and community combined, just as they did in Edward's education or the debates on transubstantiation in the homes

---

[164] Andrew Pettegree, *Foreign Protestant communities in sixteenth-century London* (Oxford, 1986), pp. 85–94; and his *Emden and the Dutch revolt: exile and the development of reformed Protestantism* (Oxford, 1992), pp. 87–91.

[165] Pettegree, *Foreign Protestant communities*, pp. 85–6.

[166] SP 10/7 fo. 39r (William Rogers to Thomas Smith, 14 May 1549; Knighton 222).

[167] Lamb, ed., *Letters, statutes, and other documents*, p. 110, with my emphasis.

[168] Haddon and Wilson, *Vita et obitus*, sigs. K1r–K3r.

of William Cecil and Richard Moryson in 1551 (see below, chapter 5, pp. 151–3). From Walter Lynne to John Cheke, Edwardians felt that they had to explain, demonstrate, prove, and persuade, because Reformation demanded historical and scholarly application. Print was a crucially important vehicle, and this was something the subjects of the crown recognized with distinction.

5

An evolving polity 1549–1553

The four years between 1549 and 1553 were absolutely formative in the evolving and emerging kingship of Edward VI. The political structures of court and Council began to mould themselves around a maturing king in a complex and sophisticated response to Edward's age, ability, and personality. But the Dudley years come with some heavy historiographical baggage, and any interpretation that reconstructs the gradual emergence of personal monarchy in the early 1550s runs headlong into two deeply ingrained traditions in the secondary literature: the idea of Edward as a king manipulated and controlled by the men around him, and the notion – which actually sits quite awkwardly with John Dudley's appalling historical reputation – that the last years of the reign represented a period of rescue and preservation for the institutional Privy Council (see above, chapter 1, pp. 25–7). In a letter written to Dudley in the late summer of 1552, William Cecil quoted Proverbs 11:14, *ubi non sunt consilia cadit populus* – 'Where no good counsel is, there the people decay' – and Dudley replied that it should be 'often had in mynde emonge us'. For his part, he would with 'all reverens' be ready to do his duty without weariness 'so longe as lyfe shall be in my bodye, for there I shalbe suer to see thoner of my master and my contrye preservyd'.[1] Historians have often found it difficult to dissociate Dudley from the politics of envy and manipulation – one predictable response to Dudley's letter to Cecil might be 'did he really *mean* what he wrote?' – but some of the same historians have also claimed that his reliance on the Privy Council laid the foundation for the Council's 'Elizabethan heyday'.[2]

---

[1] SP 10/15 fo. 1r (3 Sept. 1552; Knighton 711).
[2] G.R. Elton, *Reform and reformation: England 1509–1558* (London, 1987 edn), pp. 353–4; cf. Dale Hoak, 'Rehabilitating the duke of Northumberland: politics and political control, 1549–53', in Jennifer Loach and Robert Tittler, eds., *The mid-Tudor polity c. 1540–1560* (London and Basingstoke, 1980), p. 50.

In order to reconcile these conflicting notions – John Dudley as a
thoroughly disreputable man playing by the rules of Thomas Cromwell's
conciliar reforms of the 1530s – historians regularly argue that he sought
to use the power of the formal, proper, and bureaucratic Tudor state to
underpin his personal ascendancy. There is an alternative interpretation
of the Dudley years, an interpretation that embraces a more positive
model of politics for the 1550s and recognizes an emerging, engaged,
and active personal monarchy – at least as an ideal. This chapter builds
itself around four themes and a single question. The essential stability of
the Edwardian polity, even during the difficult months of the autumn of
1549 and spring and early summer of 1550, is the first theme. The second
is the critical importance in uncovering the networks of men around the
king, closely connected to the third theme, the political significance of
family. The fourth is the nature of the Edwardian 'Establishment', at
the centre and in the localities. And the question is this: how did the
Edwardian political establishment adapt to the reality of a maturing
king?

POLITICS AND PATRONAGE

The Dudley years were always meant to be different. In December 1552
the duke of Northumberland reminded his colleagues of 'the wyllfull government of the late duke of Somersett who tooke apon him the protector-
shyppe and government of his owne auctoryte'.[3] Edward Seymour, the
argument ran, had abused his power by alienating himself from his colleagues. Rejecting their wisdom and advice was the cause of his downfall
and a symptom of a polity out of order (see above, chapter 3, pp. 69–73).
The result of the *coup d'état* of October 1549 was devastatingly simple.
Edward Seymour was removed from his offices of governor of the king's
person and the protector of his realms. In October and November the
most important men of the protectorate were detained and sent to the
Tower of London. Seymour himself was sent away from court. At first
glance 1549 represented a definitive end to the old regime, a clear and
natural point of change in Edward's reign.

Although the politics of this transition were restless, uncomfortable,
and unsettling, it is nevertheless possible to overrate the significance
of 1549. The *coup* undoubtedly administered a shock to the Edwardian

---

3 SP 10/15 fo. 149r (28 Dec. 1552; Knighton 789).

polity, but the rhythm of the body politic re-established itself with surprising speed. There were certainly rumours of conspiracy, some resentment at Somerset's enduring popularity at court, and a generally sour relationship between Edward Seymour and John Dudley. But this was not a period of purge or revolution, and some members of the regime negotiated the testing time of 1549 and 1550 with a confident inventiveness. William Paget, Protector Somerset's *éminence grise*, detained Seymour's household servants at Windsor Castle in October 1549.[4] Edward Seymour himself was difficult to exclude from the politics of his nephew's reign. After a short period of internal exile he emerged in the late spring of 1550 as a changed and better man. In an epistle to the reader of *A Spyrytuall and moost precyouse Pearle*, published in May, Seymour referred to 'oure greate trouble, whyche of late dyd happen unto us (as all the worlde doth knowe) when it pleased God for a tyme to attempte us wyth hys scourge, and to prove if we loved hym'.[5] In the same month Seymour was readmitted to the Privy Chamber and the king's Privy Council.[6]

After 1549 the Edwardian regime redefined and restructured itself. In this there were certainly losers. Characters like Michael Stanhope and John Thynne failed to recover positions of power and influence in the regime. Although Somerset's household men were released from imprisonment, some of them faced near permanent political emasculation. Even a royal servant, principal secretary Thomas Smith, suffered because of allegation and association. Smith's presence at Windsor, and the suspicion that he had collaborated with Seymour and Stanhope, meant that his career, planned so carefully, collapsed with the loss of royal office and his lectureship in civil law at Cambridge.[7] But there were winners too. John Ponet's translation of *A tragoedie or Dialoge* by Bernardino Ochino was in press when the protectorate collapsed (see above, chapter 4, pp. 115–16). Its references to Edward Seymour were politically unacceptable after October 1549 because in the book Somerset was presented as the king's 'Christian protectour', an instrument of God, 'a very valiant manne both in noblenes, and in upryghtnes of mynde, and a singuler lover and frende of right religion'.[8] And yet Ponet's career was

[4] British Library, Cotton MS Caligula B 7 fo. 421v (10 Oct. 1549).

[5] *A Spyrytuall and moost precyouse Pearle. Teachyng all men to love and imbrace the crosse, as a mooste swete and necessary thyng, unto the sowle, and what comfort is to be taken thereof* (London, 1550; *STC* 25255), sig. {A7v}.

[6] British Library, Cotton MS Nero C 10 fo. 21v (14 May 1550).

[7] *APC 1547–50*, p. 393 (17 Feb. 1550).

[8] Bernardino Ochino, *A tragoedie or Dialoge of the unjust usurped primacie of the Bishop of Rome, & of the just abolishynge of the same*, trans. John Ponet (London, 1549; *STC* 18770), sig. YI r.

also one of the great ecclesiastical success stories of the Dudley years. In Lent 1550, as a chaplain to Cranmer, he preached before the king and court (see above, chapter 2, pp. 33–7). By June 1550 he was bishop of Rochester and by March 1551 bishop of Winchester. Just over a year later, in September 1552, the transition was complete. In spite of the clash of personality between his mentor Archbishop Cranmer and John Dudley, Dudley supported Ponet's efforts to produce a Latin and English catechism for schoolchildren 'partlie at my requeste', and he asked William Cecil 'to be a meane for the Kinges majestes lycens for the printinge of the same'.[9]

Another good case study in the transitional politics of 1549 and 1550 lies in the flowering career of Cecil himself. Within the space of eleven months, he moved from service in Edward Seymour's household to a position as principal secretary to the king from September 1550, with a short period of imprisonment in between. One of the interesting and important features of Cecil's transition is the fact that he did not break his links with Somerset in the autumn of 1549 or even during the uncertain months of spring and summer 1550. Cecil managed to demonstrate his loyalty to the restructured regime and still serve in the ducal household. There were two keys to this success. The first was that, with some help from Richard Whalley, the chamberlain of Somerset's household, he managed to convince John Dudley of his talents as a political manager. The second key was the part Cecil played in helping Dudley to recapture political initiative by preparing articles against Bishop Stephen Gardiner of Winchester. Cecil courted the attention of John Dudley by distancing himself from his own master; Dudley became, in the words of Whalley, Cecil's 'veare synguler goode lorde'.[10] This confident reinvention of himself rested in part on Dudley's feelings of vulnerability and insecurity in the months immediately following the collapse of the protectorate, because Dudley believed that Edward Seymour was trying to recover his position by courting Gardiner and working for his release from the Tower. By June 1550 Dudley believed that Seymour 'Takethe and aspyerethe to have the selfe and same ordre and Auctoryte to the dyspacche and dyreccion of the proceadinges ther as his grace hadde beinge protector'. But Dudley also professed love for the duke of Somerset, and in the interview with Richard Whalley he even shed tears.[11] This was the perfect

---

[9] SP 10/15 fo. 5r (7 Sept. 1552; Knighton 713).
[10] SP 10/10 fos. 21r–22r (Richard Whalley to William Cecil, 26 June 1550; Knighton 442); quotation at fo. 21v.
[11] SP 10/10 fo. 21r.

opportunity for Cecil to dissociate himself from Seymour's political strategy and mark himself out as his own man – and it worked.

William Cecil became 'soche A ffaiethffull servant and by that Terme most wytte Cowncelor, as unto the kynges majeste and his proceadinges, as was scarse the lyk within this his Reallme'.[12] But he was still firmly anchored in Edward Seymour's household, attendant on the duke, actively representing his master in correspondence, and acting as a point of contact for men and women who had been closely associated with the protectorate. In April 1550 John Thynne wrote on behalf of the suit of one Lok, one of the duke of Somerset's 'old chapleins'.[13] Five months later, in a letter 'To myn assurid ffrende Master William Cicill Esquier oon of the kinges Majestes Two principall Secretaries at the Courte', he asked Cecil to negotiate an end to his stewardship of Somerset's household.[14] Similarly, Katherine Brandon worked through Cecil and Edward and Anne Seymour to secure preferment for her cousin.[15] In a letter of October 1550 Katherine commented that Cecil's career had 'cum to a good markette': his wares were 'so good & salable' but the rate of exchange had of course been high. The Tower had been a painful experience and yet, in the end, he was 'no lossere'. The duchess assured Cecil that she was happy to become his partner, who would abide all adventures in his ship in fair weather or foul.[16]

Historians have for some time recognized the close relationship between John Dudley as the pre-eminent political figure of the second half of Edward's reign and William Cecil as his conciliar man of business.[17] Between 1550 and 1553, Cecil served his apprenticeship as an obsessive scribbler of memoranda, and during some long periods of illness or absence from court, Dudley himself left a substantial paper trail: letters he often wrote himself or to which he added postscripts, revealing an extremely busy and politically engaged man – and letters Cecil endorsed and filed. This meant a degree of administrative autonomy. In one good example from the first fortnight of Cecil's conciliar career, Dudley, away from court, asked Cecil to discuss with the duke of Somerset and William Herbert the preparation of a proclamation '& then send me the instrument yf it nede my hand and I wyll subscrybe to yt as ye doo'.[18] Ability,

[12] SP 10/10 fos. 21v–22r.   [13] SP 10/10 fo. 7r (24 Apr. 1550; Knighton 437).
[14] SP 10/10 fo. 68r (14 Sept. 1550; Knighton 464).
[15] Knighton 459 (3 Sept. 1550), 467 (18 Sept. 1550), and 493 (19 Nov. 1550).
[16] SP 10/10 fo. 83r (2 Oct. 1550; Knighton 474).
[17] For example, Hoak, 'Northumberland', pp. 40–1, 43.
[18] SP 10/10 fo. 7or ([?15] Sept. 1550; Knighton 465); cf. D.E. Hoak, *The King's Council in the reign of Edward VI* (Cambridge, 1976), p. 154.

discretion, and self-reliance marked Cecil as a talented man of business. Although modern analogies can be misleading – particularly when it comes to comparing Tudor government to modern government – there may be some profit in comparing Cecil as king's principal secretary to the modern Cabinet Secretary, sharing with William Petre the organization of meetings of the Privy Council, supported by its clerks; but also, as principal private secretary to a prime minister, enjoying physical access and proximity to Dudley, and thus to political power. Cecil played an important part in the governance of the later Edwardian polity: certainly not a modern civil servant but a key member of the complex network of men around the king in his court, the Council, its members, and John Dudley.

Cecil was a conduit. In November 1552 Philip Hoby thanked him for procuring 'the Signature at the Kinges Majestes handes' of his bill for the former monastery of Bisham. The land, with the advowson of its parish church, was granted to Hoby three months later.[19] When, in August 1551, Thomas Cranmer wanted to complete the consecration of Miles Coverdale because of Coverdale's 'long attendaunce, and of the greate lacke that the west parties have of hym', he asked Cecil to show the bishop elect of Exeter his 'gentill assistaunce for the obtayning of his sute' concerning Coverdale's first fruits.[20] The word used by Hoby and Cranmer was 'procurement'. Equally, in 1552 Lord Chancellor Thomas Goodrich wrote to Cecil about a prebend at Carlisle. His original candidate was Dr Belassyor, but Belassyor had died. He recommended instead Emmanuel Tremellio, the reader in Hebrew at Cambridge, but understood that Cecil had already 'mocyonid the matter'.[21] Often Cecil shuffled papers to the top of the conciliar in-tray, oiling wheels that were already in motion. Sometimes he appears to have presented suits directly to the king – physically possible because as a principal secretary Cecil could, and did, maintain personal contact with Edward. In the same month that Bishop Goodrich recommended Tremellio for the prebend at Carlisle, Cecil discussed with the king the subject of 'the ayde of the Emperor'. Together they prepared on paper a rhetorical examination *pro* and *contra*.[22] Edward worked closely with the royal secretariat (see below, pp. 165–6). Equally, other men near to the king became useful contacts. Edward's tutor, John Cheke, was approached by Richard Scudamore

---

[19] SP 10/15 fo. 111r (27 Nov. 1552; Knighton 765); *CPR 1553*, p. 192 (6 Mar. 1553).
[20] Longleat House Library, Wiltshire, Portland Papers 1 fo. 65r (13 Aug. 1551).
[21] British Library, Lansdowne MS 2 fo. 201r (5 Sept. 1552).
[22] British Library, Cotton MS Nero C 10 fo. 73r–v.

to obtain for his master Philip Hoby a brace of mastiffs for Charles V's *maître d'hôtel*, Monsieur Monfauconet. Cheke 'promysed to move the kynges majestie for them'.[23] Edward appears to have been willing to bestow royal favour. Roger Ascham recalled in 1552 how, teaching Edward penmanship in his Privy Chamber, the king had gently promised Ascham 'to do me good'.[24]

Combinations of men near to Edward were particularly attractive. In September and October 1551 Cecil and Cheke together secured for Bartholomew Traheron the deanery of Chichester (see above, chapter 4, p. 132). In 1552 Roger Ascham thanked Cecil, Richard Moryson, and Cheke 'for moving, fordering, and obteyning' a suit made to the king.[25] In 1551 Edward Lord Clinton asked Cecil to keep an eye on a suit for one of Clinton's chaplains 'in case any in my absence shall sew for it'. Clinton assured Cecil that Cheke and Thomas Wroth, a principal gentleman of the Privy Chamber, knew the details of the king's grant.[26] In May 1553 Bishop Nicholas Ridley of London sent separate letters to Cecil and John Gates, vice-chamberlain of the royal household and a principal gentleman of the king's Privy Chamber. Cheke was ill but, Ridley wrote, if he 'were amonges you, I would suerlie make him in this behaulf, one of Christes speciall Advocates, or rather, one of his principall proctors, and suerlie I would not be saide nay'.[27] Ridley had deployed the same sort of strategy six months earlier in a joint letter to Gates and Cecil, responding to the rumour of Edmund Grindal's candidacy for the projected bishopric of Newcastle.[28] Ridley complained that although he had 'dailie nede of Learned mennes Counsaill and conference', none of the prebends he had bestowed was in his own household. He named some suitable candidates and asked Gates and Cecil to present his request to the king.[29] This awareness of access and communication was not limited to the great and the good and the influential of the Edwardian establishment. William Cecil asked George Day, the former bishop of Chichester, to write to him after the 'Comunication, whiche it pleased you of Late to have with me' concerning the communion. Day could

[23] Susan Brigden, ed., 'The letters of Richard Scudamore to Sir Philip Hoby, September 1549–March 1555', *Camden Miscellany XXX* (Camden Society, fourth series, 39; London, 1990), p. 110 (18 Jan. 1550).
[24] British Library, Lansdowne MS 3 fo. 3v (27 Sept. 1552).
[25] British Library, Lansdowne MS 3 fo. 5r (Ascham to Cecil, 28 Nov. 1552).
[26] SP 10/13 fo. 32r (14 May 1551; Knighton 513).
[27] British Library, Lansdowne MS 3 fo. 52r (Ridley to Cecil, 29 May 1553).
[28] British Library, Lansdowne MS 2 fos. 220r–v, 221v (18 Nov. 1552). Cf. Patrick Collinson, *Archbishop Grindal 1519–1583: the struggle for a reformed church* (London, 1979), pp. 63–5.
[29] British Library, Lansdowne MS 2 fo. 220r.

not in his conscience accept the abolition of the altar, and he asked for Cecil's and Cheke's intercession. This request was expressive of personal relationships. Cecil, Cheke, and Day had St John's College, Cambridge in common. Also, in 1529, Cheke's father Peter appointed Day the supervisor of his will, and he became Cheke's mentor and protector.

John Cheke was one of the more obvious political survivors of the years of transition. In January 1550 the king's liberality extended to granting his tutor the former priory of Spalding in Lincolnshire and land in Suffolk.[30] In late May of the same year, at a time when Cheke was supervising his pupil's work on Cicero's *De finibus* and Edward's composition of Greek orations, Cheke was granted the manor of Downton Waylate in Essex, the advowson of its church, the manor of Preston and Hoo in Sussex, and an annual pension. These had all been granted in 1476 to Thomas Wylmote, vicar of Ashford, and to his successors. In the spring of 1550 John Ponet transferred them to Cheke in preparation for his elevation to the bishopric of Rochester.[31] Cheke's ability to navigate the difficult waters of 1549 and 1550 probably rested on the relative political neutrality of his duties. He worked in the Privy Chamber with the king but was not a gentleman of it. His duties were 'political' in the sense that he was close to the king, but he was also cushioned by his relationship with Edward. At the same time, Cheke's professional life was impossible to disentangle from the court and royal authority. His provostship of King's College, Cambridge survived the collapse of the protectorate and became a model in the regime's efforts to secure conformity at Oxford and Cambridge in the early 1550s. Cheke served as a heresy commissioner, and testified at the trial of Stephen Gardiner in 1550 and 1551. He also worked on two of the projects patronized very closely by Archbishop Cranmer. He was one of the men chosen to redraft the canon law and commissioned by Cranmer to turn the text of the statement of doctrine into the best humanist Latin (see below, pp. 150–1).[32] In September 1552 Cranmer informed William Cecil that he had sent the articles of religion to Cheke to 'set in a bettre order than it was'. 'I pray you considre wel the articles with Master Cheke', he added, '& whether you thynke best to move the Kynges majestie therin before my commynge, I refere that unto your ij wisedomes.'[33]

Family connections were critically important in the careers of the men around the king. William Cecil's father-in-law, Anthony Cooke, was an

[30] *CPR 1549–51*, p. 113.   [31] *CPR 1549–51*, p. 187 (19 May 1550).
[32] Diarmaid MacCulloch, *Thomas Cranmer* (New Haven and London, 1996), p. 524.
[33] Longleat House Library, Wiltshire, Portland Papers 1 fo. 71r (19 Sept. [1552]).

important royal servant. Like Cheke, Cooke served as a heresy commissioner; like Cecil, he was nominated as a 'civilian' in Cranmer's campaign to reform the canon law (see below, pp. 150–1). John Cheke, as tutor to the king, had access to the Privy Chamber; Cooke was a gentleman of the king's Privy Chamber by February 1551, and after 1550 he appears to have helped Cheke to teach Edward.[34] The Cooke family connection became one of the defining features of the Elizabethan political establishment. Thomas Hoby, the half-brother of William Cecil's close friend Philip, married Elizabeth Cooke in June 1558, and Catherine Cooke followed her sister in 1565 by marrying the diplomat Henry Killigrew. Relatives of Anthony Cooke became Cecil servants: Thomas Ogle, for example, the son of Anthony Cooke's sister Beatrix, who served Cecil from the middle 1550s to his death in 1574. These marriages and arrangements clearly cemented close relationships and friendships of the late 1540s and early 1550s, but they were primarily Marian and Elizabethan. During the reign of Edward, however, William Cecil's marriage to Mildred was the Cookes' principal political marriage, perhaps complemented by that of Nicholas Bacon of the court of wards to Anne Cooke by 1553. For Cecil, the marriages of his sisters-in-law in the Cheke family were just as important. Alice Cheke's husband was Dr John Blythe, Cambridge's first regius professor of physic. Their daughter, Anne, married Peter Osborne, the Lincoln's Inn-trained lawyer who served as the lord treasurer's remembrancer in the Exchequer and clerk to the principal gentlemen of the Privy Chamber after 1552. The appearance of Osborne as clerk during the financial programme of 1551–52, organized by William Cecil, may have been more than coincidence.[35]

Cecil's relatives from his first marriage joined his Marian and Elizabethan households, but the most important Edwardian kinship connection was his brother-in-law Lawrence Eresby, the husband of Magdalen Cheke. Eresby held the key to some of William Cecil's earliest Edwardian property transactions: in 1549 Thomas Smith had defended criticisms of his own actions by comparing himself to Cecil and Eresby.[36] Eresby's name opens up an important network of influence at the centre of power and in the eastern counties of England. In September 1551 Richard Goodrich and the inhabitants of Louth in Lincolnshire received

[34] Thomas Wilson, *The rule of Reason, conteinyng the Arte of Logique, set forth in Englishe* (London, 1551; *STC* 25809), sig. {A5v}.

[35] Dale Hoak, 'The secret history of the Tudor court: the king's coffers and the king's purse, 1542–1553', *Journal of British Studies*, 26 (1987), pp. 220–9.

[36] John Gough Nichols, ed., 'Some additions to the biographies of Sir John Cheke and Sir Thomas Smith', *Archaeologia*, 38 (1860), p. 124.

a royal grant for the establishment of a grammar school in the town. Eresby was appointed as its warden.[37] Goodrich was the prime mover; Cecil appears to have been the principal contact at court, with Eresby carrying letters between them in early September – just over a week before the final royal grant.[38] The foundation of the school was certainly not unique. Six months earlier, for example, Walter Mildmay and his brother Thomas (both important officers of the court of augmentations), Cecil's secretarial colleague William Petre, and Henry Tyrrell had received a similar grant for the establishment of a school in Chelmsford.[39] But the foundation of the school in Louth was still an important project, because it reinforced the Lincolnshire interests of Goodrich, Cecil, and Eresby. Like his father, Richard, William Cecil was firmly rooted in the county, and Goodrich certainly owned property there.[40] William Rede, the vicar of Grantham, referred in October 1552 to Goodrich's purchase from the king of chantry houses in the town.[41] In 1547 Thomas Cranmer had granted the reversion of land in Sleaford to Goodrich and his wife Mary. In 1550 they transferred it to another influential Lincolnshire landowner, Edward Lord Clinton, the nephew of John Dudley.[42] Eresby the gentleman servant was a commissioner for inquisitions *post mortem* for Lincolnshire and Lincoln in 1548, and in October 1550, as William Cecil's 'brother', he was nominated a chantry commissioner in Grantham.[43]

Men of rank and political influence in the late medieval and early modern English polities had important responsibilities in their local 'countries'. This was particularly significant during the Edwardian Reformation, when men like Cecil, Goodrich, and Eresby, representing the authority of the crown, could alter beyond recognition the face of local communities, sanctioning the destruction of chantry chapels and defacing the images of saints. But even at the best of times good governance demanded a close relationship between the regime and the representatives of royal power in the localities, working in county communities as commissioners, JPs, and local law officers. A man like William Cecil, with important responsibilities at court and in Council and a high profile in Lincolnshire, had to be mobile. In the summer of 1552, for

[37] *CPR 1550–53*, pp. 119–22 (21 Sept. 1551).   [38] Knighton 538 (9 Sept. 1551).
[39] *CPR 1550–53*, pp. 116–17 (March 1551).
[40] Jointly purchased by Goodrich and William Breton of London, along with property in Huntingdonshire, Cambridgeshire, and London: *CPR 1547–48*, pp. 32–5 (6 Aug. 1548).
[41] Knighton 482 (12 Oct. 1550).
[42] *CPR 1547–48*, pp. 18–19 (1 Sept. 1547); *CPR 1549–51*, p. 357 (13 Oct. 1550).
[43] *CPR 1548–49*, p. 136 (1548); Knighton 482 (12 Oct. 1550).

example, Cecil recorded an exhausting circuit of visits to Cambridge, Stoke-by-Clare in Suffolk, the house of his colleague William Petre at Ingatestone Hall in Essex, Romford, London, his own house at Wimbledon, Nonsuch, and the court at Guildford. But before this tour he had discharged his responsibilities in Lincolnshire. Cecil combined a tour of his properties with visits to his neighbours and the supervision of the execution of justice in his home town. He went to Sempringham (the home of Edward Lord Clinton), met Katherine Brandon duchess of Suffolk at Grimsthorpe and John Dudley at Burghley, attended the quarter sessions at Stamford, and toured Tinwell, Greatford, Lyddington, Peterborough, Casterton, Pickworth, Pinchbeck, and Boston – all within the space of a fortnight.[44]

Influence in London clearly enhanced Cecil's standing in Lincolnshire. As the recorder of Boston, in 1550, he was asked by the mayor and burgesses to pursue the town's interests in London and to secure from the king 'Letters of Lycence'. For Cecil, the material benefits of this sort of mediation were not substantial. In 1548 Anthony St Leger had sent him a dozen marten skins for his trouble in pressing a suit (see above, chapter 3, p. 83); in 1550 the worthies of Boston enclosed with their letter 'a pore remembraunce in wyldfowle to make mery with this Christmasse'. But the significance of the exchange should not be underestimated. Having Cecil as a senior local law officer allowed Boston to engage the services of one of the king's principal secretaries, and in return it enabled Cecil to consolidate his reputation in Lincolnshire. The mayor and his colleagues signalled their intention to visit Cecil in London to receive his 'advyce and councell' on a local matter 'dependyng in the starre chambre'. It was the intention of the mayor and burgesses to make Cecil 'prevye and of councell in all our matters and affares concernyng the commen welthe of this Towne'.[45] Two years later, they thanked him for his 'grate paynes & travayll' in securing redress for the destruction of buildings and houses in Boston. The principal offender was one John Brown, who, thanks to Cecil, had received a letter from the Privy Council. On opening it, the mayor and burgesses added with relish, Brown had visibly paled, with 'a countenance verrye lyght'.[46] William Cecil was their 'ryght worship-ffull' master, a form of address that triggered some important associations: of lordship, protection, worldly advancement, kinship, and friendship.[47] Cecil and his contemporaries were aware of these inherited

[44] Knighton 688.   [45] SP 10/11 fo. 28r–v (20 Dec. 1550; Knighton 500).
[46] SP 10/15 fo. 109r (27 Nov. 1552; Knighton 764).
[47] K.B. McFarlane, *The nobility of later medieval England* (Oxford, 1997 edn), p. 113.

associations. In 1550, writing in the context of ecclesiastical patronage, the bishop of Salisbury left Cecil to the 'tuition of Almighty God, whom I beseech always to preserve you in health with increase of worship'.[48] Katherine Brandon referred to 'my neighbours and the worshipful of the shire'.[49] Cecil the worshipful master and Cecil the principal secretary to the king could combine to powerful effect.

One of the fascinating features of the reign of Edward is the complexity of its networks of influence and power. Here Richard Goodrich – Lincolnshire gentleman, patron of the king's grammar school in Louth, and kinsman of Archbishop Cranmer – comes into his own. Goodrich was a common lawyer, educated at Jesus College, Cambridge and admitted to Gray's Inn in 1532. As a student of law in London he was the contemporary of Nicholas Bacon and John Spelman. His career began in the court of wards and liveries, where Bacon formally replaced him as attorney in January 1547 and Goodrich moved to an attorney-ship of the newly remodelled court of augmentations and revenues of the king's crown.[50] Goodrich was the fifth officer of the court; the sixth was John Gosnold, another lawyer trained at Gray's Inn.[51] Cecil and Goodrich had overlapped at Gray's Inn and the relationship between the two men remained close. In 1550 Goodrich offered to negotiate for Cecil the purchase of William Paget's house in Cannon Row.[52] In 1552 he worked with Cecil to buy property for Anthony Cooke in Somerset and Devon.[53] Goodrich, Anne Cooke, and ten-year-old Thomas Cecil stayed with Cooke at Gidea Hall in August 1552.[54] And it was Mildred Cecil who invited Goodrich to join her husband to take the waters at Bath in the same month.[55] During Cecil's peregrinations of July 1552 Goodrich had been with him at Wimbledon and visited Nonsuch with Cecil and Philip Hoby of the Privy Chamber.[56] Hoby worked with Goodrich a couple of months later, when, on the instructions of the Privy Council, the two men examined a prisoner.[57] Goodrich was a heresy commissioner in 1551 and a visitor to the Savoy in the same year.[58]

---

[48] Knighton 436 (25 Mar. 1550).
[49] SP 10/14 fo. 104r (Brandon to Cecil, June 1552; Knighton 669).
[50] *Letters and papers, foreign and domestic, of the reign of Henry VIII*, ed. J.S. Brewer, J. Gairdner, R.H. Brodie *et al.*, 21 vols. and *Addenda* (London, 1862–1932), XXI:2 no. 771 (13).
[51] *Letters and papers*, ed. Brewer, Gairdner, Brodie, *et al.*, XXI:2 no. 1.
[52] Knighton 471 (30 Sept. 1550); Knighton 479 (5 Oct. 1550).
[53] Knighton 708 (28 Aug. 1552).   [54] Knighton 697 (20 Aug. 1552).
[55] SP 10/14 fo. 144A (Goodrich to Cecil, 22 Aug. 1552; Knighton 701).   [56] Knighton 688.
[57] *APC 1552–54*, p. 124 (Sept. 1552).
[58] *CPR 1549–51*, p. 347 (18 Jan. 1551); *CPR 1550–53*, p. 123 (19 Sept. 1551).

Why was Richard Goodrich so deeply embedded in the later Edwardian regime? In part his responsibilities reflected the office he held in
augmentations. As a commissioner for the sale of the king's lands and a
surveyor of Church goods in London he was clearly working within his
area of expertise.[59] Goodrich the evangelical lawyer, nephew of Bishop
Goodrich of Ely and kinsman and friend of Cranmer, felt at home in a
regime which used the destruction of idolatry to raise crown revenue.[60]
But the timing of Richard Goodrich's career is significant. The construction of the case against Stephen Gardiner in the summer of 1550 enabled
Goodrich's friend William Cecil to establish himself in the counsels of
John Dudley (see above, p. 139), and it also gave Goodrich the opportunity to make his mark. In July 1550 the Privy Council resolved that
William Herbert and William Petre should visit Gardiner in the Tower
of London but, 'for the more autentike procedyng with him', they should
take with them 'a devine and a temporall lawier': the divine was Bishop
Nicholas Ridley of London, the common lawyer Goodrich.[61] Ridley,
Petre, and Cecil prepared articles for Gardiner to sign; Herbert, Petre,
and Goodrich travelled to the Tower two days later. Gardiner did not
know Goodrich in July 1550, but he was a familiar face by the end of the
year. Goodrich and his colleague in augmentations John Gosnold, the
civil lawyers John Oliver and Griffith Leyson, Cranmer, Ridley, Bishop
Goodrich of Ely, Bishop Holbeach of Lincoln, Principal Secretary Petre,
and James Hales of the court of common pleas were the royal commissioners appointed to hear the case against Gardiner in December 1550.[62]

Depriving Stephen Gardiner of his bishopric was a defining moment
for the Edwardian regime. When Richard Goodrich and his colleagues
declared the bishopric of Winchester 'to all effectes and purposes, to be
voyde' they marked a definitive end to the career of a bishop whose presence – let alone his publications, preaching, and appearances before the
king's councillors – had reminded the regime of a powerful case against
Reformation during royal minority (see above, chapter 2, pp. 57–60).[63]
The trial of Gardiner was a cathartic experience and an important measure of the regime's determination to destroy conservative opposition. It
was also a show of strength that allowed the Edwardian political establishment to demonstrate some of the fundamental continuities of the reign.
Members of the pre- and post-1549 regimes presented themselves before

---

[59] *CPR 1553*, p. 411 (23 May 1552); SP 10/14 fo. 144Ar (Aug. 1552).
[60] MacCulloch, *Cranmer*, pp. 366–7.
[61] John Foxe, *Actes and Monuments of these latter and perillous dayes* (London, 1563; *STC* 11222), p. 768.
[62] Foxe, *Actes and Monuments*, pp. 776–7.   [63] Foxe, *Actes and Monuments*, pp. 866–7.

the royal commissioners to offer important and sometimes damning testimony: from John Dudley, William Herbert, William Paget, William Parr, and John Russell to William Cecil, Thomas Chaloner, John Cheke, Richard Cox, Edward North, Ralph Sadler, Thomas Smith, and Anthony Wingfield.

If the careers of men like Richard Goodrich demonstrate one thing, it is that the Edwardian regime was shaped by networks of individuals who combined personal friendship and commitment to Reformation, and who were prepared, more importantly, to sit on commissions, try men like Stephen Gardiner, strip the altars of parish churches, participate in the counsels of their king, and perform the business of local and central governance. The world of Edwardian politics and governance was small – even incestuous – populated by men closely connected to one another: an organic, stable governing elite of men sympathetic to the regime. One good example is the group of common and civil lawyers who transacted the regime's business in public and in private in the early 1550s. The ubiquitous Goodrich was one of them, but there were a dozen or so of his colleagues in the law who helped to remove conservative bishops like George Day and Nicholas Heath (after observing in person the proceedings against Gardiner), and who also sat as commissioners to examine and reform the canon law – one of Archbishop Cranmer's most cherished projects. The civil lawyers who heard the sentence against Stephen Gardiner at Lambeth were Richard Lyell, Geoffrey Glynn, William Jeffrey, Richard Standish, and David Lewis; and the common lawyers Francis Morgan, William Stamford, Robert Chidley, John Caryll, and James Dyer.[64] Lyell of All Souls College, Oxford was a heresy commissioner, a canon and precentor of Wells in 1552, and, with Chidley and Stamford, a commissioner to hear Day and Heath in 1551.[65] A month later Lyell was proposed as a visitor to the University of Oxford.[66] John Caryll of the Inner Temple was one of eight common lawyers called on by Cranmer 'to resolve uppon the reformacion of the Cannon Lawes' in October 1551. Three of the others – James Hales, Goodrich, and Gosnold – had been Gardiner's judges. Significantly, the promotions of Stamford and Caryll as sergeants of law and the godly John Gosnold as general solicitor of augmentations were important enough for Edward VI to record them in his journal.[67]

[64] Foxe, *Actes and Monuments*, p. 867.   [65] Knighton 549 (Sept. 1551).
[66] Knighton 565 ([Oct. 1551]).
[67] British Library, Cotton MS Nero C 10 fo. 61r; W.K. Jordan, ed., *The chronicle and political papers of King Edward VI* (Ithaca, NY, 1966), p. 122.

John Caryll, John Gosnold, William Stamford, and their colleague Thomas Gawdy appear to have been rewarded professionally for their services to the crown. All four men were chosen to reform the canon law, along with James Hales, Richard Goodrich, Thomas Bromley, the recorder of London Robert Brooke, and master of requests John Lucas of the Inner Temple (all common lawyers) and three other groups of experts – bishops, divines, civil lawyers. It was a formidable team, wholly expressive of the Edwardian regime at its most connected and evangelical. The seven bishops were Ridley of London, Ponet of Winchester, Goodrich of Ely, Coverdale of Exeter, Hooper of Gloucester, Barlow of Bath and Wells, and Scory of Rochester – plus, of course, Cranmer. Dean of Lincoln John Taylor, Richard Cox, Matthew Parker, Hugh Latimer, Anthony Cooke, Peter Martyr, John Cheke, and John a Lasco were the theologians. The civil law was represented by William Petre, William Cecil (strangely: he was a common lawyer by training), Thomas Smith, Rowland Taylor, William May, Bartholomew Traheron, Richard Lyell, and Anthony Skinner.[68] A month after the Privy Council's instruction to establish a commission of thirty-two, Cranmer, Bishop Goodrich, Richard Cox, Peter Martyr, William May, Rowland Taylor, John Lucas, and Richard Goodrich became members of a sub-committee to draw up the preliminary survey.[69] Two days before this commission, on 9 November 1551, Richard Goodrich was granted a life annuity of £100.[70]

COURT, KINGSHIP, AND MAJORITY

Network, elite, establishment: all three words are expressive of the extent to which personal friendship could underpin professional office, and how relationships built on expertise and trust could shape the small but complex political world of the Edwardian regime. Common experiences of life and a shared sense of mission were just as significant. In November and December 1551 some of the commissioners named to reform the canon law met a small group of old friends and colleagues – holders of ecclesiastical and royal office, Cambridge academics, gentlemen of the king's Privy Chamber – in the London homes of William Cecil and Richard Moryson. On two occasions John Cheke, Anthony Cooke, Edmund Grindal, Francis Knollys, William Parr marquess of

---

[68] *APC 1550–52*, p. 382 (6 Oct. 1551). The king's draft of February 1552 revealed some fairly superficial alterations: British Library, Cotton MS Nero C 10 fo. 53v (Jordan, ed., *Chronicle*, p. 110). See also Gerald Bray, ed., *Tudor church reform: the Henrician canons of 1535 and the Reformatio legum ecclesiasticarum* (Church of England Record Society, 8; Woodbridge, 2000), pp. xlv–liv.

[69] *CPR 1550–53*, p. 114 (11 Nov. 1551).   [70] *CPR 1550–53*, p. 195.

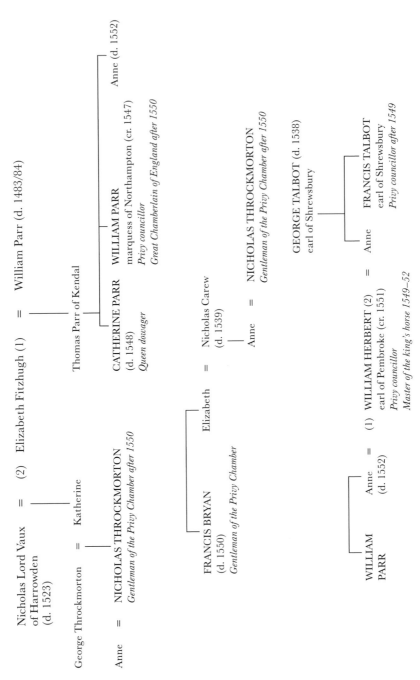

Fig. 8   The families of Herbert, Parr, Talbot, and Throckmorton.

Northampton, Lord Francis Russell, Nicholas Throckmorton, Thomas Wroth, and others debated the sacrament.[71] Both Winthrop Hudson and John Guy have pointed to the significance of these meetings for establishing a 'Cambridge connection' between the regimes of the 1550s and 1560s and the close relationship between the form and nature of the Edwardian Reformation and the ecclesiastical settlement of 1559.[72] But even from the immediate perspective of Edward's reign it is clear that these men helped to bind together the regime, giving to it its shape and character. And, of course, they prepared the way for the second Edwardian Book of Common Prayer of 1552, a rather more unambiguous Protestant statement than its predecessor.

Close connections of career and family bound together the men around the king, and here the Privy Chamber is critical. Some of the men who attended Edward in his private rooms may well have been John Dudley's political associates, admitted, like Nicholas Throckmorton, in the spring months of 1550. But they had other qualifications too, quite apart from their commitment to Protestantism and a closeness to the king. Throckmorton is a good example. He was related to some of the major families of the court (see Fig. 8). His grandmother, Elizabeth Fitzhugh, had married twice: first to William Parr, the father of William Baron Parr of Horton and Thomas Parr of Kendal; and, after Parr's death, to Nicholas Lord Vaux of Harrowden. Throckmorton was a grandson of Elizabeth's second family, because his father George had married Katherine Vaux. So Nicholas Throckmorton's cousins were the Queen Dowager Catherine, William Parr marquess of Northampton, and Anne, the first wife of William Herbert earl of Pembroke – family relationships reinforced by Throckmorton's service in the households of Catherine and William Parr in the 1540s. His own marriage further bound him into the late Henrician and Edwardian establishment. Although Throckmorton's father-in-law, Nicholas Carew, had been executed for treason during the reign of Henry VIII, Carew's wife Elizabeth was the sister of Francis Bryan, a gentleman of Edward's Privy Chamber between 1547 and his death in 1550.

Nicholas Throckmorton is just one example of how the shape of these family relationships helped to shape the Edwardian elite. The godly Anthony Denny was, through his sister Mary, the brother-in-law of John Gates (see Fig. 9). Both men served as chief gentlemen of the Privy

---

[71] Corpus Christi College Cambridge, Parker MS 102 fos. 253–8, 259–66.
[72] Winthrop S. Hudson, *The Cambridge connection and the Elizabethan settlement of 1559* (Durham, NC, 1980), esp. pp. 25–60, 90–109; John Guy, *Tudor England* (Oxford, 1988), pp. 224, 253–4.

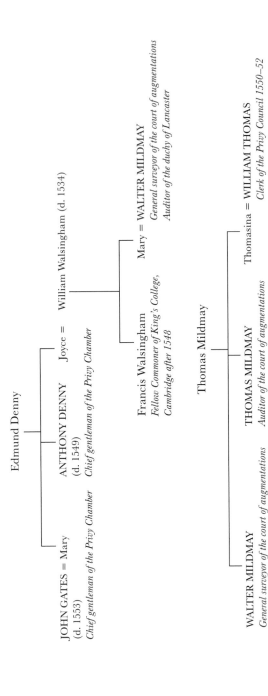

Edmund Denny

JOHN GATES = Mary   ANTHONY DENNY   Joyce =   William Walsingham (d. 1534)
(d. 1553)   (d. 1549)
Chief gentleman of the Privy Chamber   Chief gentleman of the Privy Chamber

Francis Walsingham   Mary = WALTER MILDMAY
Fellow Commoner of King's College,   General surveyor of the court of augmentations
Cambridge after 1548   Auditor of the duchy of Lancaster

Thomas Mildmay

WALTER MILDMAY   THOMAS MILDMAY   Thomasina = WILLIAM THOMAS
General surveyor of the court of augmentations   Auditor of the court of augmentations   Clerk of the Privy Council 1550–52
Auditor of the duchy of Lancaster

Fig. 9   The families of Denny, Gates, Mildmay, and Walsingham.

Chamber until their deaths (Denny's in 1549 and Gates' in 1553), and both men represented a link between the Edwardian present and the Henrician past. Denny's other sister Joyce married William Walsingham, the father of Christian, Francis, and Mary. Mary Walsingham married Walter Mildmay, a general surveyor of the court of augmentations. At some point between 1551 and 1553, Mildmay's sister Thomasina married William Thomas, a clerk of the Privy Council. John Tamworth married Christian Walsingham in 1562, but one 'Master Tamworth' had commissioned Thomas to write his *Principal rules of the Italian grammer* (1550), and in turn showed the manuscript of the book to Walter Mildmay, 'who thinkyng it a necessarie thyng for all suche of our nacion, as are studiouse in that tong, caused it thus to be put in printe for their commoditee'.[73] Connections like these naturally extended out even further. During his clerkship of the Council, William Thomas acted as an intermediary between the earl of Pembroke and Mildmay's friend William Cecil over the wardship of Cecil's sister. By 1552 Thomas had known Herbert 'a good while', and claimed to be in a position to be able to assure Cecil that the earl was never more 'bent to any man of your degree than I perceave'.[74]

Two of the defining features of the Tudor political establishment – close family ties and reciprocal interests – are marked themes in the political relationships of the second half of Edward's reign. The overwhelming impression is one of continuity and coherence. In spite of the upheavals of 1549, many of the men around the teenage king had served in his Privy Chamber from the beginning of the reign, and some even before that. Thomas Wroth, a contemporary of William Cecil at Cambridge and Gray's Inn, protégé of Thomas Cromwell, and the son-in-law of Richard Rich (lord chancellor between 1547 and 1551), was a gentleman usher to Edward in 1546.[75] The collapse of the protectorate only enhanced his position: Wroth was appointed a chief gentleman of the Privy Chamber in October 1549 and continued to enjoy the benefits and responsibilities of office – to the extent of his close involvement with the important commissions of March 1552 (see below, pp. 161–4).[76]

Continuity was quite compatible with the 'new' court and Council elite of the Dudley years. Even the career of Henry Sidney represented a continuity of sorts in service to the king. Although he entered the Privy

[73] *Principal rules of the Italian grammer, with a dictionarie* (London, 1550; *STC* 24020), 'The occasion'.
[74] SP 10/14 fo. 134r (14 Aug. 1552; Knighton 695). In 1549 Thomas had dedicated *The vanitee of this world* to Pembroke's wife Anne: *STC* 24023, sig. A2r.
[75] *Letters and papers*, ed. Brewer, Gairdner, Brodie, *et al.*, XXI:2 no. 199/68.
[76] D.O. Pam, *Protestant gentlemen: the Wroths of Durants Arbour Enfield and Loughton Essex* (Edmonton Hundred Historical Society Occasional Paper New Series, 25; London, 1973), pp. 4–5.

Chamber in the early days of John Dudley's ascendancy, and married Dudley's daughter Mary four months before his promotion to chief gentleman, Sidney's position was also expressive of a tradition of family service to Edward Tudor: his father William had been chamberlain and then steward to Edward's household as prince of Wales after 1544.[77] Of the more experienced gentlemen John Gates, of course, became a figure of authority in the Privy Chamber; Wroth was a chief gentleman; and William Fitzwilliams served as a point of contact between the king and his Council (see below, pp. 166–7). Many gentlemen remained in the Privy Chamber after the collapse of the protectorate: Maurice Berkeley, Francis Bryan, Thomas Cawarden, Thomas Darcy, William Fitzwilliams, John Gates, William Herbert, Philip Hoby, Peter Mewtas, Thomas Paston, Edward Rogers, Ralph Sadler, Anthony St Leger, Thomas Speke, and of course John Dudley himself. Edward's education proceeded at a consistent and demanding pace. John Cheke was still royal tutor, and Jean Belmaine continued to teach the king French. Anthony Cooke, commonly recognized as a supplementary tutor to the king, became a gentleman of the Privy Chamber in February 1551. The 'new' men blended in extremely well. Henry Nevill, received into the Privy Chamber on the same day as Henry Sidney in April 1550, maintained a high court profile. Nevill, Sidney, William Cecil, and John Cheke were all knighted on the day Edward elevated John Dudley to the dukedom of Northumberland.[78] A couple of months later the duke of Northumberland's son John, earl of Warwick, Henry Gates (the brother of John of the Privy Chamber), and Henry Sidney, and Nevill entertained the king in a tournament decorated with 'suche olde stuf' from the royal office of the revels.[79]

Although it has been pointed out that John Dudley surrounded Edward with men sympathetic to his personal ascendancy, perhaps the most important feature of the royal establishment of the early 1550s was that there was no real distinction between service to the king and a commitment to the regime. Edward felt comfortable with the men attendant on him. Some had served him as prince of Wales or at least from the beginning of his reign; or had been taught alongside him, worked with him, and lived with him in his suite of rooms. Later Edwardian monarchy depended for its essential stability on the establishment of a court which

---

[77] *Letters and papers*, ed. Brewer, Gairdner, Brodie, *et al.*, XVI, no. 1489 (1541); XIX:1, no. 864 (1544).
[78] 11 Oct. 1551: British Library, Cotton MS Nero C 10 fo. 44r (Jordan, ed., *Chronicle*, p. 86).
[79] Albert Feuillerat, ed., *Documents relating to the revels at court in the time of King Edward VI and Queen Mary* (Louvain, 1914), p. 56 (24 Nov. 1551); Jordan, ed., *Chronicle*, p. 97.

at once reflected Edward's personality and helped to preserve the political relationships that bound together the regime governing on his behalf. Of course 'governing on his behalf' is a suggestive phrase. How should we understand the nature of Edward's participation in governance after the collapse of the protectorate? Did the royal establishment adapt itself to the reality of a growing and maturing king?

Intellectually and practically, Edward VI's minority certainly presented a number of difficulties for his leading subjects. Minority fell short of the monarchical ideal of the king in his court, operating at the heart of the polity, capable of acting with full sovereign independence. In chapter 2, I argued that Edwardians found it difficult to reconcile the location or source of power in their polity – the king, passive – with the exercise of that power – the king, active and governing. Counsel was offered as a compensation, for the practical limitations of minority – the king acting on counsel or with his councillors – and formulations like John Cheke's 'king's majesty *etc*' (in 1549) revealed a rather serious weakness (see above, pp. 62–3). The early modern English notion of governance demanded an active and engaged monarch who could act with full and definitive sovereign independence but use the counsel and advice of his principal subjects to inform this absolute authority. But royal minority did not exist in a form of stasis, and political relationships and institutions inevitably changed as Edward VI grew into his kingship. He was nine years of age at his accession and fifteen at his death, six crucial years of physical and intellectual development for Edward and half a decade of evolution in the political culture of his reign.

The notion of even the middle teenage Edward as an operational king is of course problematic. Some historians have embraced it; some flinch at the mere possibility; and others (perhaps wisely) have decided to sit between the two extremes. The twentieth-century historiography balanced an articulate puppet against a mature, precocious, and essentially adult king (see above, chapter 1, pp. 22–4). But lurking behind these disagreements was a more fundamental and difficult issue: the nature of the middle Tudor 'constitution', or, more specifically, the precise relationship between the king and his councillors. For W.K. Jordan, Edward's political maturity could be measured in bureaucratic terms, and the degree to which the king participated in (and even began to reform) the 'administrative procedures' of the Privy Council.[80] When Dale Hoak challenged the arguments for Edward's political independence, he

---

[80] Jordan, ed., *Chronicle*, p. xxix.

worked within an identical intellectual framework. The king's bureaucratic Council appeared as a self-governing, autonomous mechanism defined by its own forms and traditions, prepared, as Edward grew up, merely to indulge the king in superfluous meetings staged especially for him.[81] In turn, this interpretation reflects a familiar preoccupation in the secondary literature on Tudor politics. But the notion that the Edwardian polity inherited the model of a formal and bureaucratically coherent Privy Council encouraged historians to impose on the 1550s a rather distorted model of politics.

A personal monarchy demanded a personal monarch, and an active king of course needed men to represent him in his governance of the realm. But kingship in the sixteenth century was not primarily an exercise in bureaucracy. Historians may enjoy shuffling paper or sitting in faculty committees; monarchs generally did not. Some medievalists have even argued that the *institutional* royal Council was a fairly late innovation, perhaps more suited to periods of monarchical incapacity than to fully operational kingship.[82] Royal governance demanded two closely connected but separable actions: a decision to act and the execution of that decision. An institutional identity for this process – particularly the part of it that involved debate and decision – was optional. The distinction rests on the linguistic confusions (or possibilities) of late medieval and early modern English. Was a king 'coun*cilled*' or 'coun*selled*'? Was the ideal formal and bureaucratic or merely informal? Or did it much matter? John Watts has exposed for the fifteenth century a tension between counsel as 'an informal dialogue between the king and his leading subjects' and the appearance and disappearance of groups of councillors bearing an institutional identity. Dr Watts has turned the institutional model on its head, questioning whether 'bureaucratic decisions' and 'political counsel' were even mutually compatible. For Watts, the officers who administered the Privy Seal Office, the Chancery, and the Exchequer 'were frequently to be found about the king and were often regarded as his counsellors because of their responsibilities' – but this did not mean that they represented 'a council as such'.[83] For Tudor historians this is the world turned upside down: the notion that the Council as an institution was fundamentally and culturally incompatible with the proper exercise of kingly power in its adult form is deeply heretical.

[81] For example, Hoak, *King's Council*, pp. 120–2.
[82] John L. Watts, 'The counsels of King Henry VI, *c.* 1435–1445', *English Historical Review*, 106 (1991), pp. 279–98; Christine Carpenter, *The Wars of the Roses: politics and the constitution in England, c. 1437–1509* (Cambridge, 1997), pp. 90–2.
[83] Watts, 'Counsels of King Henry VI', p. 282.

The political culture of the sixteenth century was different. Tudor governors were perhaps more able than their predecessors to imagine that sovereign power could be exercised on conciliar authority, but this did depend heavily on the monarchical context. A council could offer a solution (at least on paper) to the collapse of Elizabethan monarchy. And yet it was not an issue of preference. The leading subjects of the later Tudor crown were profoundly troubled by fears of dynastic insecurity, and a body exercising sovereign power was preferable to royal interregnum (see below, chapter 6, pp. 204–6).[84] The circumstances of Edward's reign were rather different. But there is some evidence to suggest that, by the early 1550s, the structures of the Council – and the dynamics of offering counsel – were beginning to change because Edward was growing into his kingship. A 'counsel for the estate', projected in 1552 (see below, pp. 162–5), represented an important political and cultural comment on the notion of the royal estate embracing the public affairs of a kingdom governed by a king counselled. Edward himself wrote that the temporal governance of his realm consisted in 'well ordering, enriching, and defending the hole bodye politique of the commenwelth', a statement that set him at the heart of the governance of his kingdom.[85] And rightly so: after all, the Edwardian model of kingship was active, engaged, and dynamic (see above, chapter 2, pp. 32–46).

How should we begin to read Edward's gradual emergence as an operational king? Should we measure his performance in terms of his involvement with the institutional Council? Did he succeed in freeing himself from the influence of the men around him? First of all it is possible to endorse Edward's developing grasp of the business of kingship *and* accept the still powerful political presence of John Dudley and his colleagues. This rests on a distinction between the cultural expectations of Edward's kingship and the political dynamics of the second half of the reign. The structures of, and relationships in, the bureaucratic Council and the royal household began to adapt themselves to the *implications* of the king's age; whether Edward actually *became* a fully executive and operational king is a different – but of course important – matter. The significant point to grasp is that the dynamics of power at the centre were capable of reshaping themselves because the men around the king accepted that, in the circumstances, they should. It is possible to acknowledge flexible and adaptive change at the Edwardian court and in

---

[84] Patrick Collinson, 'The Elizabethan exclusion crisis and the Elizabethan polity', *Proceedings of the British Academy*, 84 (1993), pp. 87–92; Stephen Alford, *The early Elizabethan polity: William Cecil and the British succession crisis, 1558–1569* (Cambridge, 1998), pp. 112–15, 225–8.

[85] British Library, Cotton MS Nero C 10 fo. 113v (Jordan, ed., *Chronicle*, p. 160).

Council but not necessarily jump to the conclusion that by 1553 Edward had assumed full kingly power.

One incident in particular suggests that by his early teens Edward had absorbed some of the core principles, and vocabularies, of kingly authority. In October 1551 Lord Chancellor Richard Rich received from the king a signet letter challenging Rich's return of a letter addressed to the lord chancellor by the Privy Council because it bore only eight signatures.[86] The message of the signet letter was simple. Edward thought his authority 'to be su[ch] that what so ever we shall do by the advise of the nombre of our Counsell attending upon our person' had more 'strength and efficacye than to be put into question or doubt of the validite therof'. The number of counsellors 'or any parte of them' did not make the king's authority. He was prepared to listen favourably – to 'inclyne' himself – to the advise of any number of counsellors; but he was not bound by them.[87] Equally, as king, Edward could instruct the men around him. He recorded in his journal that he 'marveled' at the lord chancellor's refusal to deliver a letter 'willed by any on[e] about me to write'. Edward did not need to summon all his councillors, either to make a decision or to turn that decision into action. Once again, in private, he wrote that it was 'a great impediment for me, to send to al my councell, and i shuld seme to be in bondage'.[88] He appears to have felt himself limited in two ways. First, by the practical nuisance of gathering together privy councillors for the transaction of the routine business of governance. And second, by the assault on his authority.

When Edward asked a servant – perhaps William Cecil, who endorsed the draft of the letter – to write to royal commissioners it was an instruction that would have been unremarkable in a normal, adult monarchical context. In 1551, however, it presented itself as an important measure of the transition from potential to active kingship, with Edward's sense of his own authority beginning to outgrow the protective limits imposed on a king's power during his minority. But was this sense of development complemented by physical or structural change at court or in Council? In the letter to Lord Chancellor Rich of October 1551, the king referred to 'our Counsellours here . . . presently attending upon our persone'.[89] A month earlier Richard Goodrich had received a commission from Edward to visit the Savoy and, with his colleagues, to report the findings to the king '*or his privy council attendant upon his person*'.[90] So had the monarch's leading

---

[86] Hoak, *King's Council*, pp. 139–40.   [87] SP 10/13 fo. 110r (1 Oct. 1551; Knighton 555).
[88] British Library, Cotton MS Nero C 10 fo. 43r (Jordan, ed., *Chronicle*, p. 85).
[89] SP 10/13 fo. 110r.   [90] *CPR 1550–53*, p. 123.

subjects finally transformed themselves more obviously into their *king's* counsellors? The answer to this question is, predictably, difficult and complex. Dale Hoak used the king's letter to Rich of 1551 to explore the administrative distance between a group of institutional councillors in London and some of their colleagues at Hampton Court with the king. For Professor Hoak the incident represented a procedural glitch, the result of the practical difficulty of transacting business during the king's progress.[91] But just as significant is the fact that by this point in the reign it was necessary to have men attendant on the king, any number of whom, according to Edward, could allow him to fulfil his kingly duties.

One of the most revealing and important phases in the evolution of the lines of communication around the king began early in 1552, only a few months after the exchange between Edward and Richard Rich. In January the regime established a commission to inquire into the nature and the amount of revenue administered by all the financial courts. The work of these commissioners – Bishop Goodrich of Ely, John Russell earl of Bedford, William Petre, Robert Bowes, and Walter Mildmay – was continued later in the year, with a second commission on debts to the crown in July.[92] But the important month was March 1552, when Edward himself took an interest in this and some other commissions and, more importantly, explored their implications for the shape of the Privy Council. The king began his own text of the commissions of 1552 with 'The names of the hole councel', followed by 'Those that be now callid into commission' – men outside the institutional Council, from the already busy Mildmay to Bishop Ridley of London, Bishop Thirlby of Norwich, Thomas Wroth, Richard Cotton, Edward Griffith, John Gosnold, William Cooke, and John Lucas.[93] The membership of the commission on the state of the financial courts was enlarged to include Lord Chamberlain Thomas Darcy, Thirlby, Wroth, Cotton, and Gosnold.[94] But there were other groups of commissioners, described by Edward as 'several commissions, and charges'. Ten counsellors were given responsibility to hear suits 'wiche were wont to be brought to the hole borde'. Eleven more were chosen to review penal laws and proclamations and supervise their execution in the counties. And the

---

[91] Hoak, *King's Council*, pp. 139–41.
[92] W.C. Richardson, ed., *The report of the royal commission of 1552* (Morgantown, VA, 1974), pp. xxiii, xxiv.
[93] British Library, Cotton MS Nero C 10 fo. 84r.
[94] Richardson, ed., *Royal commission*, p. xxvi and n. 56; British Library, Cotton MS Nero C 10 fo. 85v.

three principal men of the household – Thomas Darcy (chamberlain), Thomas Cheyne (treasurer), and Anthony Wingfield (comptroller) – assumed responsibility for bulwarks.[95]

This all looks thoroughly administrative and procedural, but the political implications were immense. The most significant of these 'commissions' was a group 'For the state', composed of members of the institutional Council with a special responsibility 'to attend the matters of the state' and to meet the king once a week for Edward 'to here the debating of thinges of most importaunce'. This council (or counsel) for the estate was more than another commission. It bound together the other groups working on suits, effectively fusing the men of the Privy Council, the Privy Chamber, and the royal household into a core group working with and around the king. It even, in Edward's first draft, challenged institutional boundaries. The king included two members of the commission on the state of the financial courts without formal conciliar status: Walter Mildmay of augmentations and the godly common lawyer John Gosnold. Their names were deleted but the principle stood. The governance of the kingdom was becoming more obviously focused on the person of its king.

One critical feature of the counsel for the estate was its composition. Initially Edward outlined a core group of fifteen men, all but two of them institutional councillors.[96] This core group included all the officers of state, the three principal gentlemen and two other gentlemen of the king's Privy Chamber, the most senior officers of the royal household, Edward's secretariat, and Mildmay and Gosnold. The counsel for the estate was finally expanded to include eight of the members of the institutional Council. The relationship between the counsel for the estate and the other commissions is also important. Key members of the commissions of 1552 – commissions Edward suggested should meet apart and separately – were used to bind the groups working on suits, penal laws, debts, and bulwarks. Three of the men in daily attendance on the king in his Privy Chamber were added to the first lists of the commissioners: principal gentlemen Thomas Darcy (suits, but in the first draft for penal laws, suits, the financial courts, and bulwarks) and Thomas Wroth (a commissioner for the financial courts but added to the group working on penal laws) and gentleman Philip Hoby (added to the commissions on suits and penal laws). Darcy and Hoby were counsellors for the estate.

[95] British Library, Cotton MS Nero C 10 fos. 84v, 85v.
[96] British Library, Cotton MS Nero C 10 fo. 85r; Hoak, *King's Council*, p. 316 nn. 100, 107.

Some of the men who sat on these commissions brought to their charge a particular expertise. William Cooke and John Lucas, the masters of requests, were natural choices for the group given responsibility to screen suits; Mildmay and Gosnold were the second and fifth officers of the court of augmentations. Some of the commissioners were talented amateurs, but it would be a mistake to dismiss them (as one historian of Tudor administration did) as 'politicians' rather than 'civil servants'.[97] To read Tudor royal governance as a civil service bureaucracy is a mistake. These men were chosen because they were close to the king physically and personally. When the names of the commissioners of 1552 are set down in columns, side-by-side, what becomes clear is the strategic importance of the men who acted as links between the commissions and the counsel for the estate. The one man who sat on all the commissions was Lord Chamberlain Thomas Darcy, a principal gentleman of the Privy Chamber. Three others – Keeper of the Privy Seal John Russell earl of Bedford, Philip Hoby of the Privy Chamber, and Dr Nicholas Wotton – combined work on suits and penal law with membership of the counsel for the estate. Only one man in the core group of the counsel for the estate was neither a gentleman of the Privy Chamber nor an officer of state nor a household official: William Cecil, a member of the royal secretariat, who appeared on Edward's list before his technically more senior colleague William Petre.

Of course Edward's draft, like other political documents from the reign, was not written in a vacuum. In it, Edward suggested that the members of the institutional Council who were not named to the counsel for the estate should travel back to 'their countrees' after parliament (the fourth session ended on 15 April 1552). Others, he noted, were 'sore sike, that they shal not be able to attend to any thing'. The draft appears to suggest that this second group of councillors, and perhaps also the men sent to their counties, 'when they come shal be admitted, of the counsell'.[98] The commissions of 1552 were an administrative response to the regime's genuine concerns for the fiscal health of the kingdom, but the *shape* of that response is extremely significant. So was Edward's draft for the counsel for the estate, outlining a core group of counsellors responsible for executing a number of different tasks and briefing him

[97] Richardson, ed., *Royal commission*, p. xxvi n. 58.
[98] British Library, Cotton MS Nero c 10 fo. 85v. The punctuation of the paragraph is confusing. The text is also incomplete, and has been since at least 1680: Gilbert Burnet, 'A Collection of Records, and Original Papers' (1680), which supplements *The History of the Reformation of the Church of England*, 2 vols. (London, 1679–81), II, p. 86.

on the governance of the kingdom, merely a nod in the king's direction or a fundamental recognition of the new reality of a more operational monarch?

The first point to make is that March 1552 does appear to have altered the shape of Edwardian politics. The counsellors for the estate closely match the members of the institutional Council who regularly administered the governance of the realm after the spring of 1552, and the group actually began to meet the king once a week.[99] But the 'counsel for the estate' presents a number of problems – mainly because it is difficult to reconcile its existence with accounts of the administrative structures of the Tudor polity. In *The King's Council in the reign of Edward VI* – the standard institutional study of the politics of the reign – Dale Hoak suggested that the 'historical role of the council for the state' was, primarily, the accommodation of Edward at meetings staged especially for him. It seemed to follow on from this contention that the composition of the counsellors for the estate reflected John Dudley's 'political alliances'.[100] An interpretation like this was an understandable response to a simple problem. Edward's draft did not fit the administrative and procedural model of the king's Privy Council. Professor Hoak effectively sidestepped the problem. He argued that these gatherings were not 'bona fide meetings of the Privy Council – that is to say, they were not actual working sessions of the council'.[101]

So the broad political significance of the counsel for the estate has been overlooked because it does not fit the administrative requirements of the 'Tudor constitution'. Here politics collides with bureaucracy. The draft for the counsel for the estate was a proposal for inclusion. It was designed, very clearly, to focus the consideration of the public affairs of the realm more intensely on the person of the king, and in this sense the counsel for the estate demonstrates the ambiguity between 'council' and 'counsel'. In its final corrected form (but not of course initially) the members of this group were all institutional councillors; and yet many of them were also senior members of the royal household and gentlemen of the king's Privy Chamber, perfectly able to engage the king in daily, informal conversation. This was not centralization or rationalization. It was instead a reflection of the serious and developing need for the establishment of an attendant group to support a maturing king. And so, quite naturally, the counsel for the king's estate comprehended the formal, institutional mechanics of communication between a king and his subjects,

---

[99] Hoak, *King's Council*, pp. 110–11.   [100] Hoak, *King's Council*, pp. 135, 136.
[101] Hoak, *King's Council*, p. 121.

Fig. 10   Richard Grafton's idealized representation of Edward taking counsel, from
the title-page of *The union of the two noble and illustre famelies of Lancastre & Yorke* (1548)
by Edward Hall. This is not a representation of the king attending a meeting
of the institutional Privy Council. Although the image dates from the earliest
years of Edward's reign it may offer an insight into the physical dimensions
of the 'counsel for the estate' after 1552 (see pp. 162–6).

the operation of his own household, and Edward's experience of daily
companionship and attendance. Primarily the group fulfilled a king's
need for *counsel* – of the presence of men around the king who could
allow him to practise the informal and formal dimensions of kingship.
The counsel for the estate certainly challenges the notion that, in the
political history of the Tudors, household government and conciliar responsibility – formality versus informality, 'intimacy' versus 'distance' –
are discrete and separable categories or even conflicting notions.[102] The
counsel for the king's estate was the creation of an adaptive and sophisticated political culture.

Edward met the men named in his draft once a week but this did
not limit contact between the king and his leading subjects at court.

[102] Cf. the important comments by David Starkey, 'Tudor government: the facts?', *Historical Journal*,
31 (1988), p. 930.

Edward certainly sat down with one of his principal secretaries, William Cecil, to collaborate on papers, including at least one written discussion of England's relationship with the Empire written *in utramque partem*, in two rhetorical parts *pro* and *contra* – a point of contact between an emphatically rhetorical education directed by John Cheke and the practical business of kingship.[103] Even the apparently conventional accounts presented by Edward and William Petre for the 'reorganization' of the Privy Council's work in 1553 reveal an important degree of collaboration between monarch and principal secretary and, more significantly, a recognition of the king's direct authority over his privy councillors. The intention was to set aside the working week (from Monday afternoon to Friday morning) for debate on timetabled business established by the king in private consultation with his principal secretaries. The king initiated debate – and sanctioned resolution – in the public affairs of the realm and on private suits.[104]

The Privy Chamber was another point of contact between the king and the institutional Council. On one occasion a clerk of the Council, William Thomas, communicated privately with the king in a sealed packet of letters delivered to Edward by a gentleman of the Privy Chamber 'as it were a thinge from the Counsaill'. The year was very probably 1551, when Thomas had to hand the letter to William Fitzwilliams because his usual contact in the Privy Chamber, Nicholas Throckmorton, was absent from court. Thomas' record of his correspondence with the king suggests that the channels of communication to and from Edward could be quite informal, even on Council business. Equally, contact could be initiated at royal discretion: Edward, for example, asked Throckmorton to declare his pleasure, and also deliver private notes, to Thomas.[105] It was assumed for some years that royal minority deprived the Edwardian Privy Chamber of its purpose, but this notion falls seriously short of the reality. In 1982 Dale Hoak admitted that one of the assumptions which had underpinned *The King's Council in the reign of Edward VI* – that John Dudley's dominance in the Privy Council had allowed him to infiltrate the departments of the household – should really be reversed: dominating

[103] British Library, Cotton MS Nero C 10 fo. 73r–v.
[104] British Library, Cotton MS Nero C 10 fos. 86r–88r, 89v (Edward's text); SP 10/1 fo. 56r–v (Petre's text; Knighton 805). Cf. F.G. Emmison, 'A plan of Edward VI and Secretary Petre for reorganizing the Privy Council's work, 1552–1553', *Bulletin of the Institute of Historical Research*, 31 (1958), pp. 203–10.
[105] British Library, Cotton MS Vespasian D 18 fo. 28r–v; E.R. Adair, 'William Thomas', in R.W. Seton-Watson, ed., *Tudor studies* (London, 1924), p. 142.

the king was the key to securing the 'machinery of government'.[106] Five years later, John Murphy offered a more developed account of the political dimensions of the Privy Chamber.[107]

For Murphy, the removal from power of Protector Somerset and his men 'inaugurated a period of reform' that re-established the Privy Chamber as a focus for government and politics and as an administrative and financial centre. Like Hoak, Murphy argued that the 'purge' of the Privy Council in early 1550 was a consequence of the 'packing of the Privy Chamber, and not vice versa'.[108] According to Murphy, 'traditionalists' – 'religious conservatives' – were excluded from office and service in the inner chambers of the royal palaces.[109] The new men of the Privy Chamber shared the two characteristics of the king's religion and the king's personal favour. A compelling thesis in Murphy's essay is the notion that this close relationship between Privy Council and Privy Chamber after 1550 created two sorts of councillor: men with direct access to the king in his Privy Chamber and men without. Privy Council and Privy Chamber drawing more closely together represented, for Murphy, a 'political coherence', bestowing on some of the king's institutional councillors an enhanced status 'which must have created a natural leadership within the Council'.[110]

This account of the later Edwardian Privy Chamber has much to recommend it. The chief impression is one of cohesion, of an increasingly close relationship between the king and the process of governance carried out in his name. This meant an effective end to distinctions between the 'household' dimensions of Edwardian political life and the 'formal' and bureaucratic – if, of course, they had ever really existed at all. The men who rarely attended meetings of the institutional Privy Council were not counsellors for the estate. The man who attended nearly 90 per cent of Council meetings between April 1552 and June 1553 was Lord Chamberlain Thomas Darcy, a key member of the commissions of 1552 and a counsellor for the estate.[111] Boundaries began to blur – and perhaps consciously so. John Guy has suggested that an Elizabethan 'ordre for redresse of the state of the Realme', a document which outlined the effective fusion of court and state office, was an Edwardian blueprint recycled

---

[106] Hoak, 'Privy Chamber', p. 87.
[107] John Murphy, 'The illusion of decline: the Privy Chamber, 1547–1558', in David Starkey, ed., *The English court: from the Wars of the Roses to the Civil War* (London and New York, 1987), pp. 119–40.
[108] Murphy, 'Privy Chamber', pp. 127–8; cf. Hoak, 'Northumberland', pp. 36–40.
[109] Murphy, 'Privy Chamber', p. 128.   [110] Murphy, 'Privy Chamber', p. 130.
[111] Cf. the tables in Hoak, *King's Council*, p. 111, and Hoak, 'Privy Chamber', p. 101.

for 1559.[112] One reason for attributing the source of this document to the reign of Edward is that it must have been more achievable in an exclusively male Privy Chamber, principally because women could not act as a barrier between monarch and Privy Council. But the most compelling reason is this: the core group of the counsel for the estate – the lord chancellor, the lord treasurer, the duke of Northumberland, the lord privy seal, the marquess of Northampton, the earl of Pembroke, the lord admiral, the king's chamberlain, the vice-chamberlain, the king's two principal secretaries, the dean of Canterbury and York, and Philip Hoby – corresponds almost exactly to the 'prevy counsaill' of 'An ordre for redresse of the state of the Realm'.[113] It reflects the direction in which the Edwardian polity appeared to be moving – and, above all, a sense of the structure and the potential of Tudor adult male monarchy.

John Dudley's control of the men around Edward, and the early appearance of the king's wasting illness to explain the manipulation of a talented and precocious boy by the most powerful man in the kingdom, are deeply embedded in the literature, repeated again and again in accounts of the reign in the seventeenth and eighteenth centuries. The Dudley years are still haunted by the suspicion of manipulation and self-interest. Surely the regime that collapsed in 1553 – and collapsed precisely because it was so fiercely determined to preserve itself – *must* have relied for its authority on a fragile legitimacy? Either the men who agreed to the change of succession did so at the behest of John Dudley or (as Sharon Turner argued in the early nineteenth century) it was a declaration of corporate self-interest.[114] These are, of course, legitimate positions to take on the politics of the Dudley years, but it is also possible to challenge some of these assumptions. First of all, the traditional accounts of the politics of Edward's final years rest so heavily on a seriously (even perversely) distorted historiography. And second, they express a Namierite hatred for

---

[112] Huntington Library, San Marino, California, Ellesmere MS 2625 fos. 1r–6v; Guy, *Tudor England*, p. 256.

[113] In 1552 the 'prevy counsaill' of 'An ordre' would have looked like this: lord steward (in 1552 John Dudley as lord great master of the household); the king's chamberlain (Thomas Darcy); the treasurer of the household (Thomas Cheyne); the comptroller of the household (Anthony Wingfield); the master of the horse (William Herbert earl of Pembroke); the vice-chamberlain (John Gates); the secretary (in 1552 William Cecil and William Petre); the captain of the guard (in 1552 John Gates); the dean and almoner (in 1552 Dr Nicholas Wotton as dean of Canterbury and York); the lord chancellor (Thomas Goodrich); the lord treasurer (William Paulet marquess of Winchester); the keeper of the privy seal (John Russell earl of Bedford); the lord great chamberlain (William Parr marquess of Northampton); and the lord admiral (Edward Lord Clinton). Huntington Library, San Marino, California, Ellesmere MS 2625 fo. 1r.

[114] Sharon Turner, *The history of the reigns of Edward the Sixth, Mary, and Elizabeth*, 2 vols. (London, 1829), I, pp. 335–6.

any sort of professed political principle, and generally ground themselves on the assumption that only self-interest mattered to the men around the king. Again, this reflects some of the concerns of the great backlash against the later Edwardian regime after its collapse in 1553 (discussed above, chapter 1, pp. 7–9) but as political analysis it is rather weak.

It is the duty of a historian to ask testing questions, but it is also necessary to maintain a sceptical sympathy for the 'mental world' of the political culture he or she is trying to reconstruct. Can we accept that Edwardians felt themselves bound by something other than self-interest in their political lives? Did John Dudley really understand the significance of Proverbs 11:14, quoted by (and back to) William Cecil in 1552 – 'Where no good counsel is, there the people decay' – and work seriously for the honour of his royal master and the preservation of his country? It is certainly worth thinking about the seriousness with which writers and historians have taken the politics of the second half of Edward's reign. The exercise of political power, particularly during the peculiar conditions of minority, so clearly underpinned the Edwardian political consciousness that it seems perverse to argue that the men around the king operated in an amoral bubble, unaware of what was and was not politically acceptable. Less philosophically, the practical demands of governance in England in the sixteenth century required a king. Physically and intellectually Edward VI became the focus of court and Council. He was not Henry VI. He appears to have been intelligent, aware, and capable. But even if the subversion of the king's will was a conscious political aim of the men around the king after 1550, it must have been a subversion of real subtlety – probably too subtle, given the nature of life and conversation at court, to leave evidence in the historical record.

Notions of faction and party inevitably intrude here, but Edwardian political life was not endemically factional. There was in fact an impressive degree of stability and coherence to the reign – a sort of self-righting mechanism after periods of political stress and uncertainty. The execution of Edward Seymour duke of Somerset early in 1552 may well have been the exception that proved the rule, actually underpinning the rather stable and maturing political arrangements of the Dudley years. But why, if the Edwardian polity was so stable, was Somerset executed in the first place? The answer probably lies in the difficult relationship between Seymour and John Dudley. Dudley sensed – correctly – that Edward Seymour wanted more than a seat at the Council board. From the spring of 1550, when Seymour took advantage of John Dudley's absence from the king and the Privy Council to court Stephen Gardiner, to the forced symbolism of a Seymour–Dudley marriage in June – and from the instinctive process of reconciliation in early 1550 to the rumours of a breakdown in the fragile 'amity' between the two men in February 1551 – even John Dudley the servant to the king and his country (rather than John Dudley the ambitious faction leader) found it difficult to believe that Somerset did not want to recover his political authority.[115]

The trial and execution of Edward Seymour may have been morally inexcusable, but it was the political strategy Seymour himself had deployed at the beginning of 1549 against his own brother. And there was a case to be made for the death of Somerset in 1552. Politically, he was a man determined to control and direct. He wanted recognition and authority. His style before 1549 had been abrasive and arrogant. Dudley referred in late 1552 to the career of a man marked by a wilful incompetence.[116] How compatible was this with the evolution of a kingly establishment supported by a small cadre of important royal servants regularly attendant on the king? Particularly when that elite was unequivocably committed to the service of the king and bound by ties of loyalty to Dudley? Was Edward Seymour really prepared to accommodate himself to the implications of maturing kingship? Diarmaid MacCulloch has described John Dudley as 'a politician who traded on normality, and the keynote of most aspects of his policy was achieving stability and reconstruction'.[117] But stability, authority, and service to a maturing king were difficult to balance against the powerful political presence of an erstwhile protector. Seymour and the finely tuned corporate consensus of the Dudley years were, ultimately, incompatible.

It is interesting that the counsel for the estate evolved after Somerset's execution. Before 1552 attempts to seal the Privy Chamber had reflected concerns for the security of the king and the establishment set up around him. After October 1549 six men of the Council and Privy Chamber were attendant on the king 'to give order for the good gouvernement of his most royall person, and for the honorable educacion of his Hieghnes in thies his tender yeres in learning and vertue' – the corporate alternative

---

[115] For the marriage of John Lord Lisle to Anne Seymour, see Jordan, ed., *Chronicle*, p. 32, and Brigden, ed., 'Letters of Richard Scudamore', p. 134 (Scudamore to Hoby, 1 June 1550). For the tensions of February 1551, see British Library, Cotton MS Titus B 2 fo. 29r (17 Feb. 1551); Jennifer Loach, *Edward VI*, ed. George Bernard and Penry Williams (New Haven and London, 1999), pp. 101–2.

[116] SP 10/15 fo. 149r (to the Privy Council, 28 Dec. 1552; Knighton 789).

[117] Diarmaid MacCulloch, *Tudor church militant: Edward VI and the Protestant Reformation* (London, 1999), p. 55.

to Somerset's governorship of Edward.[118] When Somerset had been taken back into the Privy Chamber, in May 1550, Edward Lord Clinton, John Dudley's nephew, also entered the king's private apartments at the head of two hundred armed yeomen.[119] The counsel for the estate, however, reflected the more settled rhythm of the exercise of monarchical authority. Royal governance rested on contact and communication, and nothing was more natural than for a king to be surrounded by the men who supported his governance of the realm. The Dudley years were still years of minority, but a middle-teenage minority quite different in its political dynamics from the earlier years of Edward's reign.

The important age for Edward, both conceptually and practically, was fourteen. In 1526 his cousin, the fourteen-year-old James V of Scotland, had been declared to be of an age to exercise his royal authority personally.[120] For Edward the change was less formal but still significant. In January 1552, three months after his own fourteenth birthday, Edward drafted 'Ceirtein pointes of waighty matters to be immediatly concluded on by my counsell', to which his principal secretary William Cecil added a note that 'These remembrances within written wer delyvered by the kynges Majestie to his privee Counsell' in the inner Privy Chamber at Greenwich, and handed to Lord Treasurer Winchester in the presence of the officers of state and the officers of the royal household.[121] These were matters of business Edward symbolically delivered to *his* Privy Council in *his* Privy Chamber, once again blurring the distinctions between the formal and the informal.

The weeks leading up to the death of Edward in July 1553 were similarly expressive of the power of personal monarchy in binding together the political establishment at court, in Privy Council, and in Privy Chamber. Edward was at the centre of the plan to divert the royal succession away from his half-sisters Mary and Elizabeth, and to leave the crown to (in the words of Diarmaid MacCulloch) 'a reliable evangelical dynasty'.[122] This dynasty was at best notional. It lay in the Suffolk line, through the heirs male of Frances, the daughter of Henry VIII's younger sister Mary, and then the heirs male of Frances' daughters Jane, Catherine, and Mary Grey. 'My devise for the succession' was drafted by

[118] *APC 1547–50*, p. 344 (15 Oct. 1549); Jordan, ed., *Chronicle*, p. 18.
[119] Hoak, 'Privy Chamber', pp. 93–4.
[120] Jamie Cameron, *James V: the personal rule 1528–1542* (East Linton, 1998), p. 9.
[121] British Library, Cotton MS Vespasian F 13 fo. 273r–v (18 Jan. 1552), printed in J.G. Nichols, ed., *The literary remains of King Edward VI*, 2 vols. (Roxburghe Club; London, 1857), II, pp. 489–90.
[122] MacCulloch, *Tudor church militant*, pp. 39–40; quotation at p. 39. Cf. Loach, *Edward VI*, ed. Bernard and Williams, pp. 163–7.

Edward, and in it the king wrote Jane herself into the royal succession (and her mother out of it) by skilful editing. The line which gave the crown 'To the L[ady] Fraunceses heires masles' and then 'For lakke of such issu to the L[ady] Janes heires masles' read, after correction, 'To the L[ady] Fraunceses heires masles, *if she have any* such issu *befor my death* to the L[ady] Jane *and her* heires masles'. The crown simply went to Jane by default.[123] For centuries this has been read as the supreme example of Dudley cunning, because John Dudley's son, Lord Guildford, married Jane Grey on 21 May 1553. But although Dudley enforced the king's will, it was Edward himself who set out to preserve his godly legacy and, implicitly, his political establishment. It is likely that Edward took fairly wide counsel from the men around him – men like Thomas Wroth and Henry Sidney of the Privy Chamber, John Cheke, and perhaps William Petre. Petre drafted part of Edward's will, which perhaps reflected Cheke's relationship with the king by making significant provision for Cheke's old Cambridge college, St John's, and exhorted the king's executors to 'travayle to cause godly ecclesiasticall lawes to be made and sett forthe' after his death.[124] Of the twenty-four men who signed the engagement to maintain the succession as limited by Edward, fifteen were counsellors for the estate (sixteen if the name of John Gosnold is counted) and one (Cheke) was the king's tutor. Two of the signatories (Edward Griffith as solicitor and John Lucas as master of requests) had been called into commission to work with privy councillors and gentlemen of the king's Privy Chamber just over a year earlier. Corporate identity and solidarity underpinned their commitment to ensuring that the will of the king was enforced.[125]

Also built into 'My devise for the succession' is a key to how Edward, in the final weeks of his life, understood (and arguably experienced himself) the gradual emergence of adult kingship out of minority. The first part of the 'devise' established the order of the royal succession after Edward's death. In the second half (much of it deleted, but still extremely significant) Edward explored forms of governance for a future Suffolk king. If over the age of eighteen at accession, full power and authority was his. But in providing for a royal minority, Edward divided governance between the king's mother and a council of twenty. This 'gouvernres' could

[123] Inner Temple Library, London, Petyt MS 538 vol. 47 fo. 317; John Gough Nichols, ed., *The chronicle of Queen Jane, and of two years of Queen Mary* (Camden Society, 48; London, 1850), p. 89.
[124] Nichols, ed., *Chronicle of Queen Jane*, pp. 101–2.
[125] Nichols, ed., *Chronicle of Queen Jane*, pp. 90–1.

do nothing without the 'th'advise and agrement' of six members of the council. If she died before her son reached the age of eighteen, the governance of the realm would be directed by this council. But the crucial age (again mirroring Edward's own experience) was fourteen, because he wrote in the provision that 'after he be 14 yere al great matters of importaunce [should] be opened to him'. In a deleted paragraph, Edward offered a mechanism for the election of councillors. If four councillors died during the female regency, a gathering of the council, assembled on the authority of the governess' letters patent, would choose four more 'wherin she shal have thre voices'. But if the governess was dead, 'the 16 shal chose among themselfes', *until* the king was fourteen years old (changed from eighteen) '*and then he by ther advice shal chose them*'.[126] The 'devise' suggests that Edward imagined for a male successor under the age of eighteen a minority of two stages. The first – like his own – would be governance on the king's behalf, but by his mother rather than a protector, supported but at the same time limited by the council established by Edward's will. The second stage necessarily involved the king not only in the business of governance but in the choice of the minority council. The clause survived in Edward's letters patent of 21 June 1553, and it was mixed governance at its best.[127] But it was also, interestingly, a mark of the possibility of emerging operational kingship after the age of fourteen.

The great irony of 1553 is that without Edward, the boy-king, the regime crumbled. Without the person of the king – the practical focus of authority and legitimacy – the body politic was headless, and a political establishment marked by a sophisticated coherence in the final years of the reign collapsed. The corporate consensus of the signatories of Edward's letters patent cracked in the difficult days of the summer of 1553, and it did so because of mixed and conflicting loyalties. In the traumatic weeks of July 1553 the boundaries between the lawful and the unlawful – and the dynastically and politically acceptable and unacceptable – blurred. The power of dynastic succession – of the long shadow cast by Henry VIII's will, complemented by the surprising energy of Mary Tudor's mobilization of the localities – triumphed over the attempt to preserve the Edwardian political and ecclesiastical establishment after

---

[126] Nichols, ed., *Chronicle of Queen Jane*, pp. 89–90, with my emphasis.
[127] Nichols, ed., *Chronicle of Queen Jane*, pp. 97–8.

the death of the king.[128] But it is important not to measure the successes or failures of the Dudley years by the collapse in July 1553 of the regime constructed in the name of Jane Grey. Yet, in a strange way, the death of Edward was final proof of the potency of his kingship and the commitment of the men around him to operational personal monarchy. The Edwardian polity had evolved, with the king at the centre of it. From his earliest years, Edward VI had been trained in kingship. Governance and politics, political culture, the court, and the bureaucratic machine met in his person. He represented the public body of the kingdom as well as the private, physical body of a king, and by the early 1550s he was effectively supported in his kingdom. Counterfactual history is a difficult and perhaps dangerous business, but it is possible to imagine that, had the king lived, the Dudley years would have allowed Edward VI to operate at the heart of one of the most radical, dynamic, and personal adult male monarchies of the Tudor century.

[128] Loach, *Edward VI*, ed. Bernard and Williams, pp. 170–9; Diarmaid MacCulloch, ed., 'The *Vita Mariae Angliae Reginae* of Robert Wingfield of Brantham', *Camden Miscellany XXVIII* (Camden Society, fourth series, 29; London, 1984), pp. 181–301; Robert Tittler and Susan L. Battley, 'The local community and the crown in 1553: the accession of Mary Tudor revisited', *Bulletin of the Institute of Historical Research*, 57 (1984), pp. 131–9.

6

Beyond 1553: the Edwardian legacy

Writing this book has convinced me of three things. The first is that there is so much still to discover about the reign of Edward VI. The second is that any account of the Edwardian polity has to be written as the history of the men and women who shaped and bound together this tightly knit political community. And the third is that the culture of politics in Edward's reign – the nature of his kingship in theory and in practice and the outlooks and assumptions of the men around the king – is both reconstructable and centrally important for our understanding of 1547–53. People and ideas matter, but reconciling the two – showing how Edwardians were influenced by, and how they themselves influenced, the culture of the reign – is an obligation that the writer of a book like this cannot avoid for too long. How can we be sure, just to use one example, that court sermons did indeed shape expectations of Edward's kingship? Or, to take another, prove that Edwardians responded positively to the iconography of godly royal supremacy? This chapter tries to answer questions like these, but it does so from outside the reign of Edward. It moves beyond 1553.

This is a conclusion and an introduction: a conclusion to a book that has tried to explore the nature of the Edwardian polity, but also an introduction to a political world and culture shaped by the legacy of 1547–53. For five years after the death of Edward, men and women had to accommodate themselves to – or resist and challenge – the Catholic queenship and rule of Mary. Those who chose to resist in print inherited from the Edwardian years strong notions of what it was to be a monarch, and they helped to transform the model of godly, reforming, Protestant kingship into a radical and fundamental test of the powers that claimed authority to govern. But even those who merely disengaged themselves from the Marian regime – who stayed in England, for example, or toured Italy – represented a bridge between an Edwardian past and an Elizabethan future, a compact, organic elite remarkable for the continuity of its membership and its essential resilience. Some familiar characters will reappear in this chapter, all of whom lived and interpreted the Edwardian inheritance in different and distinctive ways. John Ponet, protégé of Thomas Cranmer, one of Edward's favourite preachers, bishop of Rochester and Winchester, and the translator of *A tragoedie or Dialoge* (see above, chapter 4, pp. 101–15), reappears as Ponet the exile, author of the deeply subversive and dangerous book *A shorte treatise of politike power.*[1] Two other Cambridge men, Edmund Gest and Anthony Gilby, have both appeared briefly already: Gest, of King's College, a friend and colleague of Edward's tutor John Cheke, and Gilby the author of 'A prayer for the kynge' in 1551.[2] By 1558 Gilby was an embittered Marian exile in Geneva and Gest, more conventionally, chaplain to Archbishop Parker of Canterbury and almoner to Elizabeth I. Richard Goodrich, the godly lawyer of augmentations and friend of William Cecil, blended in seamlessly with the Elizabethan political establishment (see above, chapter 5, pp. 145–51). So did Walter Haddon, Latinist, civil lawyer, and editor of memorial verse to Charles and Henry Brandon in 1551, who became master of requests to Elizabeth and a public apologist for her regime.

Two characters who have not made an appearance so far are John Knox and Christopher Goodman, generally thought of as radical political theorists but, until 1553, solid members of the Edwardian establishment. Knox served his Edwardian apprenticeship as a minister in Berwick (1549) and Newcastle (1551). In October 1552 he put his name to the forty-five articles of religion as a chaplain to the king, along with colleagues like William Bill, Robert Horne, and Edmund Grindal.[3] He had certainly caught the eye of John Dudley who, in the same month, wrote to William Cecil that 'I wold to god yt moght pleas the kinges majeste' to appoint Knox to the bishopric of Rochester.[4] Knox famously irritated Dudley so much that, by early December 1552, the duke refused 'to have to do with men whiche be nether gratfull nor plesable'.[5] Goodman was an academic, an undergraduate of Brasenose College, Oxford in the 1530s, senior student (a fellow in other colleges) of Richard Cox's Christ Church between 1547 and 1553, and Lady Margaret

[1] John Ponet, *A shorte treatise of politike power, and of the true Obedience which subjectes owe to kynges and other civile Governours, with an Exhortacion to all true naturall Englishe men* (Strasburg, 1556; *STC* 20178).
[2] Anthony Gilby, *A commentarye upon the Prophet Mycha. Wrytten by Antony Gilby* (London, 1551; *STC* 11886), sig. {07r–v}.
[3] SP 10/15 fo. 65v ([20 Oct.] 1552; Knighton 739).
[4] SP 10/15 fo. 79r (28 Oct. 1552; Knighton 747).
[5] SP 10/15 fo. 137r (Dudley to Cecil, 7 Dec. 1552; Knighton 779).

Professor of Divinity in Oxford after 1551 until the death of Edward. Goodman, like Knox, spent the Marian exile in a number of European cities but lived principally in Geneva. Both men published: Goodman in 1558 and Knox, more broadly, between 1554 and 1558.[6] Read with *A shorte treatise of politike power*, Goodman's *Superior powers* and (mainly, but not exclusively) Knox's *First blast of the trumpet* help to sketch the radical afterlife of Edwardian kingship.

KINGSHIP, IDOLATRY, AND EMPIRE

On a Sunday morning in 1557, Christopher Goodman preached before the English exile congregation of Geneva. His text was from Acts of the Apostles 4:18–19, and it dealt with the conflict between obedience to human authority and obedience to God:

> And they [the Sanhedrin] called them and commaunded them that in no wyse they should speake or teache in the name of Jesu. But Peter and John aunswered to theym and sayd: whether it be ryght in the syght of God to obey you more then God, judge ye.[7]

Goodman, Ponet, and Knox identified themselves with Christ's apostles. They turned the traditional notion of obedience to 'the powers that be ordained of God' on its head, and argued instead that governors were as accountable to their subjects as they were to God. The model for this 'godly' government was Edwardian, because Goodman, Knox, and Ponet took some of the core texts and assumptions from Edwardian court preaching and biblical commentary and applied them to the political conditions of the second half of the 1550s. All three men agreed, in different ways, with Psalm 118:9, printed on the title-page of *A shorte treatise of politike power*: 'It is better to trust in the Lorde, than to trust in Princes.' The godly kingship of Edward became the key to revealing the acceptability to God of those in political authority.

According to John Ponet, human authority was heavily informed and constrained by the divine. The authority and power to make and execute

---

[6] John Knox, *On rebellion*, ed. Roger A. Mason (Cambridge, 1994) prints extracts from the 1558 tracts – *The first blast of the trumpet, The letter to the Regent, The appellation to the nobility and estates, The letter to the commonalty* – and other important texts for the period 1557–64. See also Roger A. Mason, 'Knox on rebellion', in his *Kingship and the commonweal: political thought in Renaissance and Reformation Scotland* (East Linton, 1998), pp. 139–64; and J.H. Burns, *The true law of kingship: concepts of monarchy in early-modern Scotland* (Oxford, 1996), pp. 122–52.

[7] William Whittingham's introduction to Christopher Goodman, *How superior powers o[u]ght to be obeyd of their subjects: and Wherin they may lawfully by Gods Worde be disobeyed and resisted* (Geneva, 1558; *STC* 12020), sig. {a2v}.

laws proceeded from God. In scripture governors were called gods, and because of the authority they received from God as his ministers on earth to rule and govern His people, the people should in turn obey, honour, and reverence them according to God's ordinance.[8] But for Ponet, the accountability of those in authority more than offset the power they exercised over subjects, and the radical thrust of *A shorte treatise* came from his willingness to push to its logical conclusion the complex relationship between the power of temporal rulers and the restrictions placed on that power by the laws of God and the 'positive laws' and customs of their countries.[9] God was the highest power. All people were His servants, made to serve and glorify Him – even kings and princes.[10] Kings and princes were 'but members' of the commonwealth. Commonwealths could flourish without kings, but without a commonwealth there could be no king. Commonwealths could live when their heads were cut off. They could put on a new head – make a new governor – when they saw that their old head sought his own will and not the wealth of the whole body, for which he was ordained.[11]

John Ponet worked from some of the major assumptions of Edwardian commentators on kingship. The king was, above all, an accountable public officer with profound responsibilities to God for the governance of His people (see above, chapter 2, pp. 38–44). The vital point of departure between Ponet and the Edwardian inheritance was his rejection of the 'absolute' power of monarchs. For Edward VI, and the men around him, his absolute power was indistinguishable from his power as an emperor. Edwardian commentators emphasized the *responsible* exercise of this absolute power. Ponet simply dismissed it, and argued that the 'absolute power' of human governors was merely 'a fulnesse of power, or prerogative to doo what they lust', to dispense with the laws, freely and without correction, to do contrary to the law of nature, to break God's laws and the positive laws and customs of their countries, and to treat their subjects like men treat animals.[12]

The texture and the vocabulary of *A shorte treatise* are quite different from Christopher Goodman's *How superior powers o[u]ght to be obeyd of their subjects* and John Knox's *A first blast of the trumpet against the monstrous regiment of women*. All three books are polemic, but *A shorte treatise* is more subtly disguised as coherent political theory rooted in a European tradition of writing on the nature of temporal power. The examples Ponet used

---

[8] Ponet, *Shorte treatise*, sigs. {A5v}–{A6r}.   [9] Ponet, *Shorte treatise*, sig. B3r; also sig. {C7v}.
[10] Ponet, *Shorte treatise*, sig. {D2v}.   [11] Ponet, *Shorte treatise*, sig. {D7r}.
[12] Ponet, *Shorte treatise*, sig. {B3r}.

were as diverse as the punishment by God of Saul, Jezebel, and Joram and the text of Justinian on a prince's subjection to the law.[13] His models of tyranny were Dionysius of Syracuse, Caligula, and Nero.[14] His European history extended to the representative nature of the councils, diets, and parliaments of western Europe.[15] And he offered an account of the English high constable, who had the authority to summon the king personally before parliament or other courts of judgement and even commit him to ward.[16] He took his examples of 'politike' deposition from England, Denmark, Hungary, and Portugal. And he explained that the Council of Constance (1414–18) had removed popes Gregory, John, and Benet and the Council of Basle Pope Eugenius.[17]

For John Ponet the origin of 'Politic power' lay in scripture. The authority for men to make laws was instituted after the Flood by the law of God set down in Genesis 9:6: 'He that Sheadeth the bloud of man, his bloud Shal be Shead by man. For man is made after the ymage of God.'[18] But in spite of the scriptural foundation of *A shorte treatise*, Christopher Goodman and John Knox were perhaps even more recognizably Edwardian in their critique of the human powers apparently ordained by God to govern. The model of kingship constructed and refined during the reign of Edward was powerful, providential, and driven by Old Testament texts and exemplars. Josiah and Hezekiah, obvious examples of reforming zeal, were as familiar to Knox and Christopher Goodman as they had been to preachers before the king between 1547 and 1553. Goodman and Knox were biblically driven in their condemnation of female monarchy and their promotion of godly governance. They sat themselves in 'Christ's chair', just as Hugh Latimer, John Hooper, William Bill, and Thomas Lever had done during the reign of Edward, in order to examine – and hold to account – the kingdom's magistrates (see above, chapter 2, pp. 41–3).

Before the pieces are able to fall into place, and in order to understand why it is so useful to set Knox and Goodman in the context of the Edwardian legacy, we need first to travel on a short textual journey. In 1549 Hugh Latimer used as the foundation for his first two Lenten sermons Deuteronomy 17:14–20, the account of God's declaration of His Law to Moses. After explaining the relationship between temporal

---

[13] Ponet, *Shorte treatise*, sigs. {C3v}–C4r; {C6r–v}.
[14] Ponet, *Shorte treatise*, sigs. {B7r}–C1r; cf. Desiderius Erasmus, *The education of a Christian prince*, ed. Lisa Jardine (Cambridge, 1997), p. 26.
[15] Ponet, *Shorte treatise*, sig. {A6v}.   [16] Ponet, *Shorte treatise*, sig. {G5v}.
[17] Ponet, *Shorte treatise*, sig. G3r–{v}.   [18] Ponet, *Shorte treatise*, sig. {A4r}.

and spiritual powers, and recognizing the role of preachers in guiding and admonishing kings, Latimer presented an exposition of the second half of the chapter, because it explained the election and choice of a king. The text in the edition of the sermon printed by John Day and William Seres in 1549 presented the words of God to Moses:

> When thou arte come unto the Lande whiche the Lorde thy God geveth the[e], & enjoyeste it, and dwelleste therin: If thou shalt say, I wil set a kynge over me: lyke unto al the nacions that are aboute me: Then thou shalt make him kynge over the[e], whome the Lorde thy God shall chose.
> One of thy brethren muste thou make Kynge over the[e], and mayste not set a stranger over the[e], whiche is not of thy brethren. But in any wyse, let him not holde to[o] manye horsses, that he bringe not the people agayne to Egypt, thorowe the multitude of horsses, for as muche as the Lorde hath sayd unto you: ye shall hence forth go no more agayne that waye.[19]

In the first sermon Latimer explored the implications of this 'doctryne fyt for a kynge'.[20] He contrasted God's prescription of an 'order' for the Israelites' choice of a king '& what manner a man he shoulde be' with their own 'wyll and fantasye'.[21] Latimer effectively and efficiently defined a 'godly' ruler: quite simply he was a minister of whatever title – patriarch, judge, or king – who had his 'authorytie of God'.[22] Deuteronomy 17 became a model for godly kingship. Commenting on God's injunction to Moses to avoid the rule of foreigners (17:15), Latimer presented Edward as his subjects' 'naturall liege kynge and Lorde, of oure owne nation an Englysh man, one of our owne religion'.[23] The great danger of foreign rule was that a people governed 'in the true relygion' would once again fall victim to 'all abomynacyon, and popery'.[24] God's prohibition of an excessive number of horses for the king (17:16) prompted Latimer to claim that 'God is great grand mayster of the Kynges house, & wil take accoumpt of every one that beareth rule therin.'[25] God taught what honour was decent for a king.[26] He required 'in the king and al magistrates a good herte, to walke directlye in hys wayes'.[27] A king's wife (17:17) should stand as a model of godliness.[28] And although gold and silver and sufficient treasure were fundamental to kingly authority

---

[19] Hugh Latimer, *The fyrste Sermon of Mayster Hughe Latimer, whiche he preached before the Kynges Maiest[y] wythin his graces palayce at Westmynster M.D.XL.IX. the viii. of Marche* (London, 1549; *STC* 15270.7), sig. B1 r–{v}.

[20] Latimer, *Fyrste Sermon*, sig. B2r.   [21] Latimer, *Fyrste Sermon*, sigs. {B3v}–B4r; Deuteronomy 17:15.

[22] Latimer, *Fyrste Sermon*, sig. {B6v}.   [23] Latimer, *Fyrste Sermon*, sig. {B7r}.

[24] Latimer, *Fyrste Sermon*, sig. {B7v}.   [25] Latimer, *Fyrste Sermon*, sig. C2r–{v}.

[26] Latimer, *Fyrste Sermon*, sig. C3r.   [27] Latimer, *Fyrste Sermon*, sigs. {C3v}–C4r.

[28] Latimer, *Fyrste Sermon*, sigs. {C4v}–{C6v}.

(17:17), so was the king's fair treatment of his subjects.[29] Kingly honour was an honour defined by godliness. 'It is the kynges honoure that his subjectes bee led in the true religion.'[30]

Deuteronomy 17 established the prototype for the godly king. In the first sermon of Lent 1549 Hugh Latimer sketched the character and behaviour of a king, exploring the broad parameters of a monarchical authority endorsed by God. In the second sermon, a week later, Latimer explored the implications of the last few verses of the chapter. Once the king was set on the seat of his kingdom, explained Latimer, quoting the text *verbatim*, 'he shall wryte hym out a boke & take a copy of the pryestes or Levites'. The king should 'read in it' all the days of his life, learning to fear God and His laws; not turning from God, neither to the right hand nor to the left. So this was a kingship of application and effort. Deuteronomy 17 presented itself as a model of active, attentive, and (perhaps most importantly of all) scripturally driven monarchy. It established a clear relationship between the king, the will of God communicated through scripture, the responsibilities of kingly ministry, and the governance of the kingdom.

It also provided a foundation for, and a context in which to read and understand, the godly monarchs of the Old Testament. In his epistle of dedication to Edward in *The Byble* printed by John Day and William Seres in the year of Latimer's Lenten sermons, Edmund Becke explained his dedication of 'Goddes boke' to a prince. For Becke, kingly interest and title depended on the politic statutes, laws, and ordinances of men 'ratefyed & confyrmed by the infallible woord of God' expressed in Deuteronomy 17, which, like Latimer, he quoted at length. Becke supported his contention with an example: the 'puysant prynce, that valeant and doughthy' Joshua who, after Moses, was charged with the safe conduct of God's people (Joshua 1:6–8). In 'God's commission', argued Becke, a king was commanded diligently to study God's book and to practise it in his outward living and conversation; in this way the nobility and commons of his realm would be moved to imitate his virtuous example. Becke again deployed Joshua, who had taken it to be 'parsel of hys function, charge, and office' to lead God's people to the promised land – a resonant phrase for Edward's evangelical subjects – and to offer himself, in his leadership, as a paragon of 'godly conversation and lyvyng', procuring for his people the preaching of God's word. Like other Edwardian commentators, Becke believed in a kingship of effort and

---

[29] Latimer, *Fyrste Sermon*, sig. {c8v}.   [30] Latimer, *Fyrste Sermon*, sig. {d3v}.

application, of 'industrye and diligent endevour' employed by the king himself and encouraged in others, from the lord chancellor down to the local constable.[31] Equally, Walter Lynne's representation of Edward in Cranmer's Catechism (1548), with the king imperially enthroned, handing the Bible to his bishops, was underpinned by the text of Joshua 1:8, supported by the second half of Deuteronomy 17 (see above, chapter 2, p. 42, Fig. 1).

In *The first blast of the trumpet* John Knox paired Deuteronomy and Joshua to make precisely the same point as Becke and Cranmer. It was the responsibility of the king or the chief magistrate, argued Knox, 'to know the will of God, to be instructed in His law and statutes and to promote His glory with his whole heart and study'. The sword was committed to the magistrate to punish vice and maintain virtue.[32] This was a conventional enough claim, but clearly more contentious was Knox's emphasis on the punishment of the vice of idolatry – ideally by the secular governor – embedded in a book absolute in its denunciation of female monarchy and bitter in its condemnation of Mary Tudor. Becke's and Knox's biblical texts were the same but the implications of what they had to say, and the circumstances in which they were written, were radically different. The years 1549 and 1558 were worlds apart politically. And yet both men proceeded from the same basic assumption. The king or governor was the minister of God responsible for the preservation of His people and the promotion of His law. This office at once enhanced the dignity of a king and placed him under profound obligation. So from the 1540s Tudor monarchy became measurable. In presenting polemical, often biblically driven, arguments for resistance to (and the removal of) unacceptable governors, the Marian exiles presented the king or his equivalent as an accountable public officer.

Perhaps the best expression of this important mutation of Edwardian values of kingship and political authority survives in the work of Christopher Goodman. Once again – it is hard to avoid the text – Deuteronomy 17:14–20 underpinned Goodman's presentation of the appointment and duties of a king. Goodman argued that the people of God should, in their election of a king, diligently follow His laws, because godliness preserved – and ungodliness destroyed – nations. God's law was the guide, not man's phantasy – Hugh Latimer had said exactly the same thing before Edward and his court in 1549.[33] Goodman outlined the tests

---

[31] *The Byble, that is to say all the holy Scripture* (London, 1549; *STC* 2077), sig. AA5v.
[32] Knox, *On rebellion*, ed. Mason, p. 29; cf. p. 88.   [33] Latimer, *Fyrste Sermon*, sig. {A8r}.

(or 'notes') that could be applied to a king to make sure that he was truly chosen by God. The first was by the 'expresse commandement and promesse' made to a special man: to David, for example, or Solomon. The second 'note' was perhaps more measureable. In his Word, God revealed His will and appointment. Scripture endorsed a king who had the fear of God before his eyes, a king who, with the zeal of David and Josiah, studied to promote God, hating all papistry and idolatry. Even a man anointed or elected as king and governor 'by civile policie' had to be 'a promoter & setter forthe of Godds Lawes and glorie, for which cause chieflie, this office was ordeyned'.[34]

So for Goodman, secular governorship and the promotion of godliness were inseparable. By the ordinance of God the people should only choose a king or ruler who sought His honour and glory, and who commanded nothing that conflicted with His Law. Kings had a double charge, because they were God's lieutenants: to fear God themselves and to see that their people feared Him also.[35] If rulers applied themselves with diligence to the Law of God they would learn to obey Him; and, referring to Deuteronomy 17, Goodman presented the examples of 'the Godlie kings and Rulers, having the boke of the Lorde ever with them', reading and studying it day and night like Joshua, Josiah, and Jehoshaphat. Only then was it possible to build a relationship between ruler and subject of love and preservation.[36]

In 1558 Bartholomew Traheron, the Edwardian associate of John Cheke and William Cecil, sketched Mary Tudor's character. She was 'despiteful, cruel, bloodie, wilful, furious, gileful, stuffed with painted processes, with simulation, & dissimulation, void of honestie, void of upright dealinge, voide of al semelie vertues' – the antithesis of the godly governor.[37] For Goodman, her ungodliness had poluted the polity and its governors. 'Miserable' England's counsellors were ungodly and careless. The kingdom's rulers and magistrates, from the highest to the lowest, ruled without the fear of God and colluded in the destruction of the godly.[38] There was no excuse for this, because the obligation to uphold the Laws of God rested with subjects both collectively and individually.[39] God endorsed the rule of kings so long as they reigned for and with, rather

---

[34] Goodman, *Superior powers*, p. 51.   [35] Goodman, *Superior powers*, p. 58.
[36] Goodman, *Superior powers*, p. 105.
[37] Bartholomew Traheron, *A warning to England to repente, and to turne to god from idolatrie and poperie* ([?Wesel,] 1558; *STC* 24174), sig. {A5r}.
[38] Goodman, *Superior powers*, p. 91.
[39] Jane Dawson, 'Trumpeting resistance: Christopher Goodman and John Knox', in Roger A. Mason, ed., *John Knox and the British Reformations* (Aldershot, 1998), p. 149.

than against, God and His people. An individual's obligation to obey human authority was removed when God's Laws had been betrayed.[40] For the exiles, political power had to be considered in its broadest context. 'The end of all offices', argued Goodman, was the promotion of God's Law. God did not give to counsellors, noblemen, rulers, justices, mayors, sheriffs, bailiffs, constables, and gaolers their 'dignitie' to fight against Christ; instead they should humble themselves in His presence, promote His glory, and defend all those committed by Him to their charge.[41] Although the Marian governors of England had betrayed this trust this did not mean for Goodman or Knox that their office had become irrelevant. Quite the opposite, in fact – particularly for Knox, who was more unwilling than Goodman to accept the capacity for individuals to disobey and resist authority.[42] Governorship did not, when push came to shove, reside solely in the person of the king or chief magistrate. It was the responsibility of all men in positions of authority, from Goodman's counsellor to his constable, to represent and enforce God's Law. Knox, writing in his *Appellation* (1558), argued from Romans 13 that the nobility and estates of Scotland were the 'powers ordeined by God', bearing the sword given to them by God for the maintenance of the innocent and the punishment of wrongdoers.[43]

These two themes – the promotion of a godly kingship underpinned by a profound obligation to God, and the responsibility of all men in authority to maintain God's Law – survived beyond the Marian exile. Perhaps the best, and certainly one of the most enduring, examples is the Geneva Bible. In the first edition of 1560 'The Argument', or summary, printed at the beginning of the book of Deuteronomy explained how God had raised up kings and governors for the promotion of God's Word and the preservation of His Church, giving them a special charge 'for executing thereof: whome therefore he willeth to exercise them selves diligently in the continual studie and meditacion of the same'. They should fear the Lord, love their subjects, and abhor covetousness, vice, and anything that offended the majesty of God.[44] Just as explicit was the editors' letter of dedication to Elizabeth I. She was exhorted to reform, to resist the 'craftie persuasion' of man, of worldly policy, of natural fear, and to

---

[40] Jane E.A. Dawson, 'Resistance and revolution in sixteenth-century thought: the case of Christopher Goodman', in J. van den Berg and P.G. Hoftijzer, eds., *Church, change and revolution* (Leiden, 1991), pp. 74–5; Dawson, 'Trumpeting resistance', pp. 151–2.

[41] Goodman, *Superior powers*, p. 95.   [42] Dawson, 'Trumpeting resistance', pp. 131–53.

[43] Knox, *On rebellion*, ed. Mason, pp. 84–5; Dawson, 'Trumpeting resistance', pp. 138–9.

[44] *The Bible and Holy Scriptures conteyned in the Olde and Newe Testament* (Geneva, 1560; *STC* 2093), p. 80r.

recognize that 'The grounde of true religion' was the destruction of idolatry. These high expectations – expectations one suspects Elizabeth would not have shared – came with a price. Asa (1 Kings 15:9–23; 2 Chronicles 14–16) 'began to be colde in the zeale of the Lord' and oppressed the people; God, the Epistle stated simply, 'sent him warres, & at length toke him away by death'. Similarly, the diligence and zeal of Jehoshaphat, Josiah, and Hezekiah were by the providence of God left as an example to all godly rulers to reform their countries and to establish the Word of God with all speed 'lest the wrath of the Lord fall upon them for the neglecting thereof'.[45] The notion of kingship inherited from the Marian exile – a notion which underpinned the assumptions of members of the Elizabethan political elite – was demanding and uncompromising in its expectation of continuing and zealous Reformation as the only secure foundation for the governance of the people.

Elizabeth had little sympathy with this sort of uncompromising Reformation. Her instincts were conservative, and the first thirty years of her reign were marked by bitter divisions over the reform and structure of the Elizabethan Church. Elizabeth and her counsellors could not have been more at variance in their responses to reform in, and of, the English Church; their mental worlds were utterly different. In 1559 William Cecil claimed that England had 'by exaltyng our soverayn lady to this kyngdom abandoned Idolatry and brought our salvior Christ Jesus into this kingdom'. Elizabeth interpreted her prerogative powers to block change and reform.[46] And yet the model of godly kingship entered the mainstream political culture of the Elizabethan polity. The letter of dedication in the Geneva Bible was reprinted in 1576 by Christopher Barker – and, six years later, by Barker as royal printer.[47] The authors of the first *Admonition* to parliament in 1572 claimed that they meant not 'to take away the authoretie of the civill Magistrate and chief governour' but, in seeking the restoration of Christ to His kingdom, see that 'the Prince may be better obeyed, the realme more florish in godlines'.[48] Elizabeth would have none of it. Like Archbishop Whitgift, in 1593, she believed that those who sought further Reformation challenged the temporal jurisdiction of the crown, 'to bring ev[e]ne Kinges and princes under there Censure'.[49] In a polity riven in the 1570s and 1580s by a corrosive debate on governance in church and polity, some

[45] *The Bible and Holy Scriptures*, sig. {∗∗ 2v}.   [46] SP 52/1 fo. 147r (28 July 1559).
[47] *STC* 2117 (1576); *STC* 2133 (1582).
[48] *An admonition to the Parliament* ([?Hemel Hempstead,] 1572; *STC* 10847), sig. B2r.
[49] British Library, Additional MS 28571 fo. 172r (28 Feb. 1593).

members of the political establishment – Barker and two men who supported him, William Cecil and Francis Walsingham – were perhaps
more at ease with the implications of godly monarchy than Elizabeth
herself.[50]

There are of course difficulties and dangers in imposing a neat sym-
metry on the ecclesiastical and political dynamics of the Marian and
Elizabethan decades. Marian exiles like Goodman and Knox inherited
a model of godly kingship, and, in exploring its political implications
for the 1550s, they established a series of tests of the godliness of earthly
rulers. Knox planned in a 'second blast of the trumpet' to explore four
propositions. The first was that it was 'not birth onely nor propinquitie
of blood, that maketh a kinge lawfully to reign above a people professing
Christe Jesus' but his election by the ordinance of God. Similarly, no
'idolater nor notoriouse transgressor of gods holie preceptes' should be
promoted to any form of 'publike regiment'. Oaths and promises did
not bind subjects to obey and maintain tyrants against God. And, if an
ungodly governor had been chosen, it was possible for subjects to depose and punish him.[51] This was not seamless, coherent political theory.
Knox, for example, wrote for two audiences in 1558 – one English and
the other Scottish – and (as Jane Dawson has pointed out) there are
dangers in reading his *First blast, The letter to the Regent, The appellation,* and
The letter to the commonalty of Scotland as a 'unified whole' or 'composite
unit' representing his 'political thought'.[52] Knox's promotion of the role
of magistrates, expressive of the notion of the 'two kingdoms' of separate
temporal and secular jurisdictions, did in some ways sit awkwardly with
the English (and certainly Edwardian) model of royal supremacy; it rested
more comfortably in a Scottish tradition of writing by men like Henry
Balnaves and in the world of the Lords of the Congregation – the world of
magistrate, kirk, and covenant Knox himself helped to shape.[53] And yet
the transformation of kings, councillors, and magistrates into agents and
protectors of Reformation profoundly influenced 'mainstream' political
debate in England and Scotland.

---

[50] H.G. Aldis *et al.*, eds., *A dictionary of printers and booksellers in England, Scotland and Ireland, and of foreign
printers of English books 1557–1640* (Bibliographical Society; London, 1910), pp. 18–20.

[51] John Knox, *The appellation of John Knoxe* (Geneva, 1558; *STC* 15063), pp. 77v–78r; Knox, *On
rebellion*, ed. Mason, pp. 128–9.

[52] Jane E.A. Dawson, 'The two John Knoxes: England, Scotland and the 1558 tracts', *Journal of
Ecclesiastical History*, 42 (1991), pp. 555–76; quotation at p. 555. Cf. Burns, *True law of kingship*,
pp. 128–9.

[53] James Kirk, 'Ministers and magistrates', in his *Patterns of reform: continuity and change in the Reformation
kirk* (Edinburgh, 1989), pp. 232–79.

In 1565 Bishop Edmund Gest of Rochester prepared four justifications for a military campaign by Elizabeth against her cousin Mary Stewart, the queen of Scots.[54] For Gest it was the duty of every prince internationally to defend Christ's religion. He endorsed the right of 'inferiour magistrates' to fight against their own prince 'for the defence of goddes religion', and used this argument to buttress his claim that 'mich more one prince maye fight against an other prince' for the same cause. Even more significant was Gest's defence of the withdrawal of support for an ungodly and destructive monarch. Gest offered an alternative reading of Romans 13. St Paul did not put a blanket ban on resistance to human authority: rather, disobedience to, or the withdrawal of support for, the prince depended on context and circumstance. Gest used Romans 13 to argue that the prince was God's minister by His ordinance. Consequently the prince ruled 'by goddes order appoynted & taught in his worde in defendinge his honor & all right, & in *punnishinge idolaterye* & all wronge'.[55] A year earlier, in 1564, this had been the line argued by John Knox in his debate with William Maitland of Lethington in the Scottish General Assembly. Knox distinguished between the authority written about by St Paul and the *persons* placed in that authority. Subjects, he argued, were not bound to obey their princes if the princes commanded unlawful things. According to Knox, the power written about in Romans 13 should only be understood in terms of the 'just power' God had given His magistrates and lieutenants to punish sin and maintain virtue. Vengeance and damnation would be the reward of any man who tried to take from the hands of a lawful judge a malefactor. This was not so if men 'in the fear of God' opposed the 'fury and blind rage of princes' because – and the line could have come from Edmund Gest's text 'pro defensione relligionis' – 'they resist not God, but the devil, who abuses the sword and authority of God'.[56] Gest the English bishop and almoner to Elizabeth and Knox the self-appointed prophet of God shared a common ground in the ideologically charged environment of Anglo-British politics after 1558.

The radical implications of political authority with a godly edge revealed themselves during the first two Elizabethan decades. In Elizabeth I's fourth parliament, in 1572, Edmund Gest's colleagues on the bench of bishops presented reasons 'to proove' that the English queen

---

[54] For the context of Gest's paper, see Stephen Alford, *The early Elizabethan polity: William Cecil and the British succession crisis, 1558–1569* (Cambridge, 1998), pp. 130–8.
[55] British Library, Lansdowne MS 8 fos. 83r–85v (Sept. 1565).
[56] Knox, *On rebellion*, ed. Mason, pp. 191–2; quotation at p. 192.

was 'bound in conscience to proceed' against her cousin Mary Stewart queen of Scots. In 1564 John Knox had challenged Mary as an idolatrous monarch occupying the throne of Scotland. A year later Gest constructed the case against her as ungodly foreign prince challenging the security and integrity of the English crown. By 1572 she had conspired against Elizabeth – but she was also, significantly, in English custody. The bishops prefaced their 'Reasones' with an account of the duties of their prince. The Word of God taught that 'godlye princes or magistrates' should administer justice in duty and conscience because God in his wisdom and providence had ordained magistrates to repress the wickedness of mankind.[57] The earthly ministers of God were ordained to punish offenders and to praise the good; if the magistrate did not do this, God threatened 'heavie punishmente'. So for the bishops, Elizabeth was obliged to act because of Mary Stewart's challenge to the religion of God and the crown of England *and*, just as importantly, because of Elizabeth's ministerial duty.[58]

In 1572 the bishops shared with Christopher Goodman a visceral hatred of idolatry. In *Superior powers* Goodman argued that every person, high and low, was charged by God to maintain the absolute condemnation of idolatry expressed in Deuteronomy 13:6–11. For Goodman the obligation to destroy idolatry rested with individuals. If the rulers and magistrates did not execute God's Law against idolaters 'the people are not discharged'.[59] For the bishops the agent of execution was Elizabeth; and yet, like Goodman, they argued that there were no exemptions from the Law. A king, a queen, or an emperor, 'either openly or prively knowne to be an idolatrer', could not escape punishment.[60] So their assumptions were the same. Goodman's position on Mary I was as uncompromising as the English bishops' condemnation of the queen of Scots. Mary Stewart, they argued, had done her best to seduce the people of God in England from the true religion and she had been the instrument of the adversaries of God in their efforts to overthrow the gospel. Christians feared God's just plague on magistrates and subjects because slackness and 'remiss justyce' had threatened the overthrow of God's glory and truth. Mary's behaviour only reinforced the bishops' presentation of the duty of every good prince to punish by death 'all such as does seeke to

[57] T.E. Hartley, ed., *Proceedings in the parliaments of Elizabeth I*, 3 vols. (Leicester, 1981–95), I, p. 274.
[58] Hartley, ed., *Parliaments of Elizabeth I*, I, p. 275.
[59] Goodman, *Superior powers*, pp. 182–3.
[60] Goodman, *Superior powers*, pp. 182–4; cf. Gerald Bowler, '"An axe or an acte": the parliament of 1572 and resistance theory in early Elizabethan England', *Canadian Journal of History*, 19 (1984), pp. 349–59.

seduce the people of God from his true worshippe unto supersticion and idolatrye'.[61]

Some years ago, Patrick Collinson argued that although Elizabeth I was not actively resisted by her Protestant subjects 'it does not follow that there was no ideological capacity for resistance'. Professor Collinson reconstructed these 'weapons of resistance theory': the notion that monarchy was a ministry exercised under God on His behalf; that the monarch was a public officer accountable to God and perhaps also to others exercising public offices of magistracy; and that there was a difference between monarchy and tyranny.[62] In this sense, John Knox and Edmund Gest, and Christopher Goodman and the English bishops of 1572, shared a common culture. As models of ungodly queens Jezebel (1 Kings 18, 19, 21; 2 Kings 9) and Athalia (2 Kings 8, 11; 2 Chronicles 21, 22) were as accessible to Elizabethan bishops as they had been to Knox and Goodman, writing in the late 1550s. Marian exile was profoundly formative, but at its core was an Edwardian inheritance.

Political debate is always dynamic because it rests so heavily on the immediate concerns and impulses of those engaged in it. But there were, in the sixteenth century, some constants: notions, assumptions, legacies, and ideas which, often in surprising ways, mutated or responded to different political environments – and yet nevertheless maintained a strong degree of intellectual integrity. Elizabethan Protestants shared with their predecessors a scriptural database of godly and ungodly monarchs and a set of assumptions about the proper exercise of power in polity and church. At the core of the exiles' understanding of kingly and godly ministry was the Edwardian presentation of monarchy. Preachers like Hugh Latimer and John Hooper exhorted the subjects of the crown to obey their governors, but the Edwardian regime believed itself to be godly. The rebels of 1549 were condemned because they challenged the people's leaders chosen by God (see above, chapter 2, pp. 40–1, 60). Obedience to kingship was mandatory – and Edward, as writers and preachers maintained with a remarkable persistence, was definitively godly. But John Ponet, John Knox, Christopher Goodman, the editors of the Geneva Bible, Edmund Gest, and the Elizabethan bench of bishops explored the other, equally compelling, dimension of kingship. The king was a minister, no more and no less. His office could be reconstructed from scripture, and it was informed by Word of God. It was an office of power, responsibility, and

---

[61] Hartley, ed., *Parliaments of Elizabeth I*, I, p. 276.
[62] Patrick Collinson, 'The monarchical republic of Queen Elizabeth I', in John Guy, ed., *The Tudor monarchy* (London, 1997), p. 120.

accountability. Deciding whether the king was accountable on earth or in heaven was perhaps *the* great issue of the 1550s. The reign of Edward did not give the inheritors of its legacy the answer, but it did point them in the direction.

The texts and biblical exemplars of the reign of Edward presented themselves in the years after his death as models of behaviour for the godly prince. But the notion that royal supremacy was a natural vehicle for evangelical change did not survive the 1550s intact. In 1551 Anthony Gilby included in his commentary on Micah a prayer celebrating the providential wonders of Edward's minority. Seven years later he was less certain of the relationship between godly Reformation and supremacy.[63] For Gilby, in 1558, the Reformation of Henry VIII had been a 'deformation'.[64] Henry the tyrant and lecherous monster had displaced Christ as head of the Church 'who oght alone to have this title'. He was no better than the Roman Antichrist who had also made himself a god, sat in the consciences of men, and banished the Word of God. Gilby challenged supremacy. He also condemned the imperfect Reformation of Edward's reign. Rather ambiguously, he marked it as a time when England had tasted the sweetness of the Word of God, abjured Antichrist and idolatry, and professed Christ, but he also denounced it as a period of greed cloaked by religion. Economic and political self-interest threatened to react violently against the 'liberty' of court preachers. So supremacy and incontrovertible godliness – twin pillars of the public construction of Edwardian kingship – were directly challenged by Gilby. The thrust of his 'Admonition' was radically different from an account from 1548 of the king's and Christ's joint headship of the Church.[65] It was different too from the Edward who purged his subjects' consciences of Antichrist in John Ponet's translation of *A tragoedie or Dialoge* (see above, chapter 4, pp. 108–10).

Anthony Gilby's 'Admonition' was a violent reaction to the death of Edward and the perversion of his Reformation. But the essay was binocular rather than monocular: it was a call for repentance to England and Scotland and it tracked the separate, but closely related, trajectories of godly Reformation in both kingdoms. For Gilby England and Scotland

---

[63] Gilby, *Mycha*, sig. {o7r–v}; Roger A. Mason, 'Knox, resistance, and the royal supremacy', in Mason, ed., *John Knox and the British Reformations*, pp. 169–70.

[64] Anthony Gilby, 'An admonition to England and Scotland to call them to repentance', in Knox, *Appellation*, pp. 59v–77r.

[65] *Here begynneth a boke, called the faule of the Romyshe churche* ([London, 1548]; *STC* 21305.3), sig. {c6r}.

were the two sons of Christ's parable of the vineyard (Matthew 21:28–31). During the reign of Edward, England had come to the Lord's vineyard. Scotland had also been called, both by some of its own countrymen and 'by earnest travail of our English nation'. But the kingdom had 'continually refused'.[66] Gilby argued that there had been, over the years, a potential for a closer relationship between the two realms. Union through the marriage of Edward Tudor as prince of Wales to Mary Stewart had been betrayed in Scotland, and the result was war and destruction.[67] But the context was emphatically providential. Satan and his son Antichrist 'could not abyde, that Christ should grow so strong by joynynge that ile togither in perfect religion'.[68]

Anthony Gilby's 'ile' was 'Britanie', England and Scotland 'both makinge one Iland most happie'.[69] The intention of the 'pestilent generation' in Scotland that had spirited Mary Stewart away to France in 1548 had been to cut forever 'the knot of the frendship, that might have ensued betwixte England and Scotland by that godlie conjunction'.[70] Here Gilby inherited Edwardian writing on the relationship between England and Scotland. This, in turn, relied very heavily on claims Edward's father had made to superiority over the Scots. Both kings deployed print. In 1542 the royal printer Thomas Berthelet produced a rather terse twenty-nine-page statement in defence of Henry VIII's war with the Scots 'wherin alsoo appereth the trewe & right title, that the kinges most royall majesty hath to the soverayntie of Scotlande'.[71] After an account of Henry's relationship with James V, and the strained diplomacy of the very early 1540s, the *Declaration* presented as a simple historical fact that the Scots acknowledged 'the kynges of Englande superior lordes of the realme of Scotlande'. Homage and fealty were two of the keys to this traditional, feudal relationship.[72] Henry acknowledged that although two or more men of the same estate could rule the 'Isle' for the better administration of justice 'amonges rude people' there was – and had been – an alternative strategy: the governance of 'one superiour in righte, of whom the sayd astates shuld depende'. The model was Brutus, who had governed a single realm called Britain, a 'whole Isle within the Ocean sea'.[73] Before his death Brutus divided the realm between his three sons Locrine,

---

[66] Gilby, 'Admonition', p. 65r.   [67] Gilby, 'Admonition', p. 66r.
[68] Gilby, 'Admonition', p. 65r.
[69] Gilby, 'Admonition', p. 59r; for the references to 'Britanie', pp. 60r, 61r.
[70] Gilby, 'Admonition', p. 66v.
[71] *A declaration, conteynyng the just causes and consyderations, of this present warre with the Scottis* (London, 1542; *STC* 9179), title-page.
[72] *Declaration*, sig. {B4r–v}.   [73] *Declaration*, sig. {B4v}.

Albanact, and Camber. Because Locrine of England was the eldest – and because Brutus, as conqueror of the whole island, had apportioned the parts of the kingdom in the way that he did – the English king clearly exercised superiority within the island.[74]

The great Edwardian contribution to this model of the Anglo-British relationship was to slide the iron fist of superiority into the velvet glove of love and amity. In *A Declaracion of Christe and of his offyce* (1547) John Hooper celebrated Protector Somerset's military victory over the Scots as 'a sin-guler favour and mercyfull benediction, of God yeven from heven'.[75] This heavenly victory also represented a restoration of the old amity and friendship originally established by God – between England and Scotland as one realm and one island separated from the world, sharing a common race and a common language.[76] The breach of this 'Natu-rall frendshippe' was the work of the Devil, who had taught Scotland 'only disobedience unto here Naturall and Laufull prince and superiour powre the Kynges majestie of Englond'.[77] Hooper's book was a piece of private enterprise – he was still on the continent when *A Declaracion* was published – but arguments rather similar to his were deployed di-rectly by the Edwardian regime in 1547 and 1548. This was a campaign of state-sponsored print, in which the king's printer proper (Richard Grafton) and the king's printer for Latin, Greek, and Hebrew (Reynold Wolf) between them produced four books defending Protector Somer-set's military campaign in Scotland and articulating claims of English friendship and superiority. Wolf's contribution was a Latin translation of a blackletter text printed by Grafton in February 1548, *An Epistle or exhortacion, to unitie & peace*. Grafton also produced *An epitome* of Edward VI's title to Scotland and, perhaps more interestingly, *An exhortation to the Scotts* by a Scot, James Henrisoun, a merchant of Edinburgh.[78]

In 1558 Anthony Gilby endorsed this middle-Tudor policy of tough love. The Scots had only themselves to blame for resisting a 'godlie

---

[74] *Declaration*, sigs. {B4v}–C1r.

[75] John Hooper, *A Declaracion of Christe and of his offyce compylyd by Johan Hoper* (Zurich, 1547; *STC* 13745), sig. {A2v}.

[76] Hooper, *Declaracion of Christe*, sig. A3r.

[77] Hooper, *Declaracion of Christe*, sig. A3r–{A3v}.

[78] *An Epistle or exhortacion, to unitie & peace, sent from the Lorde Protector, & others the kynges moste honorable counsaill of England To the Nobilitie, Gentlemen, and Commons, and al others the inhabitauntes of the Realme of Scotlande* (London, 1548; *STC* 22268); *An epitome of the title that the Kynges Majestie of Englande, hath to the sovereigntie of Scotlande, continued upon the auncient writers of both nacions, from the beginnyng* (London, 1548; *STC* 3196); *An exhortation to the Scotts to conforme themselves to the honourable expedient and godly union betwene the two realmes of Englande and Scotland, dedicated to Edward duke of Somerset by James Harryson* (London, 1547; *STC* 12857); on Henrisoun, see Marcus Merriman, *The rough wooings: Mary queen of Scots 1542–1551* (East Linton, 2000), pp. 269–73.

conjunction' between England and Scotland.[79] Godliness was the key
to the regime's pamphlets of 1547 and 1548 – a godliness of compulsion
and a friendship imposed against the will of one of the parties, perhaps,
but amity nevertheless. Like *A declaration* of 1542, *An epitome* presented a
history of the island of Britain from the days of Brutus, in which union
was presented as a patriotic duty for the Scots.[80] *An Epistle or exhortacion,
to unitie & peace* was more concessive, but still, like the other pamphlets
of 1547 and 1548, found it hard to work out why the Scots had failed so
clearly to recognize the great benefits of union.[81] The Gospel of Christ
would be used by the Edwardian regime to save Scotland from itself.[82]
An Epistle sketched the cultural similarities of these 'twoo brethren of
one Islande of greate Britayn'.[83] It was the intention of Edward, by the
counsel of his governor and protector,

not to conquer, but to have an amitie, not to wynne by force, but to conciliate
by love, not to spoyle and kil, but to save and kepe, not to dissever and divorce,
but to joyne in mariage from high to low, bothe the realmes, to make of one Isle
one realme, in love, amitie, concorde, peace, and Charitie.

But Protector Somerset reminded the Scots that if they refused to be loved
they would be conquered, and they alone responsible for the ensuing
bloodshed.[84] James Henrisoun used *A declaration* of 1542 as one of his
sources, and from it he presented an English superiority grounded in
the rights of Locrine, supported by the principle that governance by one
king was the best sort of governance.[85] But Henrisoun also gave these
conventional points a godly and antipapal twist: he contrasted the godly
unity of two realms agreeing 'in the concorde & unite of one religion'
with the pope and his creatures who trod 'Gods word under fote, to utter
their fylthye merchaundise, & to sclander the precious ware & Jewels of
the scripture'.[86]

There are two interesting themes in the Anglo-Scottish propaganda of
1547 and 1548. The first is the presentation of Edward in the earliest years
of his kingship. In *An Epistle or exhortacion, to unitie & peace* he was effectively
written out of the authorship of a text from 'the Lorde Protector & others
the kynges moste honorable counsaill of England'. And yet, of course, the
message of conciliation was the king's, 'our Masters'.[87] James Henrisoun
dedicated *An exhortation* to Edward Seymour as a man able to mediate

---

[79] Gilby, 'Admonition', sigs. {J1v}–{J2v}.   [80] *Epitome*, sigs. {h4v}–h5r.
[81] *Epistle or exhortacion*, sigs. {A2v}–A3r).   [82] *Epistle or exhortacion*, sig. {A3v}.
[83] *Epistle or exhortacion*, sig. {A4v}.   [84] *Epistle or exhortacion*, sig. {A8r}.
[85] Henrisoun, *Exhortation*, sigs. {e8v}, {f1r–v}, {g5v}–{g6r }.
[86] Henrisoun, *Exhortation*, sig. {h4v}.   [87] *Epistle or exhortacion*, sig. {A8r}.

and represent royal power.[88] He also sketched the relationship between governor and protector and king. Edward VI was young of years but ripe in virtue to govern any kingdom. He possessed excellent gifts of nature and an inclination to all godliness. He would be nothing inferior to the honour and glory of his father.[89] But like other Edwardian writers, Henrisoun explored Edward Seymour's tutorial care for his nephew, framing his youth with 'verteous preceptes, Godly examples, and sincere educacion' (see above, chapter 3, pp. 73–4).[90]

The second feature is the extent to which these explorations of the Anglo-British relationship became expressions of Tudor empire and supremacy. When Henry VIII pronounced that he was an emperor it was a declaration both of his sovereign power and of his relationship with the English Church as God's Vicar. It was not really territorial. But built into propaganda of the 1530s were some important texts relating to claims for English supremacy over Scotland. In the 'Collectanea satis co-piosa' (*c.* 1530), the important manuscript source collection presented to Henry as proof of his imperial authority, one passage presented evidence for English overlordship of Scotland.[91] This claim was printed in *De vera differentia regiae potestatis & Ecclesiasticae* (1538) and translated into English for the Edwardian incarnation of *De vera*, *The true dyfferens between the regall power and the Ecclesiasticall power* (1548). The implication of the inclusion of this sort of material was that empire, supremacy, and even sovereignty could be given territorial expression, or could find themselves in part defined territorially. In 1542 the title-page of *A declaration, conteynyng the just causes and consyderations, of this present warre with the Scottis* claimed for Henry 'the soveraynitie of Scotlande'. *An epitome* (1547) did the same, and conceived of England as 'the onely supreme seat of thempire of greate Briteigne'.[92]

For Edward VI and his subjects this was godly empire: James Henrisoun said as much in 1547 and so did Anthony Gilby eleven years later. Early Elizabethans inherited these sophisticated and contradictory notions of dominance and amity, empire and godly friendship. These claims and assumptions formed a conceptual foundation for William Cecil's Anglo-British politics of the 1560s. An important feature of Cecil's strategic thought after 1559 was a model of England and Scotland bound

---

[88] Henrisoun, *Exhortation*, sig. a2r.   [89] Henrisoun, *Exhortation*, sig. {a6r–v}.
[90] Henrisoun, *Exhortation*, sig. {a6v}.
[91] Graham Nicholson, 'The Act of Appeals and the English Reformation', in Claire Cross, David Loades, and J.J. Scarisbrick, eds., *Law and government under the Tudors* (Cambridge, 1988), pp. 23–4.
[92] *Epitome*, sig. {A5v}.

together by amity and common political interest, united by a co-operative Protestantism organized to counter the mobilized, aggressive powers of Catholic Europe. And yet he had absorbed, and could deploy in the politics of Elizabeth's reign, the other part of the Henrician and Edwardian inheritance. The historical fact of English superiority was used to justify political and military intervention in Scotland. Elizabeth I as superior monarch – an umpire in the game of dynasty – could hear the case against Mary queen of Scots after 1568.[93] This 'British' inheritance, and the contribution of the reign of Edward to it, was influential even beyond the sixteenth century. John Hayward used his *Life, and Raigne of King Edward the Sixt* (1630) as a vehicle for his contribution to the Jacobean debate on Anglo-Scottish Union, itself a maturing of the middle- and later-Tudor notions of friendship, superiority, and English territorial imperial monarchy.[94]

FROM EDWARD TO ELIZABETH

The relationship between the Edwardian, Marian, and Elizabethan political establishments was a difficult and complex one. Some prominent Edwardians did precisely what generations of historians, from the comfort of their studies, expected them to do after 1553: as good Protestants they travelled to the continent. Anthony Cooke, Philip Hoby, and Thomas Wroth – all gentlemen of the king's Privy Chamber – went abroad during the reign of Mary. At least three of the young contributors to the memorial volumes to Martin Bucer and Charles and Henry Brandon – Nicholas Carvyle, John Seaman, and William Temple – left King's College, Cambridge for the continent after 1553. So did the godly fellows of Magdalen College, Oxford who had petitioned for the removal of Owen Oglethorpe from the presidency of their college – all of them contributors to the memorial volumes of 1551, and one at least, Michael Reniger, an Edwardian correspondent of William Cecil (discussed above, chapter 4, pp. 129–31). Cecil, Nicholas Bacon, and Matthew Parker chose to remain in England between 1553 and 1558. Some men with good Edwardian pedigrees travelled abroad only after short periods of conformity to the Marian regime.[95] And although Mary's reign allowed back

[93] Alford, *Early Elizabethan polity*, pp. 59–60, 163–4.
[94] Lisa J. Richardon, 'Sir John Hayward and early Stuart historiography', 2 vols., PhD dissertation, University of Cambridge (1999), I, pp. 208–10.
[95] Andrew Pettegree, 'Nicodemism and the English Reformation', in his *Marian Protestantism: six studies* (Aldershot, 1995), p. 98.

into political life two of the most important opponents of the Edwardian Reformation – Stephen Gardiner and Reginald Pole – men like John Mason, Walter Mildmay, and Richard Sackville continued to serve the crown between 1553 and 1558.

Historians sometimes prefer an ordered past of neat categories and tidy historical explanations, but the Marian years insist on teasing us with difficult questions. To what extent was this fragmented response to the end of Edward's reign a comment on the commitment of his subjects to godly Reformation? Why did men like Cecil act in the way that they did, and what does their behaviour have to tell us about the cohesion of the Edwardian political establishment? Loyalty to the legitimate ruler, complex rationalizations of behaviour, social and family obligations, and the availability of a 'Nicodemite option' – keeping one's faith hidden from public scrutiny – may all have been reasons.[96] Much more work remains to be done on the politically established and disestablished of the exile years, and we should resist the temptation to pronounce definitive judgement. The exile of Philip Hoby, for example, was not conventionally godly. He spent a good part of his time on the continent in Italy. In 1554 Hoby and his half-brother Thomas were in Padua with Thomas Wroth, John Cheke, Henry Nevill, John Tamworth, three sons of Anthony Denny, Anthony Cooke, and others. The Hoby brothers later travelled to Mantua with Wroth, Cooke, and Cheke. From Thomas Hoby's account of the journey it was a pleasant tour of architectural and historical interest.[97] Indeed friendship, and with it a sense of common community, survived the testing-time of the Marian years, even for the men who chose to remain on their estates. Philip Hoby himself arrived back in England over three years before the death of Mary, and in November 1557 he pestered William Cecil to make merry with their friends Walter Mildmay and John Mason – Cecil in political retirement, Mildmay and (more obviously as a privy councillor) Mason servants of Mary Tudor.[98] When Philip Hoby died in May 1558, among his executors were William Cecil and his brother Thomas. Thomas spent the rest of the summer of 1558 with the Cecils at Burghley and married Mildred's sister Elizabeth in June.[99]

[96] Pettegree, 'Nicodemism', pp. 105–6.
[97] Edgar Powell, ed., 'The travels and life of Sir Thomas Hoby, Knight, of Bisham Abbey, written by himself. 1547–1564', *Camden Miscellany X* (Camden Society, third series, 4; London, 1902), pp. 116–17.
[98] C.S. Knighton, ed., *Calendar of State Papers, Domestic Series, of the reign of Mary I* (London, 1998), nos. 663, 664.
[99] Powell, ed., 'Travels and life', p. 127.

Philip Hoby's Marian social circle was relatively unaffected by his friends' individual relationships with the regime, and these were associations that extended into Elizabeth's reign. Roger Ascham provided one of the most interesting insights into how established friendships underpinned the early Elizabethan regime. In *The scholemaster* (1570) Ascham recorded a dinner in the chamber of William Cecil at the court at Windsor, in December 1563. Ascham was present; so was Cecil, William Petre, John Mason, Nicholas Wotton, Richard Sackville, Walter Mildmay, Walter Haddon, John Astley, Bernard Hampton, and Nicasius Yetswert. Yetswert and Hampton were clerks of the Privy Council; Haddon and Astley were master of requests and master of the jewel house respectively; Sackville was treasurer of the Exchequer, Mildmay its chancellor, Petre, Mason, and Wotton all privy councillors; and Cecil was principal secretary to the queen.[100] Some of them – principally Petre and Mason but also, more humbly, Hampton and Yetswert – had served Mary Tudor. All of them, with the exception of Astley as a member of Princess Elizabeth Tudor's household, had held office under Edward.

Ascham's dinner may have been nothing more than a literary device, but it still confirms, factually or fictionally, the close relationship between the middle-Tudor and Elizabethan political establishments. When Nicholas Throckmorton composed his list of candidates for early Elizabethan office, the pool of talent in which he fished for names was, more or less, an Edwardian one.[101] Gentlemen of Edward's Privy Chamber like Thomas Wroth, Francis Knollys, Peter Mewtas, and William Fitzwilliams were recommended for ambassadorial duty or for the office of vice-chamberlain. Nicholas Wotton, Anthony Cooke, John Caryll, and James Dyer all presented themselves as candidates for the lord chancellorship. Throckmorton named Caryll and the common lawyers Nicholas Bacon and Richard Goodrich as men suitable for the mastership of the rolls. Politically at least, Caryll, Goodrich, and Dyer had cut their teeth during the reign of Edward – particularly during the Edwardian trials of conservative bishops (see above, chapter 5, pp. 150–1). Elizabeth's first secretariat, as Throckmorton sketched it, was thoroughly Edwardian in its personnel: William Cecil, re-entering

---

[100] Roger Ascham, *The scholemaster Or plaine and perfite way of teachyng children, to understand, write, and speake, the Latin tong, but specially purposed for the private brynging up of youth in Jentlemen and Noble mens house* (London, 1570; *STC* 832), sigs. B1r–B2r.

[101] J.E. Neale, ed., 'Sir Nicholas Throckmorton's advice to Queen Elizabeth on her accession to the throne', *English Historical Review*, 65 (1950), pp. 94–8.

political life in the office he had left five years earlier, supported by William Honing and Bernard Hampton as clerks, with Walter Mildmay as a possible second principal secretary. Even Thomas Parry, as a member of Elizabeth's household, was bound into a complex network of political and professional association – particularly with William Cecil, formerly the Edwardian surveyor of Elizabeth's lands. And of course there was Throckmorton himself, the cousin of Elizabeth's stepmother Catherine Parr, a gentleman of Edward VI's Privy Chamber after 1550, and an important point of contact between the king and his political elite (see above, chapter 5, pp. 152–3).

The early Elizabethan political world was populated by the subjects of the queen's late brother. Some, like William Cecil, became stars in the Elizabethan firmament. Others, like Cecil's father-in-law Anthony Cooke, transported themselves into comfortable (but, in the case of Cooke, rather irritable) retirement.[102] There were other men, younger than Cooke, who failed to reach their potential. Thomas Smith spent a miserable Elizabethan embassy in France but appears to have come (like Nicholas Throckmorton) within a cat's whisker of appointment to the Privy Council in 1565. He was appointed to the board in 1571, in his middle sixties.[103] Richard Goodrich's enemy was the grave, ending a career of real potential. In 1558 Nicholas Throckmorton considered Goodrich a candidate for attorney general, expert enough to counsel Elizabeth in the first days of her accession, but he 'was not able attend'. Throckmorton also added Goodrich's name to a list of those suitable for the mastership of the rolls 'if his health will serve'.[104] This may have been why Goodrich was out of the court of augmentations by the beginning of Elizabeth's reign. He was dead by 1562. Goodrich appears to have stayed in England between 1553 and 1558 but, like Cecil, kept his head down – in July 1561 he was granted a lease for land in return for his service to Henry VIII and Edward but not Edward's sister.[105] In the early 1550s Goodrich had sat on innumerable royal commissions, and the habit must have been a hard one to break. Goodrich reappeared in April 1559 as a commissioner to take the accounts of all persons chargeable with the goods of Edward Seymour duke of Somerset.[106] More importantly he sat with Nicholas Bacon, William Cecil, and attorney general Gilbert

---

[102] Marjorie Keniston McIntosh, 'Sir Anthony Cooke: Tudor humanist, educator, and religious reformer', *Proceedings of the American Philosophical Society*, 119 (1975), pp. 245–9.
[103] British Library, Lansdowne MS 102 fo. 111r (William Cecil to Thomas Smith, 3 June 1565).
[104] Neale, ed., 'Throckmorton's advice', pp. 94, 95.
[105] *Calendar of the Patent Rolls ... Elizabeth I 1560–63* (London, 1948), p. 31.
[106] *Calendar of the Patent Rolls ... Elizabeth I 1558–60* (London, 1939), p. 51.

Gerard on the commission for the sale of crown lands for ready money after October 1561. All four commissioners were former members of Gray's Inn, two of them (Bacon and Cecil) kinsmen by marriage, and another two (Cecil and Goodrich) close friends.

Richard Goodrich was a friend of the godly and a member of the connected, complex governing elite that was the middle-Tudor establishment. For Roger Ascham, in *The scholemaster*, he was 'Our deare frende' Master Goodrich; Nicholas Throckmorton, writing from Paris on hearing the news of Goodrich's death, also called him a dear friend.[107] *An Epytaphe upon the Death of M. Rycharde Goodricke Esquier* praised him as a man of learning and prudence, ready to defend a right and to hear a poor man's cause; the law and the realm had both lost a worthy man, 'And that whiche is the greatest gryefe/Goddes worde hath lost, a membre chiefe.'[108] The London diarist Henry Machyn recorded Goodrich's funeral. Two hundred gentlemen from the inns of court followed the coffin from Whitefriars to his grave in St Andrew's Holborn. The mourners included Archbishop Matthew Parker of Canterbury, Bishop Richard Cox of Ely, Bishop Edmund Grindal of London, and Lord Keeper of the Great Seal Nicholas Bacon. His principal mourners represented, in other words, the Edwardian establishment made good. Laurence Nowell, the dean of St Paul's, preached the funeral sermon.[109]

Richard Goodrich's Elizabethan career was over almost before it had started, and his death in early middle age robbed the regime of a man who, socially and professionally, had adapted so naturally to the political circumstances of 1558 and beyond. Walter Haddon, civil lawyer and Latinist, made a very similar transition. Haddon became one of Elizabeth's masters of requests – a match between office and officer accurately spotted by Nicholas Throckmorton in 1558.[110] Even the bare bones of Haddon's early Elizabethan career point to a political world of depth and experience. With (among others) Anthony Cooke, Thomas Smith, and Peter Osborne of the Exchequer (the husband of John Cheke's niece Anne), Haddon sat on the commission to search out heresy and vagrancy underpinned by the act of uniformity.[111] As a civil lawyer he contributed

[107] Ascham, *Scholemaster*, sig. {B2v}; *Calendar of State Papers, Foreign Series, of the reign of Elizabeth, 1562*, ed. Joseph Stevenson (London, 1867), p. 73 (Nicholas Throckmorton to Thomas Windebank, 5 June 1562).

[108] *STC* 17145.3.

[109] John Gough Nichols, ed., *The diary of Henry Machyn, citizen and merchant-taylor of London, from AD 1550 to AD 1563* (Camden Society, 42; London, 1848), p. 283.

[110] Neale, ed., 'Throckmorton's advice', p. 96; *Calendar of the Patent Rolls . . . 1558–60*, p. 28 (20 Oct. 1559).

[111] *Calendar of the Patent Rolls . . . 1560–63*, pp. 279–80 (20 July 1562).

to a number of commissions and represented the queen in foreign negotiations, and the rewards were substantial. In September 1559 Elizabeth
granted Haddon an annuity of £50 for his good counsel and
attendance.[112] Just over four years later he was given land in Norfolk.[113]
As lucrative, in January 1563, had been the grant of the wardship
and marriage of Catherine, the daughter of Thomas Farneham of the
Exchequer and the wards, and a brother-in-law of Thomas Chaloner.[114]
Haddon died, in January 1571, a wealthy man.

Walter Haddon was very publicly associated with the continuities
and personalities of the middle-Tudor decades. He was, perhaps above
all, lauded as a Latin stylist. His *Lucubrationes* were edited in 1567 by
Thomas Hatcher, a fellow of King's College, Cambridge.[115] The volume
was dedicated to William Cecil as Elizabeth's secretary and counsellor
and the chancellor of the University of Cambridge. *Lucubrationes* printed
a letter from Thomas Wilson, Haddon's friend and protégé, to Thomas
Hatcher, and the volume included university orations, his orations
on Bucer and the Brandon brothers from 1551, and Haddon's letters
to Charles Brandon, John Dudley, John Cheke, George Day, Richard
Cox, Thomas Wilson, Jerome Osorio de Fonseca, Robert Dudley earl of
Leicester, Thomas Smith, Thomas Heneage, and John Sturm. There
were dedications in another of Haddon's works, *Poemata* (1567), to
Elizabeth Tudor, her brother Edward, Henry Brandon, Roger Ascham,
Thomas Hoby, Martin Bucer, Thomas Cranmer, Matthew Parker, Anne
Heneage, and others.[116] What is more, these books were printed by
William Seres, a member of William Cecil's household, his estate
manager during the Marian years, and, by the reign of Elizabeth, a
substantial printer. The editor, Thomas Hatcher, was the son of Dr John
Hatcher of St John's College, Cambridge, a contributor to John Cheke's
memorial volume on the death of Martin Bucer and Haddon's and
Thomas Wilson's collection of verse for the sons of Katherine Brandon
duchess of Suffolk. John Hatcher was an executor of the will of Nicholas
Carr, John Cheke's successor as regius professor of Greek in Cambridge,
and a leading member of Cheke's circle; Thomas Hatcher wrote for

---

[112] *Calendar of the Patent Rolls . . . 1558–60*, p. 111.
[113] *Calendar of the Patent Rolls . . . Elizabeth I 1563–66* (London, 1960), p. 202: no. 1043 (2 Mar. 1565).
[114] *Calendar of the Patent Rolls . . . 1560–63*, p. 618.
[115] Thomas Hatcher, ed., *G. Haddoni legum doctoris, S. Reginae Elisabethae a supplicum libellis, lucubrationes
passim collectae, & editae* (London, 1567; *STC* 12596). For a bibliography of the Elizabethan editions
of Haddon's work, see Lawrence V. Ryan, 'Walter Haddon: Elizabethan Latinist', *Huntington
Library Quarterly*, 2 (1954), pp. 118–19.
[116] Ryan, 'Walter Haddon', p. 118.

the posthumous volume of Carr's work on Demosthenes, dedicated in manuscript and in print to Walter Mildmay as privy councillor and chancellor of the Exchequer.[117]

This may look like a convoluted way to prove a point, but the point is an important one. Walter Haddon was part of a spidery network of friendship, professional interest, and association. For Patrick Collinson, *The shaping of the Elizabethan regime* (1969) by Wallace MacCaffrey 'describes the coming together of a group of politicians to form a collective, quasi-organic, and, for some considerable time, stable governing group'.[118] Professor MacCaffrey had concentrated principally on Elizabeth's privy councillors, but it may well be necessary, in the light of the Edwardian inheritance, to include within this 'stable governing group' men like Richard Goodrich and Walter Haddon. These people gave to the polity its political shape, and also, in the case of Walter Haddon, an intellectual coherence. Indeed, the earliest debates on the nature of the Elizabethan settlement – between John Jewel and Thomas Harding, Robert Horne and John Feckenham, and Haddon and Jerome Osorio de Fonseca – were, in terms of the histories of the protagonists, thoroughly Edwardian affairs. Haddon undoubtedly contributed to the Elizabethan regime's public projection of itself. He revised Alexander Alesius' Latin prayer book of 1551, printed by Reynold Wolf as *Liber precum publicarum* (1560).[119] It is fairly certain that he wrote part, if not all, of *Dialogus contra Papistarum tyrannidem* (1562), composed in the context of the persecution of French Protestants by the Guise but also concerned with the false claims of papal supremacy.[120] But, above all, his debate in print with Osorio demonstrated the importance to the Elizabethan regime of defending itself in the best Ciceronian Latin possible.

Osorio's challenge was that heresy was dangerous to monarchy, and he sketched the activities of the spoilers of the Church, who had abandoned right worship and despoiled the Church of convents, monasteries, images, ceremonies and the sacraments, of papal supremacy, and freedom of the will.[121] In response, Haddon explained how the reformers had scoured and cleansed the Church, restoring to the people the gospel of

---

[117] Cambridge University Library, MS Dd.4.56: 'Orationes aliquot Demosthenis a Nicolao Carro Medicinae Doctore eloquentissime e Graeco translatae' (*c.* 1566–8), later printed as *Demosthenis, Graecorum Oratorum Principis, Olynthiacae orationes tres, & Philippicae quatuor, e Graeco in Latinum conversae, a Nicolao Carro* (London, 1571; *STC* 6577).
[118] Collinson, 'Monarchical republic', p. 116.
[119] Lawrence V. Ryan, 'The Haddon–Osorio controversy (1563–1583)', *Church History*, 22 (1953), p. 142; Ryan, 'Walter Haddon', p. 104.
[120] Ryan, 'Haddon–Osorio', p. 144.   [121] Ryan, 'Haddon–Osorio', p. 145.

Christ and the sincere worship of God according to the ancient rule and discipline of the primitive Church. He praised Martin Bucer and Peter Martyr Vermigli as models of learning and purity. And he sketched the conventional set of challenges to papal supremacy, endorsed the doctrine of election, and presented an England healthy in its reformed religion.[122] Osorio's contribution was popularly read on the continent; Haddon's reply had more difficulty finding a printer in France – perhaps not surprisingly – but senior members of the regime worked hard to present the defence of England's Reformation to a European audience. In January 1564 William Cecil sent 'Master haddons boke' to Thomas Smith in France. Cecil asked Smith to have it published 'and add some commendation of your hand wher and as yow thynk mete'.[123] Three months later he suggested two printers of experience and expertise: Reynold Wolf, who had been Edward VI's printer for Latin, Greek, and Hebrew; and Richard Jugge who, as an Etonian and a graduate of King's College, Cambridge, must have known Haddon well.[124]

The final version of the book Cecil called 'Haddon contra Osorium' is fugitive. *G. Haddoni Reformatione Anglicana epistola Apologetica ad H. Osorium, Lusitanum* appears to have been printed in Paris, and the only surviving Latin text exists in *Lucubrationes.*[125] Still, an edition in English, edited by Abraham Hartwell of King's College, Cambridge, had been printed by William Seres in 1565.[126] And yet, these problems apart, the debate between Haddon and Osorio was a battle of Ciceronian elegance, a public contest of Latin by two men of opposing theologies conducted within an identical intellectual tradition. On the continent one polemicist argued that Haddon's 'canine tongue' had dared to yelp at the Catholic Church – an assault on both his Latin and his defence of the Elizabethan Reformation.[127] In England the reply to Osorio cemented Haddon's reputation as a consummate linguist, and the text's inclusion in *Lucubrationes* was entirely appropriate. Haddon's epistles also imitated Cicero and examined subjects as diverse and familiar as the importance of studying the works of the ancients, the nature of the scholarly community, the

---

[122] Ryan, 'Haddon–Osorio', pp. 146–7.   [123] British Library, Lansdowne MS 102 fo. 56v.
[124] *Calendar of State Papers, Foreign Series, of the reign of Elizabeth, 1564–5*, ed. Joseph Stevenson (London, 1870), pp. 110–11 (14 Apr. 1564).
[125] Hatcher, ed., *Lucubrationes*, pp. 210–68; Ryan, 'Walter Haddon', p. 121.
[126] Abraham Hartwell, *A sight of the Portugall Pearle, that is, The Aunswere of D. Haddon Maister of the requests unto our soveraigne Lady Elizabeth . . . against the epistle of Hieronimus Osorius a Portugall, entitled a Pearle for a Prince* (London, 1565; *STC* 12598).
[127] Ryan, 'Haddon–Osorio', p. 149.

usefulness of learning to the individual and to the commonwealth, and the excellence of the art of oratory.[128]

In *The early Elizabethan polity*, I argued that the rhetorical and classical education William Cecil received at Cambridge in the 1530s equipped him with both method (particularly in the construction of policy memoranda in two parts *pro* and *contra*) and political identity: the *vir civilis*, the active public man, able to plead in the courts and serve in the counsels of his prince. The relationship between this classical culture and the daily demands of political life was not one of crude causation; it provided instead a complex cultural and psychological substructure upon which Cecil built his political life. His stylish italic hand and his memoranda *in utramque partem* for Edward VI and the Privy Council of the 1560s were the equivalents of the classical *sententiae* his brother-in-law Nicholas Bacon used to adorn the long gallery of his house at Gorhambury, near St Albans.[129] One dimension of this culture was the intellectual coherence of the 'Cambridge connection' of the 1530s and 1540s, the impressive group of Hellenists like John Cheke, Thomas Smith, and Roger Ascham, Latinists like Walter Haddon, and rhetoricians like Thomas Wilson and Richard Rainolde. In *The early Elizabethan polity* Haddon was a notable absentee: unfairly, because Haddon may have taught Wilson his civil law and, as professor of rhetoric in the 1540s, very probably lectured both Wilson and Rainolde in the subject. Haddon briefly appears in Wilson's *The Arte of Rhetorique*, a book which was reprinted in seven Elizabethan editions, all of them dedicated to Robert Dudley earl of Leicester (see also above, chapter 4, pp. 124–6).[130]

If the classical and rhetorical demands of Henrician Cambridge helped to form a cultural and psychological substructure for the political life of William Cecil as principal secretary to Elizabeth I, did the minority of Edward VI similarly underpin the politics of the early Elizabethan polity? This is a question with profound implications for the shape and nature of later-Tudor monarchy. Minority was not a desirable end in itself, but nor was unmarried female queenship. So did the experiences of 1547–53 – of defending Reformation by a minor and of balancing the sovereign authority of the king against the necessary involvement of his

---

[128] Ryan, 'Walter Haddon', pp. 104–5.
[129] Alford, *Early Elizabethan polity*, pp. 15–18; Patrick Collinson, 'Sir Nicholas Bacon and the Elizabethan *via media*', *Historical Journal*, 23 (1980), pp. 258–61; Elizabeth McCutcheon, ed., *Sir Nicholas Bacon's great house sententiae* (English Literary Renaissance Supplements, 3; Amherst, 1977).
[130] *STC* 25800–25806.

advisers – provide many of the same men, working in an altered set of political circumstances, with the intellectual equipment to cope with the comparable demands of female monarchy?

If the key to the political creed of Elizabeth's councillors from 1558 was the notion of 'mixed polity', then the answer to this question may well be a cautious yes.[131] One presentation of Edward VI rested on his godliness and his supremacy, but, in the main, Edwardians sketched a collaborative Reformation promoted by a king counselled, endorsed by parliament. Their difficulty in reconciling these notions was manifest (see above, chapter 2, pp. 60–4). In his response to John Knox's *First blast of the trumpet*, John Aylmer, the tutor of Lady Jane Grey, certainly associated the rule of 'boyes and women, or effeminate persons', and he defended the legitimacy of Elizabeth as queen on at least three grounds.[132] The first was God's secret purpose.[133] The second was Elizabeth's education and learning.[134] The third was more problematic but, like the first two defences of Elizabeth's queenship, it had a peculiarly Edwardian edge to it. 'That cytie is at the pits brinke, wherin the magistrate ruleth the lawes, and not the lawes, the magistrate: What could any kyng in Israell do in that common wealth, besides the pollycie appoynted by Moyses?'[135] Aylmer sketched a 'regiment' for England that was 'not a mere Monarchie' but a 'rule mixte', an arrangement represented in image and in fact by a parliament of the three estates – monarch, noblemen, burgesses and knights. In this sense, female monarchy (like royal minority?) was not a dangerous matter because the laws ruled, not the queen, and the execution of these laws was supervised by a counsel working at her elbow.[136]

To what extent were these notions influenced by the political experiences of the reign of Edward? Once again, it is worth stressing that this is an issue of substructure and of deep political and cultural assumptions. There is no evidence to suggest that Elizabethans tried to impose on politics post-1558 plans or solutions to problems constructed between 1547 and 1553 – with, perhaps, the exceptions of Edward's coronation and the parliamentary religious settlement of 1559.[137] The dynamics of

---

[131] Alford, *Early Elizabethan polity*, pp. 34–7.

[132] John Aylmer, *An harborowe for faithfull and trewe subjectes, agaynst the late blowne Blaste, concerninge the Government of Wemen* ([London,] 1559; *STC* 1005), sig. {G3v}.

[133] Aylmer, *An harborowe*, sig. B3r.   [134] Aylmer, *An harborowe*, sig. N2r–{v}.

[135] Aylmer, *An harborowe*, sig. H2r–{v}.   [136] Aylmer, *An harborowe*, sig. H3r–{v}.

[137] Dale Hoak, 'The coronations of Edward VI, Mary I, and Elizabeth I, and the transformation of Tudor monarchy', in Richard Mortimer and Charles S. Knighton, eds., *Reformation to revolution: Westminster Abbey 1540–1660* (Stamford, 2002); Winthrop S. Hudson, *The Cambridge connection and the Elizabethan settlement of 1559* (Durham, NC, 1980).

Edward's reign were rather different from those of his sister's polity. On balance, a male minority appears to have posed fewer intellectual problems (at least superficially) for the subjects of the Tudor crown than either married or single female monarchy. Mary and Elizabeth were (as the cliché puts it) women in a man's world. Edward was confidently expected by his subjects to grow into his kingship, a kingship they had helped to mould. And, of course, a boy could live in private chambers staffed by the men who sat in his institutional Council and ran his household. The practical dimensions of a queen regnant were more difficult. With Edward there was the real prospect of active and dynamic kingship; with Mary and Elizabeth there was perhaps a sense of more limited potential.

Between 1547 and 1553 the Tudor polity moved slowly in the direction of an operational personal monarchy. After 1558 the political elite appeared to be dragging political culture in the opposite direction, progressively detaching the person of the queen from the sovereignty she exercised, determined to preserve the continuities of governance and provide for the security of the realm. Sovereignty could, in extreme circumstances, be held, temporarily, by an institutional council. In 1563, and again in 1584, the Privy Council sketched plans for its transition into a privy council (or counsel) of estate and a great (or grand) council of the realm.[138] These proposals were, on the face of it, radically different from the counsel of estate of 1552, which attempted, in very practical terms, to focus the governance of the realm more personally on Edward. The Elizabethan plans defined with precision what the principal subjects of Edward VI had generally left opaque: the degree to which a council could act as the location of sovereign power in the polity. But the Elizabethan proposals for conciliar interregnum reflected the abnormal and distorted politics of Elizabeth's reign. They were not the products of a healthy political relationship between the queen and her counsellors (either in the institutional Council or in parliament) and were influenced rather more by a perception on the part of the men who framed them of danger and international crisis. But although there are serious problems in reading the extraordinary political environment of the early part of Elizabeth's reign as extensions of the politics of Edward's reign – the period between 1547 and 1553 as a portent of things to come – some connections can be made.

---

[138] Patrick Collinson, 'The Elizabethan exclusion crisis and the Elizabethan polity', *Proceedings of the British Academy*, 84 (1994), pp. 87–92; Alford, *Early Elizabethan polity*, pp. 111–15, 225–8.

The Edwardian counsel for the estate, and the explorations of advice and consultation presented in court sermons and advice literature, came very close to establishing a model political relationship between a king and his counsellors. The counsel for the estate (see above, chapter 5, pp. 162–5) embraced the public affairs of a kingdom governed by a king counselled. It had immense potential. But for most of Edward's reign the king was effectively separated from the elite governing in his name. The monarchical ideal was sovereign and kingly independence, reinforced (but in no sense limited by) the counsel and advice of his principal subjects. Instead counsel compensated for the practical limitations of the king's minority. John Cheke's defence of Reformation by the 'king's majesty etc' (see above, chapter 2, p. 62) obscured rather than clarified. It was an example of tactical imprecision, doubt, and uncertainty because it left unclear the precise relationship between the monarch and the men around him. Reconciling the regime's confident declaration of Edward's powers as king, its reliance on counsel, Council and parliament in defending Reformation, its faith in personal monarchy but the effective independence of the men around the king was a difficult business. Given the nature of English politics and political debate in the 1550s – the apparent confidence in the integrity of Mary's sovereign power in the Act concerning the Regal Power (1554), the politics of married female monarchy, and the Marian and early Elizabethan assaults on queenship – it is hardly surprising that Elizabethan political culture inherited a number of dangerously mixed messages on the nature of Tudor monarchy.

If the Tudor polity of the second half of the sixteenth century was in a period of transition – from a royal estate, where the monarch *was* the kingdom, to 'state', a polity conscious of existence beyond the life of the king or queen and capable of defining itself ideologically as Protestant – the reign of Edward was absolutely formative. It helped to establish the context of change. In constructing a polity built on the foundation of personal and dynamic monarchy, but able to compensate for its absence, the years between 1547 and 1553 allowed councillors and courtiers to engage with some of the challenges they continued to face in the following half-century of female rule. In promoting a godly Reformation of the realm, underpinned by the authority of the king-in-parliament, Edwardians transformed the Henrician royal supremacy into a vehicle for evangelical change. For forty years Elizabethans contested the implications. What was the nature of the Elizabethan royal supremacy? And what was its purpose? Was the monarch, as supreme head of the English Church, obliged to promote further Reformation? Was the Tudor supremacy merely expressed in statute or was parliament a forum for the redress of ecclesiastical abuses? The years 1547–53 left a double legacy of people and ideas: a complex set of ideas with which to decode (or confuse) the relationship between monarch and subject and polity and church, complemented by fascinating and complex networks of friendship, association, and office. Without the reign of Edward VI – and particularly the king's minority – the shape of English governance, monarchy, and political thought in the sixteenth century would have been radically different.

Bibliography

I MANUSCRIPTS

LONDON

British Library
  Additional MSS
  Cotton MSS
  Harley MSS
  Lansdowne MSS
  Royal MSS
  Stowe MSS
Inner Temple Library
  Petyt MS 538 vol. 47 (Edward VI's 'devise for the succession', 1553)
Public Record Office
  SP 10 (State Papers, Domestic, Edward VI)
  SP 11 (State Papers, Domestic, Mary I)
  SP 12 (State Papers, Domestic, Elizabeth I)
  SP 52 (State Papers, Scotland, Elizabeth I)
  SP 68 (State Papers, Foreign, Edward VI)

CAMBRIDGE

Cambridge University Library
  Dd.4.56 (Nicholas Carr's lectures on Demosthenes, *c.* 1566–8)
  Dd.9.31 (William Gray's 'sayeinges' for Edward Seymour duke of Somerset, 1549–50)
  Probate records from the Vice-Chancellor's Court
Corpus Christi College
  Parker MSS
King's College Library
  Commons Books 1547–53
  Mundum Books 1547–53
  Protocollum Book 1500–78

HATFIELD HOUSE LIBRARY, HATFIELD, HERTFORDSHIRE

Cecil Papers

HUNTINGTON LIBRARY, SAN MARINO, CALIFORNIA

Ellesmere MS 2625.

LONGLEAT HOUSE LIBRARY, WARMINSTER, WILTSHIRE

Portland Papers
Seymour Papers
Thynne Papers

II CALENDARS, REFERENCE WORKS,
AND RESOURCES

Acts of the Privy Council of England, ed. J.R. Dasent *et al.*, new series, 46 vols. (London, 1890–1964).

Aldis, H.G. *et al.*, eds., *A dictionary of printers and booksellers in England, Scotland and Ireland, and of foreign printers of English books 1557–1640* (Bibliographical Society; London, 1910).

Alumni Cantabrigienses. A biographical list of all known students, graduates and holders of office at the University of Cambridge, from the earliest times to 1900, ed. John Venn and J.A. Venn, 10 vols. (Cambridge, 1922–54).

The Bible in English, http://collections.co.uk/bie (Bell and Howell Information and Learning).

Bindoff, S.T., ed., *The House of Commons 1509–1558*, 3 vols. (History of Parliament; London, 1982).

Calendar of the Patent Rolls preserved in the Public Record Office: Edward VI, 6 vols. (HMSO; London, 1924–29).

Calendar of the Patent Rolls . . . Elizabeth I 1558–60 (HMSO; London, 1939).

Calendar of the Patent Rolls . . . Elizabeth I 1560–63 (HMSO; London, 1948).

Calendar of the Patent Rolls . . . Elizabeth I 1563–66 (HMSO; London, 1960).

Calendar of State Papers, Domestic: see Knighton, C.S., ed.

Calendar of State Papers, Foreign Series, of the reign of Elizabeth, 1564–5, ed. Joseph Stevenson (London, 1870).

Calendar of the manuscripts of the marquis of Bath preserved at Longleat, Wiltshire, 4 vols. (Royal Commission on Historical Manuscripts; London, 1904–68).

Colvin, H.M., ed., *The history of the king's works, IV. 1485–1660 (Part II)* (London, 1982).

Complete peerage, ed. Vicary Gibbs *et al.*, 13 vols. (London, 1910–40).

Duff, E. Gordon, *The English provincial printers, stationers and bookbinders to 1557* (Cambridge, 1912).

Early English Books Online, http://wwwlib.umi.com/eebo/ (Bell and Howell Information and Learning).

Fairbank, Alfred, and Bruce Dickens, eds., *The italic hand in Tudor Cambridge* (Cambridge Bibliographical Society Monograph, 5; London, 1962).

Gray's Inn: *The register of admissions to Gray's Inn, 1521–1889* (London, 1889).

Greg, W.W., *Some aspects and problems of London publishing between 1500 and 1650* (Oxford, 1956).

A history of Suffolk, ed. William Page, 2 vols. (Victoria History of the Counties of England; London, 1907–11).

Knighton, C.S., ed., *Calendar of State Papers, Domestic Series, of the reign of Edward VI 1547–1553* (HMSO; London, 1992).

Calendar of State Papers, Domestic Series, of the reign of Mary I (HMSO; London, 1998).

Leedham-Green, E.S., ed., *Books in Cambridge inventories. Book-lists from vice-chancellor's court probate inventories in the Tudor and Stuart periods*, 2 vols. (Cambridge, 1986).

Letters and papers, foreign and domestic, of the reign of Henry VIII, ed. J.S. Brewer, J. Gairdner, R.H. Brodie *et al.*, 21 vols. and *Addenda* (London, 1862–1932).

Lincoln's Inn: *The records of the Honourable Society of Lincoln's Inn*, 2 vols. (London, 1896).

MacLure, Millar, *Register of sermons preached at Paul's Cross 1534–1642*, ed. Jackson Campbell Boswell and Peter Pauls (Ottawa, 1989).

McKerrow, R.B., *Printers' and publishers' devices in England and Scotland 1485–1640* (Bibliographical Society; London, 1913).

Middle Temple: *Register of admissions to the Honourable Society of the Middle Temple*, 3 vols. (London, 1949).

A short-title catalogue of books printed in England, Scotland, & Ireland and of English books printed abroad 1475–1640, ed. W.A. Jackson, F.S. Ferguson, and Katharine F. Pantzer, 3 vols. (Bibliographical Society; London, 1976–91).

Williams, Franklin B., *Index of dedications and commendatory verses in English books before 1641* (Bibliographical Society; London, 1962).

III PRINTED SOURCES 1547–53

All suche Proclamacions, as have been sette furthe by the Kynges Majestie (and passed the Print) from the last daie of Januarij, in the firste yere of his highnes reigne (London: Richard Grafton, 1550; *STC* 7758).

Becon, Thomas, *The Fortresse of the faythfull agaynst the cruel assautes of povertie and honger newlye made for the comforte of poore nedye Christians, by Thomas Becon* (London: John Day and William Seres, 1550; *STC* 1721).

Bible: Old and New Testaments:

The Byble, that is to say all the holy Scripture: In whych are contayned the Olde and New Testamente, truly & purely translated into English, & nowe lately with greate industry & diligence recognised (London: [Steven Mierdman] for John Day and William Seres, 1549; *STC* 2077).

Bible: New Testament:
The new Testament in Englishe after the greeke translation annexed wyth the translation of Erasmus in Latin (London: Thomas Gaultier, 1550; *STC* 2821).
The newe Testament of our Saviour Jesu Christe. Faythfully translated out of the Greke. Wyth the Notes and expositions of the darke places therein (London: Richard Jugge, 1552; *STC* 2867).
Certayne Sermons, or Homelies, appoynted by the kynges Majestie, to be declared and redde, by all persones, Vicars, or Curates, every Sondaye in their churches, where they have Cure (London: Richard Grafton, 1547; *STC* 13640).
Cheke, John, *De obitu doctissimi et sanctissimi theologi doctoris Martini Buceri, Regii in celeberrima Cantabrigiensi Academia apud Anglos publice sacrarum literarum prelectoris Epistolae duae* (London: Reynold Wolf, 1551; *STC* 5108).
   The hurt of sedicion, howe greveous it is to a Commune welth (London: John Day and William Seres, 1549; *STC* 5109).
A Copye of a Letter contayning certayne newes, and the Articles or requestes of the Devonshyre & Cornyshe rebelles. M.D.XLIX (London: John Day and William Seres, 1549; *STC* 15109.3).
Coverdale, Miles, *A Spyrytuall and moost precyouse Pearle. Teachyng all men to love and imbrace the crosse, as a mooste swete and necessary thyng, unto the sowle, and what comfort is to be taken thereof* (London: [Steven Mierdman for] Walter Lynne, 1550; *STC* 25255).
Cranmer, Thomas, *An answer of the Most Reverend Father in God Thomas Archebyshop of Canterburye, primate of all Englande and metropolitane unto a crafty and sophisticall cavillation devised by Stephen Gardiner doctour of law, late byshop of Winchester* (London: Reynold Wolf, 1551; *STC* 5991).
An Epistle or exhortacion, to unitie & peace, sent from the Lorde Protector, & others the kynges moste honorable counsaill of England To the Nobilitie, Gentlemen, and Commons, and al others the inhabitauntes of the Realme of Scotlande (London: Richard Grafton, 1548; *STC* 22268).
An epitome of the title that the Kynges Majestie of Englande, hath to the sovereigntie of Scotland, continued upon the auncient writers of both nacions, from the beginnyng (London: Richard Grafton, 1548; *STC* 3196).
Erasmus, Desiderius, *The first tome or volume of the Paraphrases of Erasmus upon the newe testament, conteinyng the fower Evangelistes, with the Actes of the Apostles* (London: Edward Whitchurch, 1551; *STC* 2866).
Foxe, Edward, *The true dyfferens betwen the regall power and the Ecclesiasticall power Translated out of latyn by Henry lord Stafforde* (London: William Copland, 1548; *STC* 11220).
Gerrard, Philip, *A godly invective in the defence of the Gospell* (London: Richard Grafton, 1547; *STC* 11797).
Gest, Edmund, *A Treatise againste the prevee Masse in the behalfe and furtheraunce of the mooste holye communyon, made by Edmund Gest* (London: [William Hill and] Thomas Raynald, 1548; *STC* 11802).
Gilby, Anthony, *A commentarye upon the Prophet Mycha. Wrytten by Antony Gilby* (London: John Day, 1551; *STC* 11886).

Haddon, Walter, and Thomas Wilson, *Vita et obitus duorum fratrum Suffolciensium, Henrici et Caroli Brandoni prestanti virtute, et splendore nobilitatis ducum illustrissimorum, duabus epistolis explicata* (London: Richard Grafton, 1551; *STC* 25817).

Hall, Edward, *The union of the two noble and illustre famelies of Lancastre & Yorke* (London: Richard Grafton, 1548; *STC* 12722). The second edition of 1550 is *STC* 12723.

Henrisoun, James, *An exhortation to the Scotts to conforme themselves to the honourable expedient and godly union betwene the two realmes of Englande and Scotland, dedicated to Edward duke of Somerset by James Harryson* (London: Richard Grafton, 1547; *STC* 12857).

Here begynneth a boke, called the faule of the Romyshe churche ([London: ?Nicholas Hill, 1548]; *STC* 21305.3).

Homilies: see *Certayne Sermons, or Homelies.*

Hooper, John, *A declaracion of Christe and of his offyce compylyd / by Johan Hoper / Anno 1547* (Zurich: Augustine Fries, 1547; *STC* 13745).

A Declaratyon of the ten holy commaundementes of almyghtye God wryten Exo. xx. Deu. 5. Collected out of the scrypture Canonycall by John Houper, with certayne newe addisions made by the same maister Houper ([London: Thomas Gaultier? for] Richard Jugge, 1550; *STC* 13750.5).

A funeral oration, made the .xiiii. daye of January, by John Hoper, the yeare of oure salvatyon .M.D.XLIX. upon the texte wrytten in the Revelation of Saynt John Capi. xiiii. (London: Thomas Raynald, 1550; *STC* 13755).

Godly and most necessary Annotations in the .xiii. Chapyter too the Romaynes: Set furthe by the right vigilant Pastor, Jhon Hoper, by gods calling, Busshop of Gloucestre (Worcester: John Oswen, 1551; *STC* 13756).

A godly Confession and Protestacion of the christian fayth, made and set furth by Jhon Hooper, wherin is declared what a christian manne is bound to beleve of God, hys King, his neibour, and hymselfe (London: John Day, 1550; *STC* 13757).

An Homelye to be read in the tyme of pestylence, and a moste presente remedye for thesame (Worcester: John Oswen, [1553]; *STC* 13759).

An oversight, and deliberacion upon the holy Prophete Jonas: made, and uttered before the kynges majestie, and his moost honorable councell, by Jhon Hoper in lent last past. Comprehended in seven Sermons. Anno .MD.L. (London: John Day and William Seres, 1550; *STC* 13763).

Injunctions geven by the moste excellente Prince, Edward the .VI. by the grace of GOD, Kynge of Englande, Fraunce, and Irelande: Defendour of the Faith, & in earthe under CHRIST, of the Churche of Englande & of Irelande the supreme head: To all and singuler hys Lovinge Subjectes, aswel of the Clergie, as off the Laietie (London: Richard Grafton, 1547; *STC* 10088).

Latimer, Hugh, *The fyrste Sermon of Mayster Hughe Latimer, whiche he preached before the Kynges Majest[y] wythin his graces palayce at Westmynster M.D.XL.IX. the viii. of Marche* (London: John Day and William Seres, 1549; *STC* 15270.7).

A moste faithfull Sermon preached before the Kynges most excellente Majestye, and hys most honorable Councell, in hys Courte at Westminster, by the reverend Father Master Hughe Latimer. Anno Domi[ni] .M.D.L. (London: John Day, 1550; *STC* 15289).

A moste faithfull Sermon preached before the Kynges most excellente Majestye, and hys most honorable Councel, in his Court at Westminster, by the reverende Father Master. Hughe Latymer (London: John Day, [1553]; *STC* 15290).

A notable Sermon of the reverende father Maister Hughe Latemar, whiche he preached in the Shrouds at paules churche in London, on the .xviii. daye of January. 1548 (London: John Day and William Seres, 1548; *STC* 15291).

The seconde Sermon of Maister Hughe Latimer, whych he preached before the Kynges majestie, within his graces Palayce at Westminster the .xv. day of Marche. M.ccccc.xlix. (London: John Day and William Seres, 1549; *STC* 15274.7).

A Sermon of Master Latimer, preached at Stamford the .ix. day of October. (London: John Day, [1550]; *STC* 15293).

Lever, Thomas, *A fruitfull Sermon made in Poules churche at London in the shroudes the seconde daye of February by Thomas Lever: Anno .M.D & fiftie.* (London: John Day and William Seres, 1550; *STC* 15543).

A Sermon preached at Pauls Crosse, the .xiiii. day of December, by Thomas Lever. Anno .MD.L. (London: John Day, 1550; *STC* 15546.3).

A Sermon preached the thyrd Sondaye in Lente before the Kynges Majestie, and his honorable Counsell, by Thomas Leaver. Anno Domini. M.ccccc.l. (London: John Day, 1550; *STC* 15548).

Lynne, Walter, *The beginning and endynge of all popery, or popishe kyngedome* (London: John Herford for Walter Lynne, 1548; *STC* 17115).

A message sent by the kynges Majestie, to certain of his people, assembled in Devonshire (London: Richard Grafton, 1549; *STC* 7506).

Ochino, Bernardino, *Fouretene Sermons of Barnardine Ochyne, concernyng the predestinacion and eleccion of god: very expediente to the settynge forth of hys glorye among hys creatures. Translated out of Italian in to oure natyve tounge by A.C* (London: John Day and William Seres, 1551; *STC* 18767).

A tragoedie or Dialoge of the unjuste usurped primacie of the Bishop of Rome, and of all the just abolishyng of the same, made by master Barnardine Ochine an Italian, & translated out of Latine into Englishe by Master John Ponet Doctor of Divinitie, never printed before in any language (London: [Nicholas Hill for] Walter Lynne, 1549; *STC* 18770, 18771).

Sermons of the ryght famous and excellent clerke Master Bernardine Ochine (Ipswich: Anthony Scoloker, 1548; *STC* 18765).

Parker, Matthew, *Howe we ought to take the death of the Godly, a Sermon made in Cambrydge at the buriall of the noble Clerck .D. M. Bucer* (London: Richard Jugge, [1551]; *STC* 19293).

Parr, Catherine, *The lamentacion of a sinner, made by the most vertuous Ladie, Quene Caterin, bewayling the ignoraunce of her blind life: set furth and put in print at the instaunt desire of the righte gracious ladie Catherin Duchesse of Suffolke, & the earnest requeste of the right honourable Lord, William Parre, Marquesse of North Hampton* (London: Edward Whitchurch, 1547; *STC* 4827). The second edition (also printed by Whitchurch) is *STC* 4828.

Patten, William, *The Expedicion into Scotlande of the most woorthely fortunate prince Edward, Duke of Soomerset, uncle unto our most noble sovereign lord the kinges Majestie Edward the .VI.* (London: Richard Grafton, 1548; *STC* 19476.5).

Ponet, John, *A notable Sermon concerninge the ryght use of the lordes supper and other thynges very profitable for all men to knowe preached before the Kynges most excellent Mayestye and hys most honorable counsel in hys courte at Westmynster the 14. daye of Marche, by Mayster John ponet Doctor of dyvinity. 1550.* ([London: Steven Mierdman for] Walter Lynne, 1550; *STC* 20177).

A Proclamacion, set furth by the body and state, of the Kynges Majest[y]s privey Counsayle, concernyng the devisers, writers, and casters abrode, of certain vile, slaunderous, and moste trayterous letters, billes, scrowes, and papers, tendyng to the seducement of the kynges majesties good & lovyng subjectes (London: Richard Grafton, 10 Oct. 1549; *STC* 7829).

A Proclamacion set forth by the state and bodie of the Kynges Majest[i]es Counsayle now assembled at London, conteinyng the very trouth of the Duke of Somersets evel Government, and false and detestable procedinges (London: Richard Grafton, 1549; *STC* 7828).

Proclamations: see *All suche Proclamacions.*

Thomas, William, *The historie of Italie, a boke excedyng profitable to be redde: Because it intreateth of the astate of many and divers common weales, how thei have ben, & now be governed* (London: Thomas Berthelet, 1549; *STC* 24018).

Principal rules of the Italian grammer, with a Dictionarie (London: Thomas Berthelet, 1550; *STC* 24020).

The vanitee of this world (London: Thomas Berthelet, 1549; *STC* 24023).

Turke, John, *A lamentation of the death of the moost victorious Prynce henry the eyght late Kynge of thys noble royalme of Englande* (London: [John Day and William Seres for] John Turke, [1547]; *STC* 13089).

Vermigli, Peter Martyr, *A discourse or traictise of Petur Martyr Vermilla Florentine, the publyque reader of divinitee in the Universitee of Oxford wherin he openly declared his whole and determinate judgemente concernynge the Sacrament of the Lordes supper in the sayde Universitee* (London: [Edward Whitchurch,] 1550; *STC* 24665).

An epistle unto the right honorable and christian prince, the Duke of Somerset written unto him in Latin, awhile after hys deliveraunce out of trouble, by the famous clearke Doctour Peter Martyr, and translated into Englyshe by Thomas Norton (London: [Nicholas Hill for] Walter Lynne, 1550; *STC* 24666).

Wilson, Thomas, *The Arte of Rhetorique, for the use of all suche as are studious of Eloquence, sette forth in English, by Thomas Wilson* (London: Richard Grafton, 1553; *STC* 25799).

The rule of Reason, conteinyng the Arte of Logique, set forth in Englishe, by Thomas Wilson (London: Richard Grafton, 1551; *STC* 25809).

IV PRINTED TUDOR SOURCES 1538–47, 1553–1603

An admonition to the Parliament ([?Hemel Hempstead: ?J. Stroud,] 1572; *STC* 10847).

Ascham, Roger, *The scholemaster Or plaine and perfite way of teachyng children, to under-stand, write, and speake, the Latin tong, but specially purposed for the private bryngyng up of youth in Jentlemen and Noble mens house* (London: John Day, 1570; *STC* 832).

Aylmer, John, *An harborowe for faithfull and trewe subjectes, agaynst the late blowne Blaste, concerninge the Government of Wemen* ([London: John Day,] 1559; *STC* 1005).

The Bible and Holy Scriptures conteyned in the Olde and Newe Testament (Geneva: Rowland Hall, 1560; *STC* 2093).

Carlile, Christopher, *A discourse, Concerning two divine Positions . . . Publiquely disputed at a Commencement in Cambridge, Anno Domini 1552* (London: Roger Ward, 1582; *STC* 4654).

Carr, Nicholas, *Demosthenis, Graecorum Oratorum Principis, Olynthiacae orationes tres, & Philippicae quatuor, e Graeco in Latinum conversae, a Nicolao Carro* (London: Henry Denham, 1571; *STC* 6577).

Cheke, John, *An homilie of saint John Chrysostome . . . newely made out of Greke into latin by master Cheke, and englished by Tho. Chaloner* (London: Thomas Berthelet, 1544; *STC* 14637).

A declaration, conteynyng the just causes and consyderations, of this present warre with the Scottis, wherin alsoo appereth the trewe & right title, that the kinges most royall majesty hath to the soverayntie of Scotlande (London: Thomas Berthelet, 1542; *STC* 9179.3).

An Epytaphe upon the Death of M. Rycharde Goodricke Esquier ([London: 1562]; *STC* 17145.3).

Erasmus, Desiderius, *A very pleasaunt & fruitful Diologe called the Epicure, made by that famous clerke Erasmus of Roterodame*, trans. Philip Gerrard (London: Richard Grafton, 1545; *STC* 10460).

Foxe, Edward, *De vera differentia regiae potestatis & Ecclesiasticae, & quae sit ipsa veritas ac virtus utriusque. Opus eximium* (London: Thomas Berthelet, 1538; *STC* 11219).

Foxe, John, *Actes and Monuments of these latter and perillous dayes* (London: John Day, 1563; *STC* 11222). The two-volume second edition of 1570 is *STC* 11223.

Gilby, Anthony, 'An admonition to England and Scotland to call them to repentance, written by Antoni Gilby', in Knox, *Appellation*, pp. 59–77.

Goldyng, Arthur, trans., *A briefe treatise concerning the burnynge of Bucer and Phagius, at Cambrydge, in the tyme of Quene Mary, with theyr restitution in the time of our moste gracious soverayne lady that nowe is* (London: Thomas Marsh, 1562; *STC* 3966).

Goodman, Christopher, *How superior powers o[u]ght to be obeyd of their subjects: and Wherin they may lawfully by Gods Worde be disobeyed and resisted* (Geneva: Jean Crespin, 1558; *STC* 12020).

Grafton, Richard, *A Chronicle at large and meere History of the affayres of Englande and Kinges of the same, deduced from the Creation of the worlde, unto the first habitation of thys Islande: and so by contynuance unto the first yere of the reigne of our most deere and sovereigne Lady Queene Elizabeth* (London: Henry Denham for Richarde Tottle and Humffrey Toye, 1569; *STC* 12147).

Hartwell, Abraham, *A sight of the Portugall Pearle, that is, The Aunswere of D. Haddon Maister of the requests unto our soveraigne Lady Elizabeth . . . against the epistle of Hieronimus Osorius a Portugall, entitled a Pearle for a Prince* (London: William Seres, 1565; *STC* 12598).

Hatcher, Thomas, ed., *G. Haddoni legum doctoris, S. Reginae Elisabethae a supplicum libellis, lucubrationes passim collectae, & editae* (London: William Seres, 1567; *STC* 12596).

Holinshed, Raphael, *The First and second volumes of Chronicles*, 2 vols. (London: Henry Denham, 1597; *STC* 13569).

Knox, John, *The appellation of John Knoxe* (Geneva: [J. Poullain and A. Rebul,] 1558; *STC* 15063).

Langley, Thomas, ed., *An Abridgement of the notable worke of Polidore Vergile* (London: Richard Grafton, 1546; *STC* 24657).

Poor Pratte: see Pratte, Poor

Ponet, John, *A shorte treatise of politike power, and of the true Obedience which subjectes owe to kynges and other civile Governours, with an Exhortacion to all true naturall Englishe men* ([Strasburg: the heirs of W. Köpfel,] 1556; *STC* 20178).

Pratte, Poor, *The copie of a pistel or letter sent to Gilbard Potter in the tyme When he was in prison, for speakinge on our most true quenes part the Lady Mary before he had his eares cut of. The .xiij. of Julye* (London: [Richard Jugge for] Hugh Singleton, 1 Aug. 1553; *STC* 20188).

Stow, John, *The Annales of England, faithfully collected out of the most autenticall Authors, Records, and other Monuments of Antiquitie, from the first inhabitation untill this present yeere 1592* (London: Ralfe Newbery, 1592; *STC* 23334).

Tacitus, Cornelius, *The annales of Cornelius Tacitus. The description of Germanie*, trans. Richard Grenewey (London: [Arnold Hatfield for] Bonham and John Norton, 1598; *STC* 23644).

Traheron, Bartholomew, *A warning to England to repente, and to turne to god from idolatrie and poperie* ([?Wesel: ?P.A. de Zuttere,] 1558; *STC* 24174).

V PRINTED SOURCES 1603–1850

Anstis, John, *The register of the most noble Order of the Garter*, 2 vols. (London, 1724).

Burnet, Gilbert, 'A Collection of Records, and Original Papers' (1680), to supplement *The History of the Reformation of the Church of England*, 2 vols. (London, 1679–81), II, p. 86.

Collier, Jeremy, *An Ecclesiastical History of Great Britain, Chiefly of England*, 2 vols. (London, 1708–14).

Edward VI, K. *Edward the VI*[th] *His Own Arguments Against the Pope's Supremacy. Wherein several Popish Doctrines and Practices, contrary to God's Word, are animadverted on; and the Marks of Anti-Christ are applied to the Pope of Rome. Translated out of the Original, written with the King's own Hand in French, and still preserved. To which are subjoined some Remarks upon his Life and Reign, in Vindication of his Memory, from Dr. Heylin's severe and unjust Censure* (London, 1682).

Goodwin, James, ed., *The Gospel according to Saint Matthew and part of the first chapter of the Gospel according to Saint Mark translated into English from the Greek, with original notes, by Sir John Cheke, knight* (London and Cambridge, 1843).

Harington, John, *Nugae Antiquae: being a miscellaneous collection of original papers, in prose and verse; written during the reigns of Henry VIII, Edward VI, Queen Mary, Elizabeth, and King James*, ed. Thomas Park, 2 vols. (London, 1804).

Hayward, John, *The Life, and Raigne of King Edward the Sixt* (London, 1630; *STC* 12998).

Heylyn, Peter, *Ecclesia Restaurata; or the History of the Reformation of the Church of England* (London, 1661).

Hume, David, *The History of England under the House of Tudor*, 2 vols. (London, 1759).

Jenkyns, Henry, ed., *The remains of Thomas Cranmer*, 4 vols. (Oxford, 1833).

Kennett, White, *A Complete History of England: with the Lives of all the Kings and Queens thereof; From the Earliest Account of Time, to the Death of His late Majesty King William III*, 3 vols. (London, 1706).

Lamb, John, ed., *A collection of letters, statutes, and other documents, from the MS library of Corpus Christi College, illustrative of the history of the University of Cambridge, during the period of the Reformation, from AD MD, to AD MDLXXII* (London, 1838).

Lingard, John, *A history of England*, 8 vols. (London, 1819–30).

Nichols, John Gough, ed., *The diary of Henry Machyn, citizen and merchant-taylor of London, from AD 1550 to AD 1563* (Camden Society, 42; London, 1848).

Strype, John, *Historical Memorials, chiefly Ecclesiastical*, 3 vols. (London, 1721).

Turner, Sharon, *The history of the reigns of Edward the Sixth, Mary, and Elizabeth*, 2 vols. (London, 1829).

Tytler, Patrick Fraser, ed., *England under the reigns of Edward VI and Mary*, 2 vols. (London, 1839).

VI MODERN WORKS

Adair, E.R., 'William Thomas', in R.W. Seton-Watson, ed., *Tudor studies* (London, 1924), pp. 133–60.

Adams, Simon, 'Baronial contexts? Continuity and change in the noble affinity, 1400–1600', in John L. Watts, ed., *The end of the middle ages? England in the fifteenth and sixteenth centuries* (Stroud, 1998), pp. 155–97.

'The Dudley clientele, 1553–1563', in G.W. Bernard, ed., *The Tudor nobility* (Manchester and New York, 1992), pp. 241–65.

'Favourites and factions at the Elizabethan court', in Ronald G. Asch and Adolf M. Birke, eds., *Princes, patronage, and the nobility: the court at the beginning of the modern age c. 1450–1650* (Oxford, 1991), pp. 265–87.

Alford, Stephen, 'Between God and government', *Times Literary Supplement*, 11 Feb. 2000, p. 28.

The early Elizabethan polity: William Cecil and the British succession crisis, 1558–1569 (Cambridge, 1998).

'Politics and political history in the Tudor century', *Historical Journal*, 42 (1999), pp. 535–48.

Amos, N. Scott, '"It is fallow ground here": Martin Bucer as critic of the English Reformation', *Westminster Theological Journal*, 61 (1999), pp. 41–52.

Aston, Margaret, *The king's bedpost: Reformation and iconography in a Tudor group portrait* (Cambridge, 1993).

Barnett, Richard C., *Place, profit, and power: a study of the servants of William Cecil, Elizabethan statesman* (Chapel Hill, NC, 1969).

Batho, Gordon R., 'Syon House: the first two hundred years', *Transactions of the London and Middlesex Archaeological Society*, 19 (1958), pp. 1–17.

Beer, Barrett L., 'London and the rebellions of 1548–1549', *Journal of British Studies*, 12 (1972), pp. 15–38.

'Northumberland: the myth of the wicked duke and the historical John Dudley', *Albion*, 11 (1979), pp. 1–14.

Beer, Barrett L., ed., 'A critique of the protectorate: an unpublished letter of Sir William Paget to the duke of Somerset', *Huntington Library Quarterly*, 34 (1971), pp. 277–83.

Beer, Barrett L., and Sybil M. Jack, eds., 'The letters of William, Lord Paget of Beaudesert, 1547–63', *Camden Miscellany XXV* (Camden Society, fourth series, 13; London, 1974).

Bernard, G.W., 'The downfall of Sir Thomas Seymour', in G.W. Bernard, ed., *The Tudor nobility* (Manchester and New York, 1992), pp. 212–40.

Black, Anthony, *Political thought in Europe 1250–1450* (Cambridge, 1992).

Blayney, Peter, 'William Cecil and the Stationers', in Robin Myers and Michael Harris, eds., *The Stationers' Company and the book trade 1550–1990* (Winchester and New Castle, DE, 1997), pp. 11–34.

Bowler, Gerald, '"An axe or an acte": the parliament of 1572 and resistance theory in early Elizabethan England', *Canadian Journal of History*, 19 (1984), pp. 349–59.

Bradshaw, Christopher, 'David or Josiah? Old Testament kings as exemplars in Edwardian religious polemic', in Bruce Gordon, ed., *Protestant history and identity in sixteenth-century Europe*, 2 vols. (Aldershot, 1996), II, pp. 77–90.

Bray, Gerald, ed., *Tudor church reform: the Henrician canons of 1535 and the Reformatio legum ecclesiasticarum* (Church of England Record Society, 8; Woodbridge, 2000).

Brigden, Susan, ed., 'The letters of Richard Scudamore to Sir Philip Hoby, September 1549–March 1555', Camden Miscellany XXX (Camden Society, fourth series, 39; London, 1990).

Burns, J.H., *Lordship, kingship, and empire: the idea of monarchy, 1400–1525* (Oxford, 1992).

The true law of kingship: concepts of monarchy in early-modern Scotland (Oxford, 1996).

Bush, Michael L., *The government policy of Protector Somerset* (London, 1975).

'Protector Somerset and requests', *Historical Journal*, 17 (1974), pp. 451–64.

Cameron, Jamie, *James V: the personal rule 1528–1542* (East Linton, 1998).

Canning, Joseph, *A history of medieval political thought 300–1450* (London, 1996).

Carpenter, Christine, *The Wars of the Roses: politics and the constitution in England, c. 1437–1509* (Cambridge, 1997).

Chrimes, S.B., *English constitutional ideas in the fifteenth century* (Cambridge, 1936).

Coleman, Christopher, and David Starkey, eds., *Revolution reassessed: revisions in the history of Tudor government and administration* (Oxford, 1986).

Collinson, Patrick, *Archbishop Grindal 1519–1583: the struggle for a reformed church* (London, 1979).

The birthpangs of Protestant England: religious and cultural change in the sixteenth and seventeenth centuries (New York, 1988).

'The Elizabethan exclusion crisis and the Elizabethan polity', *Proceedings of the British Academy*, 84 (1994), pp. 51–92.

'The monarchical republic of Queen Elizabeth I', in John Guy, ed., *The Tudor monarchy* (London, 1997), pp. 110–34.

Davies, Hugh Sykes, 'Sir John Cheke and the translation of the Bible', *Essays and Studies*, 5 (1952), pp. 1–12.

Dawson, Jane E.A., 'Resistance and revolution in sixteenth-century thought: the case of Christopher Goodman', in J. van den Berg and P.G. Hoftijzer, eds., *Church, change and revolution* (Leiden, 1991), pp. 69–79.

'Revolutionary conclusions: the case of the Marian exiles', *History of Political Thought*, 11 (1990), pp. 257–72.

'Trumpeting resistance: Christopher Goodman and John Knox', in Roger A. Mason, ed., *John Knox and the British Reformations* (Aldershot, 1998), pp. 130–53.

'The two John Knoxes: England, Scotland and the 1558 tracts', *Journal of Ecclesiastical History*, 42 (1991), pp. 555–76.

Dowling, Maria, 'The gospel and the court: Reformation under Henry VIII', in Peter Lake and Maria Dowling, eds., *Protestantism and the national church in sixteenth century England* (London, 1987), pp. 36–77.

Humanism in the age of Henry VIII (London and Dover, New Hampshire, 1986).

Elton, G.R., *England under the Tudors* (London, 1955).

'The good duke', *Historical Journal*, 12 (1969), pp. 702–6.

'Government by edict?', *Historical Journal*, 8 (1965), pp. 266–71.

Reform and reformation: England 1509–1558 (London, 1987 edn).

'Tudor government: the points of contact. II. The Council', *Transactions of the Royal Historical Society*, fifth series, 25 (1975), pp. 195–211.

The Tudor revolution in government (Cambridge, 1953).

Elton, G.R., ed., *The Tudor constitution: documents and commentary* (Cambridge, 1982 edn).

Emmison, F.G., 'A plan of Edward VI and Secretary Petre for reorganizing the Privy Council's work, 1552–1553', *Bulletin of the Institute of Historical Research*, 31 (1958), pp. 203–10.

Erasmus, Desiderius, *The education of a Christian prince*, ed. Lisa Jardine (Cambridge, 1997).

Ferguson, Arthur B., 'The Tudor commonweal and the sense of change', *Journal of British Studies*, 3 (1963), pp. 11–35.

Feuillerat, Albert, ed., *Documents relating to the revels at court in the time of King Edward VI and Queen Mary* (Louvain, 1914).

Froude, James Anthony, *History of England from the fall of Wolsey to the death of Elizabeth*, 12 vols. (London, 1856–70).

Giles, J.A., ed., *The whole works of Roger Ascham*, 3 vols. in 4 (London, 1864–5).

Gunn, S.J., 'The accession of Henry VIII', *Historical Research*, 64 (1991), pp. 278–88.

Early Tudor government, 1485–1558 (Basingstoke and London, 1995).

Guy, John, 'The Henrician age', in J.G.A. Pocock, ed., *The varieties of British political thought, 1500–1800* (Cambridge, 1993), pp. 13–46.

'The rhetoric of counsel in early modern England', in Dale Hoak, ed., *Tudor political culture* (Cambridge, 1995), pp. 292–310.

'Thomas Cromwell and the intellectual origins of the Henrician Reformation', in Alastair Fox and John Guy, *Reassessing the Henrician age: humanism, politics and reform 1500–1550* (Oxford, 1986), pp. 151–78.

Tudor England (Oxford and New York, 1988).

Guy, John, ed., *The Tudor monarchy* (London, 1997).

Hall, Basil, 'Martin Bucer in England', in D.F. Wright, ed., *Martin Bucer: reforming church and community* (Cambridge, 1994), pp. 144–60.

Hartley, T.E., *Proceedings in the parliaments of Elizabeth I*, 3 vols. (Leicester, 1981–95).

Hastings, Elizabeth T., ed., 'A sixteenth century manuscript translation of Latimer's *First sermon before Edward*', *Publications of the Modern Language Association of America*, 60 (1945), pp. 959–1002.

Hindle, Steve, *The state and social change in early modern England, c. 1550–1640* (Basingstoke and London, 2000).

Hoak, Dale E., 'The coronations of Edward VI, Mary I, and Elizabeth I, and the transformation of Tudor monarchy', in Richard Mortimer and Charles S. Knighton, eds., *Reformation to revolution: Westminster Abbey 1540–1660* (Stamford, 2002).

'The iconography of the crown imperial', in Dale Hoak, ed., *Tudor political culture* (Cambridge, 1995), pp. 54–103.

The King's Council in the reign of Edward VI (Cambridge, 1976).

'The king's Privy Chamber, 1547–1553', in DeLloyd J. Guth and John W. McKenna, eds., *Tudor rule and revolution* (Cambridge, 1982), pp. 87–108.

'Rehabilitating the duke of Northumberland: politics and political control, 1549–53', in Jennifer Loach and Robert Tittler, eds., *The mid-Tudor polity c. 1540–1560* (London and Basingstoke, 1980), pp. 29–51.

'The secret history of the Tudor court: the king's coffers and the king's purse, 1542–1553', *Journal of British Studies*, 26 (1987), pp. 208–31.

Houlbrooke, R.A., 'Henry VIII's wills: a comment', *Historical Journal*, 37 (1994), pp. 891–9.

Hudson, Winthrop S., *The Cambridge connection and the Elizabethan settlement of 1559* (Durham, NC, 1980).

Ives, E.W., 'Henry VIII's will – a forensic conundrum', *Historical Journal*, 35 (1992), pp. 779–804.

'Henry VIII's will: the protectorate provisions of 1546–7', *Historical Journal*, 37 (1994), pp. 901–14.

Jack, Sybil M., 'An unknown draft of the October 8th letter from the Council at Windsor to the Council at London', *Huntington Library Quarterly*, 46 (1983), pp. 270–5.

Jackson, J.E., ed., 'Longleat papers no. 4', *Wiltshire Archaeological and Natural History Magazine*, 18 (1878–79), pp. 257–61.

Jordan, W.K., *Edward VI: the threshold of power. The dominance of the duke of Northumberland* (London, 1970).

Edward VI: the young king. The protectorship of the duke of Somerset (London, 1968).

Jordan, W.K., ed., *The chronicle and political papers of King Edward VI* (Ithaca, NY, 1966).

Kantorowicz, Ernst H., *The king's two bodies: a study in mediaeval political theology* (Princeton, 1957).

King, John N., *English Reformation literature: the Tudor origins of the Protestant tradition* (Princeton, 1982).

'Protector Somerset, patron of the English Renaissance', *Papers of the Bibliographical Society of America*, 70 (1976), pp. 307–31.

Tudor royal iconography: literature and art in an age of religious crisis (Princeton, 1989).

Kirk, James, *Patterns of reform: continuity and change in the Reformation kirk* (Edinburgh, 1989).

Knighton, C.S., 'The principal secretaries in the reign of Edward VI: reflections on their office and archive', in Claire Cross, David Loades, and J.J. Scarisbrick, eds., *Law and government under the Tudors* (Cambridge, 1988), pp. 163–75.

Knox, John, *On rebellion*, ed. Roger A. Mason (Cambridge, 1994).

Loach, Jennifer, *Edward VI*, ed. George Bernard and Penry Williams (New Haven and London, 1999).

Loades, David, *John Dudley duke of Northumberland, 1504–1553* (Oxford, 1996).

Lockwood, Shelley, 'Marsilius of Padua and the case for the royal ecclesiastical supremacy', *Transactions of the Royal Historical Society*, sixth series, 1 (1991), pp. 89–119.

MacCaffrey, Wallace T., *The shaping of the Elizabethan regime: Elizabethan politics, 1558–1572* (Princeton, 1968).

McConica, James Kelsey, *English humanists and Reformation politics under Henry VIII and Edward VI* (Oxford, 1968 edn).

MacCulloch, Diarmaid, *Thomas Cranmer* (New Haven and London, 1996).

Tudor church militant: Edward VI and the Protestant Reformation (London, 1999).

MacCulloch, Diarmaid, ed., 'The *Vita Mariae Angliae Reginae* of Robert Wingfield of Brantham', *Camden Miscellany XXVIII* (Camden Society, fourth series, 29; London, 1984), pp. 181–301.

McCullough, Peter E., *Sermons at court: politics and religion in Elizabethan and Jacobean preaching* (Cambridge, 1998).

McCutcheon, Elizabeth, ed., *Sir Nicholas Bacon's great house sententiae* (English Literary Renaissance Supplements, 3; Amherst, 1977).

McFarlane, K.B., *The nobility of later medieval England* (Oxford, 1997 edn).

McIntosh, Marjorie Keniston, 'Sir Anthony Cooke: Tudor humanist, educator, and religious reformer', *Proceedings of the American Philosophical Society*, 119 (1975), pp. 233–50.

Maitland, F.W., 'The crown as corporation', in H.A.L. Fisher, ed., *The collected papers of Frederic William Maitland*, 3 vols. (Cambridge, 1911), III, pp. 245–70.

Malkiewicz, A.J.A., 'An eye-witness's account of the *coup d'état* of October 1549', *English Historical Review*, 70 (1955), pp. 600–9.

Manzalaoui, M.A., ed., *Secretum secretorum: nine English versions* (Early English Text Society, 276; Oxford, 1977).

Mason, Roger A., *Kingship and the commonweal: political thought in Renaissance and Reformation Scotland* (East Linton, 1998).

'Knox, resistance and the royal supremacy', in Roger A. Mason, ed., *John Knox and the British Reformations* (Aldershot, 1998), pp. 154–75.

Merriman, Marcus, *The rough wooings: Mary Queen of Scots 1542–1551* (East Linton, 2000).

Miller, Helen, 'Henry VIII's unwritten will: grants of lands and honours in 1547', in E.W. Ives, R.J. Knecht, and J.J. Scarisbrick, eds., *Wealth and power in Tudor England* (London, 1978), pp. 87–105.

Muller, James Arthur, ed., *The letters of Stephen Gardiner* (Cambridge, 1933).

Murphy, John, 'The illusion of decline: the Privy Chamber, 1547–1558', in David Starkey, ed., *The English court: from the Wars of the Roses to the Civil War* (London and New York, 1987).

Neale, J.E., ed., 'Sir Nicholas Throckmorton's advice to Queen Elizabeth on her accession to the throne', *English Historical Review*, 65 (1950), pp. 91–8.

Nichols, John Gough, 'Some additions to the biographies of Sir John Cheke and Sir Thomas Smith', *Archaeologia*, 38 (1860), pp. 98–127.

Nichols, John Gough, ed., *The chronicle of Queen Jane, and of two years of Queen Mary* (Camden Society, 48; London, 1850).

The *literary remains of King Edward VI*, 2 vols. (Roxburghe Club; London, 1857).

Nicholson, Graham, 'The Act of Appeals and the English Reformation', in Claire Cross, David Loades, and J.J. Scarisbrick, eds., *Law and government under the Tudors* (Cambridge, 1988), pp. 19–30.

O'Day, Rosemary, 'Hugh Latimer: prophet of the kingdom', *Historical Research*, 65 (1992), pp. 258–76.

Pam, D.O., *Protestant gentlemen: the Wroths of Durants Arbour Enfield and Loughton Essex* (Edmonton Hundred Historical Society Occasional Paper New Series, 25; London, 1973).

Parry, G.J.R., 'Inventing "The good duke" of Somerset', *Journal of Ecclesiastical History*, 40 (1989), pp. 370–80.

Peck, Dwight C., ed., *Leicester's commonwealth: the copy of a letter written by a Master of Art of Cambridge (1584) and related documents* (Athens, OH and London, 1985).

Percy, Eustace, *The Privy Council under the Tudors* (Oxford and London, 1907).

Pettegree, Andrew, *Emden and the Dutch revolt: exile and the development of reformed Protestantism* (Oxford, 1992).

    Foreign Protestant communities in sixteenth-century London (Oxford, 1986).

    'Nicodemism and the English Reformation', in his *Marian Protestantism: six studies* (Aldershot, 1995), pp. 86–117.

Pocock, Nicholas, ed., *Troubles connected with the Prayer Book of 1549* (Camden Society, new series, 37; London, 1884).

Pollard, A.F., *England under Protector Somerset: an essay* (London, 1900).

    The history of England from the accession of Edward VI to the death of Elizabeth (1547–1603) (London, 1910).

Powell, Edgar, ed., 'The travels and life of Sir Thomas Hoby, Knight, of Bisham Abbey, written by himself. 1547–1564', *Camden Miscellany X* (Camden Society, third series, 4; London, 1902), pp. 1–144.

Redworth, Glyn, *In defence of the Church Catholic: the life of Stephen Gardiner* (Oxford, 1990).

Reed, A.W., 'Nicholas Udall and Thomas Wilson', *Review of English Studies*, 1 (1925), pp. 275–83.

Rex, Richard, 'The role of English humanists in the Reformation up to 1559', in N. Scott Amos, Andrew Pettegree, and Henk van Nierop, eds., *The education of a Christian society: humanism and the Reformation in Britain and the Netherlands* (Aldershot, 1999), pp. 19–40.

Richardson, W.C., ed., *The report of the royal commission of 1552* (Morgantown, VA, 1974).

Rose-Troup, Frances, *The Western Rebellion of 1549: an account of the insurrections in Devonshire and Cornwall against religious innovations in the reign of Edward VI* (London, 1913).

Roskell, J.S., 'The office and dignity of protector of England, with special reference to its origins', *English Historical Review*, 68 (1953), pp. 193–233.

Ryan, Lawrence V., 'The Haddon–Osorio controversy (1563–1583), *Church History*, 22 (1953), pp. 142–54.

    Roger Ascham (Stanford, 1963).

    'Walter Haddon: Elizabethan Latinist', *Huntington Library Quarterly*, 17 (1954), pp. 99–124.

Schmidt, A.J., 'Thomas Wilson, Tudor scholar-statesman', *Huntington Library Quarterly*, 20 (1957), pp. 205–18.

    'Thomas Wilson and the Tudor commonwealth: an essay in civic humanism', *Huntington Library Quarterly*, 23 (1959), pp. 49–60.

Shagan, Ethan H., 'Protector Somerset and the 1549 rebellions: new sources and new perspectives', *English Historical Review*, 114 (1999), pp. 34–63; and the subsequent debate between Shagan, Michael Bush, and George Bernard in *English Historical Review*, 115 (2000), pp. 103–33.

Skinner, Quentin, *Reason and rhetoric in the philosophy of Hobbes* (Cambridge, 1996).
Slavin, Arthur J., 'The fugitive folio and other problems: a new edition of Edward VI's writings', *Manuscripta*, 11 (1967), pp. 94–101.
'Profitable studies: humanists and government in early Tudor England', *Viator*, 1 (1970), pp. 307–25.
Starkey, David, 'Tudor government: the facts?', *Historical Journal*, 31 (1988), pp. 921–31.
Tittler, Robert, and Susan L. Battley, 'The local community and the crown in 1553: the accession of Mary Tudor revisited', *Bulletin of the Institute of Historical Research*, 57 (1984), pp. 131–9.
Watt, J.A., 'Spiritual and temporal powers', in J.H. Burns, ed., *The Cambridge history of medieval political thought c. 350–c. 1450* (Cambridge, 1988).
Watts, John L., 'The counsels of King Henry VI, C. 1435–1445', *English Historical Review*, 106 (1991), pp. 279–98.
Henry VI and the politics of kingship (Cambridge, 1996).
Williams, Penry, *The later Tudors: England 1547–1603* (Oxford, 1995).
The Tudor regime (Oxford, 1979).
Wood, Neal, *Foundations of political economy: some early Tudor views on state and society* (Berkeley, Los Angeles, and London, 1994).

VII UNPUBLISHED DISSERTATIONS

Bryson, Alan, 'The great men of the country: the Edwardian regime, 1547–53', PhD dissertation, University of St Andrews (2001).
Bush, Michael L., 'The rise to power of Edward Seymour, Protector Somerset, 1500–1547', PhD dissertation, University of Cambridge (1965).
Fisher, Rodney M., 'The inns of court and the Reformation 1530–1580', PhD dissertation, University of Cambridge (1974).
Morrison, G.R., 'The land, family, and domestic following of William Cecil, Lord Burghley c. 1550–1598', DPhil dissertation, University of Oxford (1990).
Needham, Paul S., 'Sir John Cheke at Cambridge and court', 2 vols., PhD dissertation, Harvard University (1971).
Richardson, Lisa J., 'Sir John Hayward and early Stuart historiography', 2 vols., PhD dissertation, University of Cambridge (1999).

Index